Three Case Histories

Volumes in the Collier Books edition of
The Collected Papers of Sigmund Freud

Each volume has an Introduction by the Editor,
Philip Rieff.

Three Case Histories

SIGMUND FREUD

WITH AN INTRODUCTION BY THE EDITOR

PHILIP RIEFF

COLLIER BOOKS

A Division of Macmillan Publishing Co., Inc.

NEW YORK

First Collier Books Edition 1963

20 19 18 17 16 15 14 13 12 11

ISBN 0-02-076650-5

This Collier Books edition is published by arrangement with Basic Books, Inc. Macmillan Publishing Co., Inc., 866 Third Avenue, New York, N.Y. 10022. Printed in the United States of America.

Contents

Introduction

EACH OF THE three case histories reprinted in this volume will supply the reader with a different example of Freud's supreme gift: for making a clear and yet irreducibly complex analysis of the most complicated thing in the world—a human being. Such a gift, for entertaining complexities in modes of analysis reciprocally complex, is characteristic of all first-rate scientists and artists. But in a moral scientist the intellectual gift must be compounded by one more characteristic, which need not be present in the analyst of nonmoral actions: that capacity for introspection which, transformed into sympathetic understanding, relates the moral scientist to his object as one human to another. Without this relation it would be impossible to consider psychoanalysis as at once a theory and a therapy. Religious teachers, poets, novelists, sages—many have had the gift. It was Freud's capacity to rationalize sympathetic understanding into an analytic program of therapy, under the banner of science, that accounts for a compelling quality in his thought—a quality belonging, usually, to religious exercises; that unique pull is always present in the moral sciences, rightly conceived, and always missing in the physical sciences, rightly conceived.

Implicit in these case histories is the realization that none of us, including Freud, is so very different from the wretched men here analyzed. But we are utterly different from the object of, say, Einstein's studies. We are cases; we have histories. There is no reducing us to non-cases, without histories—although this utopian and rather mad hope is not without ardent supporters nowadays.

Freud never indulged in the religion of science. On the other hand, he did not delude himself with any form of the older tradition of wishing: for some meaningful end toward which we are all, in our otherwise separate histories, tending. Therefore he was caught in the middle, between scientism and religion, a thorn in both sides. Probably the middle is the most interesting place to be; it is the one position of strength remaining, once the weakness of all positions, including its own, has been exposed by it.

Freud's is really a psychology of weakness, founded as it is upon the condition of man at the time of his formative beginnings. Neuroses are a form of denial of certain weaknesses, in a misdirected effort to stabilize them; to these weaknesses some men return, by way of symptoms or more subtle protests, when they must, for reasons neither Freud nor anyone after him has made sufficiently clear. More precisely, we do not really *return*; rather, our weaknesses, specified in our infancy and childhood, are always with us. Why some men succumb, sometimes in bizarre ways, while others, no less latently weak, are spared, remains a mystery, involving not only ourselves but possibly also our forefathers and certainly the cultures to which we are subject. What is a disease entity in one culture may be a glorious capacity in another. Freud has made a start toward getting away altogether from doctrines of disease entities toward a truer psychology of *processes* by which men become what they are.

In each of the three cases republished here, Freud examined an incredibly involved structure of weaknesses, so involved that no one else has yet appeared who is capable of writing case histories with anything like the mastery of detail that Freud achieved. The best example of this unprecedented and still unique mastery occurs in the final case, that of the "Wolf Man." On the more accessible levels in each case, Freud examines the pathetic ways in which each of the three men tried to patch over the structure of their weakness in order to keep them hidden, as far as possible, even from themselves.

Freud was called in on only two of these three cases. The third, that of a jurist named Schreber, he read about in a book. But even from Schreber's own memoir on how his own self-patching job revealed him, Freud could detect the particular places of weakness and the hidden connections between them.

I shall not use this preface to summarize for the reader the structures of weakness Freud observed in each of the cases; that, after all, is the purpose of reading the book. It is my purpose, here, merely to impress upon the reader the fact that Freud shared with the profoundly religious a sense of the weakness of man, and, moreover, shared with the profoundly scientific a will to overcome human weakness, so far as possible, unaided by even the most beautiful illusions of outside help perpetually on its way.

There remains only to make clear some dates. Freud's treatment of the "Rat Man" began on October 1, 1907, and continued for almost a year. Within a month after the case came his way, Freud reported on it to his colleagues, and again on a number of occasions thereafter. Because the patient was relieved of his symptoms, finding himself able to work and love again, Freud considered this an unambiguously successful therapy. However, another symptom, for which Freud conceived no remedy, intervened: the man fell during the First World War.

As I have said, Dr. Daniel Paul Schreber, the second subject of this volume, was a case Freud never saw. This case is remarkable among all Freud contemplated because the patient was a psychotic, a type Freud never treated. Indeed, Freud doubted that his techniques were applicable to psychotics; this is a question still being examined, empirically, by workers in the psychiatric field. During a remission of his symptoms, Schreber wrote a book, *Memoirs of My Nervous Illness,* which was published in 1903. Upon Schreber's book and some ancillary material, Freud based this case history. Apart from the fact that Freud was here probing a psychosis rather than a neurosis, and this indirectly through a literary document, the case of Schreber is notable mainly because of the way in which Freud found the links between paranoia and homosexuality. Much of the most durable (i.e., theoretical) material is in the third part of the Schreber case.

"Psychoanalytic Notes Upon an Autobiographical Account of a Case of Paranoia" also carries significant implications for the Freudian analysis of religion. To be religious, as Freud sees it in telling exaggeration here, is to be passive, compliant, dependent—all are essentially feminine traits. One feature of the intricate messianic delusion to which Schreber fell prey, while confined in a mental hospital, was the belief that he had changed his sex. Schreber's desire to be a woman submitting to a masculine God, Freud took as an exemplary case of the submissiveness which defined the religious attitude. Again, in the last of the three cases, that of the "Wolf Man," Freud explained his patient's childhood streak of piety as a projection of the boy's feminine attitude toward his own father.

The case of the "Wolf Man" may well be the greatest Freud ever wrote; certainly it is a remarkable intellectual performance, disciplining hordes of detail (in this case, the childhood sources of an adult neurosis) in a way never achieved, at least for publication, before or since. Written in 1914, "From the History of an Infantile Neurosis" was not published by Freud until 1918. The delay was not due to Freud's reluctance, as in the case of "Dora," but rather merely one of the difficulties consequent upon writing during a time of war.

The "Wolf Man" was a wealthy and completely incapacitated young Russian who, in his gratitude to Freud for helping him make life livable, became a devoted follower in the psychoanalytic movement. In a reminiscence written many years after his analysis, the "Wolf Man" emphasized how much his "new knowledge, the feeling that he had, so to speak, 'discovered' Freud, and the hope of regaining his health, made his condition rapidly improve." But the case itself indicates how little therapeutic suggestion had to do with the remission of symptoms. The historical importance of the case of the "Wolf Man" to the psychoanalytic canon is rather as a counter against Jung's theory of the libido, proposed in 1912. The libido, according to Jung, while sexual in its sources, is more than sexual. Freud's view of the specifically sexual content of the libido would be tantamount, in Jung's words, "to treating the Cologne cathedral in a textbook of mineralogy, on the ground that it consisted very largely of stones." Freud's rejection of the Jungian idea of libido as *"intentionality* in general" sealed a difference between the two schools of psychology which has been damaging for both, I think.

PHILIP RIEFF

University of Pennsylvania
1962

Three Case Histories

NOTES UPON A CASE OF
OBSESSIONAL NEUROSIS[1] (1909)

THE MATTER CONTAINED in the following pages will be of two kinds. In the first place I shall give some fragmentary extracts from the history of a case of obsessional neurosis. This case, judged by its length, the injuriousness of its effects, and the patient's own view of it, deserves to be classed as a fairly severe one; the treatment, which lasted for about a year, led to the complete restoration of the patient's personality, and to the removal of his inhibitions. In the second place, starting out from this case, and also taking other cases into account which I have previously analysed, I shall make some disconnected statements of an aphoristic character upon the genesis and finer psychological mechanism of obsessional processes, and I shall thus hope to develop my first observations on the subject, published in 1896.[2]

A programme of this kind seems to me to require some justification. For it might otherwise be thought that I regard this method of making a communication as perfectly correct

---

[1] [First published in *Jahrbuch für psychoanalytische und psychopathologische Forschungen*, Bd. i., 1909. Reprinted in Freud, *Sammlung kleiner Schriften*, iii., 1913.]

[2] "Further Remarks on the Defence Neuro-Psychoses" (II. "The Nature and Mechanism of the Obessional Neurosis"), *Early Psychoanalytic Writings*, Collier Books edition BS 188V.

and as one to be imitated; whereas in reality I am only accommodating myself to obstacles, some external and others inherent in the subject, and I should gladly have communicated more if it had been right or possible for me to do so. I cannot give a complete history of the treatment, because that would involve my entering in detail into the circumstances of my patient's life. The importunate interest of a capital city, focussed with particular attention upon my medical activities, forbids my giving a faithful picture of the case. On the other hand I have come more and more to regard the distortions usually resorted to in such circumstances as useless and objectionable. If the distortions are slight, they fail in their object of protecting the patient from indiscreet curiosity; while if they go beyond this they require too great a sacrifice, for they destroy the intelligibility of the material, which depends for its coherence precisely upon the small details of real life. And from this latter circumstance follows the paradoxical truth that it is far easier to divulge the patient's most intimate secrets than the most innocent and trivial facts about him, for, whereas the former would not throw any light on his identity, the latter, by which he is generally recognized, would make it obvious to every one.

Such is my excuse for having curtailed so drastically the history of this case and of its treatment. And I can offer still more cogent reasons for having confined myself to the statement only of some disconnected results of the psychoanalytic investigation of obsessional neuroses. I must confess that I have not yet succeeded in completely penetrating the complicated texture of a *severe* case of obsessional neurosis, and that, if I were to reproduce the analysis, it would be impossible for me to make the structure, such as by the help of analysis we know or suspect it to be, visible to others through the mass of therapeutic work superimposed upon it. What adds so greatly to the difficulty of doing this is the patients' resistances and the forms in which they are expressed. But even apart from this it must be admitted that an obsessional neurosis is in itself not an easy thing to understand—much less so than a case of hysteria. As a matter of fact we should have expected to find the contrary. The language of an obsessional neurosis—the means by which it expresses its secret thoughts—is, as it were, only a dialect of the language of hysteria; but it is a dialect in which we ought to be able to find our way about more easily, since it is more nearly related to the forms of expression adopted by our conscious thought than is the language of hysteria. Above all, it does not involve the leap from a mental process to a somatic innervation—hysterial conversion—which can never be fully comprehensible to us.

Perhaps it is only because we are less familiar with obsessional neuroses that we do not find these expectations confirmed by the facts. Persons suffering from a severe degree of obsessional neurosis present themselves far less frequently for analytic treatment than hysterical patients. They dissimulate their condition in daily life, too, as long as they possibly can, and often call in a physician only when their complaint has reached such an advanced stage as, had they been suffering, for instance, from tuberculosis of the lungs, would have led to their being refused admission to a sanatorium. I make this comparison, moreover, because, as with the chronic infectious disease which I have just mentioned, we can point to a number of brilliant therapeutic successes in severe no less than in light cases of obsessional neurosis, where these have been taken in hand at an early stage.

In these circumstances there is no alternative but to report the facts in the imperfect and incomplete fashion in which they are known and in which it is legitimate to communicate them. The crumbs of knowledge offered in these pages, though they have been laboriously enough collected, may not in themselves prove very satisfying; but they may serve as a starting-point for the work of other investigators, and common endeavour may bring the success which is perhaps beyond the reach of individual effort.

I

Extracts from the Case History

A YOUNGISH man of university education introduced himself to me with the statement that he had suffered from obsessions ever since his childhood, but with particular intensity for the last four years. The chief features of his disorder were *fears* that something might happen to two people of whom he was very fond—his father and a lady whom he admired. Besides this he was aware of *compulsive impulses*—such as an impulse, for instance, to cut his throat with a razor; and further he produced *prohibitions*, sometimes in connection with quite unimportant things. He had wasted years, he told me, in fighting against these ideas of his, and in this way had lost much ground in the course of his life. He had tried various treatments, but none had been of any use to him except a course of hydrotherapy at a sanatorium near ——; and this, he thought, had probably only been because he had made an acquaintance there which had led to regular sexual intercourse. Here he had no opportunities of the sort, and he seldom had intercourse and only at irregular intervals. He felt disgust at prostitutes. Altogether, he said, his sexual life had been stunted; onanism had played only a small part in it, in his sixteenth or seventeenth year. His potency was normal; he had first performed coitus at the age of twenty-six.

He gave me the impression of being a clear-headed and shrewd person. When I asked him what it was that made him lay such stress upon telling me about his sexual life, he replied that that was what he knew about my theories. Actually, however, he had read none of my writings, except that a short time before he had been turning over the pages of one of my books and had come across the explanation of some curious verbal associations[1] which had so much reminded him of some of his own "efforts of thought" in connection with his ideas that he had decided to put himself in my hands.

(a) THE BEGINNING OF THE TREATMENT

The next day I made him pledge himself to submit to the one and only condition of the treatment—namely, to say everything that came into his head, even if it was *unpleasant* to him, or seemed *unimportant* or *irrelevant* or *senseless*. I then gave him leave to start his communications with any subject he pleased, and he began as follows:[2]

He had a friend, he told me, of whom he had an extraordinarily high opinion. He used always to go to him when he was tormented by some criminal impulse, and ask him whether he despised him as a criminal. His friend used then to give him moral support by assuring him that he was a man of irreproachable conduct, and had probably been in the habit, from his youth onwards, of taking a dark view of his own life. At an earlier date, he went on, another person had exercised a similar influence over him. This was a nineteen-year-old student (he himself had been fourteen or fifteen at the time) who had taken a liking to him, and had raised his self-esteem to an extraordinary degree, so that he appeared

---

[1] *Zur Psychopathologie des Alltagslebens*, 1904.

[2] What follows is based upon notes made on the evening of the day of treatment, and adheres as closely as possible to my recollection of the patient's words.—I feel obliged to offer a warning against the practice of noting down what the patient says during the actual time of treatment. The consequent withdrawal of the physician's attention does the patient more harm than can be made up for by any increase in accuracy that may be achieved in the reproduction of his case history.

to himself to be a genius. This student had subsequently become his tutor, and had suddenly altered his behaviour and begun treating him as though he were an idiot. At length he had noticed that the student was interested in one of his sisters, and had realized that he had only taken him up in order to gain admission into the house. This had been the first great blow of his life.

He then proceeded without any apparent transition:

(b) INFANTILE SEXUALITY

"My sexual life began very early. I can remember a scene out of my fourth or fifth year. (From my sixth year onwards I can remember everything.) This scene came into my head quite distinctly, years later. We had a very pretty young governess called Fräulein Peter.[3] One evening she was lying on the sofa lightly dressed, and reading. I was lying beside her, and begged her to let me creep under her skirt. She told me I might, so long as I said nothing to any one about it. She had very little on, and I fingered her genitals and the lower part of her body, which struck me as very queer. After this I was left with a burning and tormenting curiosity to see the female body. I can still remember the intense excitement with which I waited at the Baths (which I was still allowed to go to with the governess and my sisters) for the governess to undress and get into the water. I can remember more things from my sixth year onwards. At that time we had another

---

[3] Dr. Alfred Adler, who was formerly an analyst, once drew attention in a privately delivered paper to the peculiar importance which attaches to the *very first* communications made by patients. Here is an instance of this. The patient's opening words laid stress upon the influence exercised over him by men, that is to say, upon the part played in his life by homosexual object-choice; but immediately afterwards they touched upon a second *motif,* which was to become of great importance later on, namely, the conflict between man and woman and the opposition of their interests. Even the fact that he remembered his first pretty governess by her surname, which happened to be a man's Christian name, must be taken into account in this connection. In middle-class circles in Vienna it is more usual to call a governess by her Christian name, and it is by that name that she is more commonly remembered.

governess, who was also young and good-looking. She had abscesses on her buttocks which she was in the habit of expressing at night. I used to wait eagerly for that moment, to appease my curiosity. It was just the same at the Baths—though Fräulein Lina was more reserved than her predecessor." (In reply to a question which I threw in, "As a rule," the patient told me, "I did not sleep in her room, but mostly with my parents.") "I remember a scene which must have taken place when I was seven years old.[4] We were sitting together one evening—the governess, the cook, another servant-girl, myself and my brother, who was eighteen months younger than me. The young women were talking, and I suddenly became aware of Fräulein Lina saying: 'It could be done with the little one; but Paul' (that was I) 'is too clumsy, he would be sure to miss it.' I did not understand clearly what was meant, but I felt the slight and began to cry. Lina comforted me, and told me how a girl, who had done something of the kind with a little boy she was in charge of, had been put in prison for several months. I do not believe she actually did anything wrong with me, but I took a great many liberties with her. When I got into her bed I used to uncover her and touch her, and she made no objections. She was not very intelligent, and clearly had very strong sexual cravings. At twenty-three she had already had a child. She afterwards married its father, so that to-day she is a Frau Hofrat.[5] Even now I often see her in the street.

"When I was six years old I already suffered from erections, and I know that once I went to my mother to complain about them. I know too that in doing so I had some misgivings to get over, for I had a feeling that there was some connection between this subject and my ideas and inquisitiveness, and at that time I used to have a morbid idea *that my parents knew my thoughts; I explained this to myself by supposing*

---

[4] The patient subsequently admitted that this scene probably occurred one or two years later.

[5] [The Austrian title of *"Hofrat"* is awarded to prominent physicians, lawyers, university professors, civil servants, etc. It is perhaps equivalent to a knighthood in modern England.—*Trans.*]

that I had spoken them out loud, without having heard myself do it. I look on this as the beginning of my illness. There were certain people, girls, who pleased me very much, and I had a very strong wish *to see them naked.* But in wishing this I had *an uncanny feeling, as though something must happen if I thought such things, and as though I must do all sorts of things to prevent it.*"

(In reply to a question he gave an example of these fears: "For instance, *that my father might die.*") "Thoughts about my father's death occupied my mind from a very early age and for a long period of time, and greatly depressed me."

At this point I learnt with astonishment that the patient's father, with whom his obsessional fears were still occupied at that actual time, had died several years previously.

The events in his sixth or seventh year which the patient described in the first hour of his treatment were not merely, as he supposed, the beginning of his illness, but were already the illness itself. It was a complete obsessional neurosis, wanting in no essential element, at once the nucleus and the prototype of the later disorder—an elementary organism, as it were, the study of which could alone enable us to obtain a grasp of the complicated organization of his subsequent illness. The child, as we have seen, was under the domination of a component of the sexual instinct, scoptophilia (the instinct of looking), as a result of which there was a constant recurrence in him of a very intense wish connected with persons of the female sex who pleased him—the wish, that is, to see them naked. This wish corresponds to the later obsessional or compulsive idea; and if the quality of compulsion was not yet present in it, this was because the ego had not yet placed itself in complete opposition to it and did not yet regard it as something foreign to itself. Nevertheless, opposition to this wish from some source or other was already in activity, for its occurrence was regularly accompanied by a painful affect.[6] A conflict was evidently in progress in the mind of this young

---

[6] Yet attempts have been made to explain obsessions without taking affectivity into account!

libertine. Side by side with the obsessive wish, and intimately associated with it, was an obsessive fear: every time he had a wish of this kind he could not help fearing that something dreadful would happen. This something dreadful was already clothed in a characteristic indeterminateness which was thenceforward to be an invariable feature of every manifestation of the neurosis. But in a child it is not hard to discover what it is that is veiled behind an indeterminateness of this kind. If the patient can once be induced to give a particular instance in place of the vague generalities which characterize an obsessional neurosis, it may be confidently assumed that the instance is the original and actual thing which has tried to hide itself behind the generalization. Our present patient's obsessive fear, therefore, when restored to its original meaning, would run as follows: "If I have this wish to see a woman naked, my father will have to die." The painful affect was distinctly coloured with a tinge of uncanniness and superstition, and was already beginning to give rise to impulses to do something to ward off the impending evil. These impulses were subsequently to develop into the *protective measures* which the patient adopted.

We find, therefore: an erotic instinct and a revolt against it; a wish which has not yet become compulsive and, struggling against it, a fear which is already compulsive; a painful affect and an impulsion towards the performance of defensive acts. The inventory of the neurosis has reached its full muster. Indeed, something more is present, namely, a kind of *delusional formation* or *delirium*[7] with the strange content that his parents knew his thoughts because he spoke them out loud without his hearing himself do it. We shall not go far astray if we suppose that in making this attempt at an explanation the child had some inkling of those remarkable mental processes which we describe as unconscious and which we cannot dispense with if we are to throw any scientific light upon this obscure subject. "I speak my thoughts out loud, without hear-

---

[7] ["Delirium" is here used in a technical sense which is explained below on p. 78.—*Trans.*]

ing them" sounds like a projection into the outer world of our own hypothesis that he had thoughts without knowing anything about them; it sounds like an endopsychic perception of the repressed.

For the situation is clear. This elementary neurosis of child-hood already involved a problem and an apparent absurdity, like any complicated neurosis of maturity. What can have been the meaning of the child's idea that if he had this lasciv-ious wish his father would have to die? Was it sheer nonsense? Or are there means of understanding the words and of looking upon them as a necessary consequence of earlier events and premises?

If we apply knowledge gained elsewhere to this case of childhood neurosis, we shall not be able to avoid the suspicion that in this instance as in others, that is to say, before the child had reached his sixth year, there had been conflicts and repressions, which had themselves been overtaken by amnesia, but had left behind them as a residuum the particular content of this obsessive fear. Later on we shall learn how far it is possible for us to rediscover those forgotten experiences or to reconstruct them with some degree of certainty. In the meantime stress may be laid on the fact, which is probably more than a mere coincidence, that the patient's infantile amnesia ended precisely with his sixth year.

To find a chronic obsessional neurosis beginning like this in early childhood, with lascivious wishes of this sort con-nected with uncanny apprehensions and an inclination to the performance of defensive acts, is no new thing to me. I have come across it in a number of other cases. It is absolutely typical, although probably not the only possible type. Before proceeding to the events of the second sitting, I should like to add one more word on the subject of the patient's early sexual experiences. It will hardly be disputed that they may be described as having been considerable both in themselves and in their consequences. But it has been the same with the other cases of obsessional neurosis that I have had the op-portunity of analysing. Such cases, unlike those of hysteria, invariably possess the characteristic of premature sexual activity. Obsessional neuroses make it much more obvious than hysterias that the factors which go to form a psychoneurosis are to be found in the patient's infantile sexual life and not in his present one. The current sexual life of an obsessional neurotic may often appear perfectly normal to a superficial observer; indeed, it frequently offers to the eye far fewer pathogenic elements and abnormalities than in the instance we are now considering.

(c) THE GREAT OBSESSIVE FEAR

"I think I shall begin to-day with the experience which was the direct occasion of my coming to you. It was in August during the manoeuvres at ——. I had been suffering before, and tormenting myself with all kinds of obsessional thoughts, but they had quickly passed off during the manoeuvres. I was keen to show the regular officers that people like me had not only learnt a good deal but could stand a good deal too. One day we started from —— on a short march. During a halt I lost my pince-nez, and, although I could easily have found them, I did not want to delay our start, so I gave them up. But I wired to my opticians in Vienna to send me another pair by the next post. During that same halt I sat between two officers, one of whom, a captain with a Czech name, was to be of no small importance to me. I had a kind of dread of him, *for he was obviously fond of cruelty*. I do not say he was a bad man, but at the officers' mess he had repeatedly defended the introduction of corporal punishment, so that I had been obliged to disagree with him very sharply. Well, during this halt we got into conversation, and the captain told me he had read of a specially horrible punishment used in the East . . ."

Here the patient broke off, got up from the sofa, and begged me to spare him the recital of the details. I assured him that I myself had no taste whatever for cruelty, and certainly had no desire to torment him, but that naturally I could not grant him something which was beyond my power. He might just as well ask me to give him the moon. The overcoming of resistances was a law of the treatment, and on no consideration could it be dispensed with. (I had explained the idea of "resistance" to him at the beginning of the hour, when he told me there was much in himself which he would have to overcome if he was to relate this experience of his.) I went on to say that I would do all I could, nevertheless, to guess the full meaning of any hints he gave me. Was he perhaps thinking of impalement?—"No, not that; . . . the criminal was tied up . . ."—he expressed himself so indistinctly that I could not immediately guess in what position— ". . . a pot was turned upside down on his buttocks . . . some *rats* were put into it . . . and they . . ."—he had again got up, and was showing every sign of horror and resistance— ". . . *bored their way in* . . ."—Into his anus, I helped him out.

At all the more important moments while he was telling his story his face took on a very strange, composite expression. I could only interpret it as one of *horror at pleasure of his own of which he himself was unaware.* He proceeded with the greatest difficulty: "At that moment the idea flashed through my mind *that this was happening to a person who was very dear to me.*"[8] In answer to a direct question he said that it was not he himself who was carrying out the punishment, but that it was being carried out as it were impersonally. After a little prompting I learnt that the person to whom this "idea" of his related was the lady whom he admired.

He broke off his story in order to assure me that these thoughts were entirely foreign and repugnant to him, and to tell me that everything which had followed in their train had passed through his mind with the most extraordinary rapidity. Simultaneously with the idea there always appeared a "sanction," that is to say, the defensive measure which he was obliged to adopt in order to prevent the phantasy from being fulfilled. When the captain had spoken of this ghastly punishment, he went on, and these ideas had come into his head,

[8] He said "idea"—the stronger and more significant term "wish," or rather "fear," having evidently been censored. Unfortunately I am not able to reproduce the peculiar indeterminateness of all his remarks.

by employing his usual formulas (a "But" accompanied by a gesture of repudiation, and the phrase "Whatever are you thinking of?") he had just succeeded in warding off *both* of them.

This "both" took me aback, and it has no doubt also mystified the reader. For so far we have heard only of one idea—of the rat punishment being carried out upon the lady. He was now obliged to admit that a second idea had occurred to him simultaneously, namely, the idea of the punishment also being applied to his father. As his father had died many years previously, this obsessive fear was much more nonsensical even than the first, and accordingly it had attempted to escape being confessed to for a little while longer.

That evening, he continued, the same captain had handed him a packet that had arrived by the post and had said: "Lieutenant A.[9] has paid the charges[10] for you. You must pay him back." The packet had contained the pince-nez that he had wired for. At that instant, however, a "sanction" had taken shape in his mind, namely, *that he was not to pay back the money* or it would happen—(that is, the phantasy about the rats would come true as regards his father and the lady). And immediately, in accordance with a type of procedure with which he was familiar, to combat this sanction there had arisen a command in the shape of a vow: "*You must pay back the 3.80 crowns[11] to Lieutenant A.*" He had said these words to himself almost half aloud.

Two days later the manoeuvres had come to an end. He had spent the whole of the intervening time in efforts at repaying Lieutenant A. the small amount in question; but a succession of difficulties of an apparently *external* nature had arisen to prevent it. First he had tried to effect the payment through another officer who had been going to the post

[9] The names are of little consequence here.

[10] [The charges in question were for the cost of the new pince-nez. In Austria a system of "payment on delivery" operates through the post office.—*Trans.*]

[11] [At that time equal to about 3s. 2d.—*Trans.*]

office. But he had been much relieved when this officer brought him back the money, saying that he had not met Lieutenant A. there, for this method of fulfilling his vow had not satisfied him, as it did not correspond with the wording, which ran: "*You* must pay back the money to Lieutenant A." Finally, he had met Lieutenant A., the person he was looking for; but he had refused to accept the money, declaring that he had not paid anything for him, and had nothing whatever to do with the post, which was the business of Lieutenant B. This had thrown my patient into great perplexity, for it meant that he was unable to keep his vow, since it had been based upon false premises. He had excogitated a very curious means of getting out of his difficulty, namely, that he should go to the post office with both the men, A. and B., that A. should give the young lady there the 3.80 crowns, that the young lady should give them to B., and that then he himself should pay back the 3.80 crowns to A. according to the wording of his vow.

It would not surprise me to hear that at this point the reader had ceased to be able to follow. For even the detailed account which the patient gave me of the external events of these days and of his reactions to them was full of self-contradictions and sounded hopelessly confused. It was only when he told the story for the third time that I could get him to realize its obscurities and could lay bare the errors of memory and the displacements in which he had become involved. I shall spare myself the trouble of reproducing these details, the essentials of which we shall easily be able to pick up later on, and I will only add that at the end of this second sitting the patient behaved as though he were dazed and bewildered. He repeatedly addressed me as "Captain," probably because at the beginning of the hour I had told him that I myself was not fond of cruelty like Captain M., and that I had no intention of tormenting him unnecessarily.

The only other piece of information that I obtained from him during this hour was that from the very first, on all the previous occasions on which he had had a fear that something would happen to people he loved no less than on the present one, he had referred the punishments not only to our present life but also to eternity—to the next world. Up to his fourteenth or fifteenth year he had been devoutly religious, but from that time on he had gradually developed into the free-thinker that he was to-day. He reconciled the contradiction between his beliefs and his obsessions by saying to himself: "What do you know about the next world? Nothing *can* be known about it. You're not risking anything—so do it." This form of argument seemed unobjectionable to a man who was in other respects particularly clear-headed, and in this way he exploited the uncertainty of reason in the face of these questions to the benefit of the religious attitude which he had outgrown.

At the third sitting he completed his very characteristic story of his efforts at fulfilling his obsessional vow. That evening the last gathering of officers had taken place before the end of the manoeuvres. It had fallen to him to reply to the toast of "The Gentlemen of the Reserve." He had spoken well, but as if he were in a dream, for at the back of his mind he was being incessantly tormented by his vow. He had spent a terrible night. Arguments and counter-arguments had struggled with one another. The chief argument, of course, had been that the premise upon which his vow had been based—that Lieutenant A. had paid the money for him—had proved to be false. However, he had consoled himself with the thought that the business was not yet finished, as A. would be riding with him next morning part of the way to the railway station at P——, so that he would still have time to ask him the necessary favour. As a matter of fact he had not done this, and had allowed A. to go off without him; but he had given instructions to his orderly to let A. know that he intended to pay him a visit that afternoon. He himself had reached the station at half-past nine in the morning. He had deposited his luggage there and had seen to various things he had to do in the small town, with the intention of afterwards paying his visit to A. The village in which A. was stationed was about an hour's drive from the town of P——. The railway journey to the place where the post office was would take three hours. He had calculated, therefore, that the execution of his complicated plan would just leave him time to catch the evening train from P—— to Vienna. The ideas that were struggling within him had been, on the one hand, that he was simply being cowardly and was obviously only trying to save himself the unpleasantness of asking A. to make the sacrifice in question and of cutting a foolish figure before him, and that that was why he was disregarding his vow; and, on the other hand, that it would, on the contrary, be cowardly of him to fulfil his vow, since he only wanted to do so in order to be left in peace by his obsessions. When in the course of his deliberations, the patient added, he found the arguments so evenly balanced as these, it was his custom to allow his actions to be decided by chance events as though by the hand of God. When, therefore, a porter at the station had addressed him with the words, "Ten o'clock train, sir?" he had answered "Yes," and in fact had gone off by the ten o'clock train. In this way he had produced a *fait accompli* and felt greatly relieved. He had proceeded to book a seat for luncheon in the restaurant car. At the first station they had stopped at it had suddenly struck him that he still had time to get out, wait for the next down train, travel back in it to P——, drive to the place where Lieutenant A. was quartered, from there make the three hours' train journey with him to the post office, and so forth. It had only been the consideration that he had booked his seat for luncheon with the steward of the restaurant car that had prevented his carrying out this design. He had not abandoned it, however; he had only put off getting out until a later stop. In this way he had struggled through from station to station, till he had reached one at which it had seemed to him impossible to get out because he had relatives living there. He had then determined to travel through to Vienna, to look up his friend there and lay the whole matter before him, and then, after his friend had made his decision, to catch the night train back to P——. When I expressed a doubt whether this would have been feasible, he assured me that he would have had half an hour to spare between the arrival of the one train and the de-

parture of the other. When he had arrived in Vienna, however, he had failed to find his friend at the restaurant at
which he had counted on meeting him, and had not reached
his friend's house till eleven o'clock at night. He told him the
whole story that very night. His friend had held up his hands
in amazement to think that he could still be in doubt whether
he was suffering from an obsession, and had calmed him down
for the night, so that he had slept excellently. Next morning
they had gone together to the post office, to dispatch the
3.80 crowns to ——, the post office at which the packet
containing the pince-nez had arrived.

It was this last statement which provided me with a starting-
point from which I could begin straightening out the various
distortions involved in his story. After his friend had brought
him to his senses he had dispatched the small sum of money
in question neither to Lieutenant A. nor to Lieutenant B., but
direct to the post office. He must therefore have known that
he owed the amount of the charges due upon the packet
to no one but the official at the post office, and he must have
known this before he started on his journey. It turned out that
in fact he had known it before the captain made his request
and before he himself made his vow; for he now remembered
that a few hours *before* meeting the cruel captain he had had
occasion to introduce himself to another captain, who had
told him how matters actually stood. This officer, on hearing
his name, had told him that he had been at the post office a
short time before, and that the young lady there had asked
him whether he knew a Lieutenant H. (the patient, in fact),
for whom a packet had arrived, to be paid for on delivery.
The officer had replied that he did not, but the young lady had
been of opinion that she could trust the unknown lieutenant
and had said that in the meantime she would pay the charges
herself. It had been in this way that the patient had come
into possession of the pince-nez he had ordered. The cruel
captain had made a mistake when, as he handed him over
the packet, he had asked him to pay back the 3.80 crowns to
A., and the patient must have known it was a mistake. In
spite of this he had made a vow founded upon this mistake,

a vow that was bound to be a torment to him. In so doing he had suppressed to himself, just as in telling the story he had suppressed to me, the episode of the other captain and the existence of the trusting young lady at the post office. I must admit that when this correction has been made his behaviour becomes even more senseless and unintelligible than before.

After he had left his friend and returned to his family his doubts had overtaken him afresh. His friend's arguments, he saw, had been no different from his own, and he was under no delusion that his temporary relief was attributable to anything more than his friend's personal influence. His determination to consult a doctor was woven into his delirium[12] in the following ingenious manner. He thought he would get a doctor to give him a certificate to the effect that it was necessary for him, in order to recover his health, to perform some such action as he had planned in connection with Lieutenant A.; and the lieutenant would no doubt let himself be persuaded by the certificate into accepting the 3.80 crowns from him. The chance that one of my books happened to fall into his hands just at that moment directed his choice to me. There was no question of getting a certificate from me, however; all that he asked of me was, very reasonably, to be freed of his obsessions. Many months later, when his resistance was at its height, he once more felt a temptation to travel to P—— after all, to look up Lieutenant A. and to go through the farce of returning him the money.

(d) INITIATION INTO THE NATURE OF THE TREATMENT

The reader must not expect to hear at once what light I have to throw upon the patient's strange and senseless obsessions about the rats. The true technique of psychoanalysis requires the physician to suppress his curiosity and leaves the patient complete freedom in choosing the order in which topics shall succeed each other during the treatment. At the fourth sitting, accordingly, I received the patient with the question: "And how do you intend to proceed to-day?"

[12] [See below, p. 78.]

"I have decided to tell you something which I consider most important and which has tormented me from the very first." He then told me at great length the story of the last illness of his father, who had died of emphysema nine years previously. One evening, thinking that the condition was one which would come to a crisis, he had asked the doctor when the danger could be regarded as over. "The evening of the day after to-morrow," had been the reply. It had never entered his head that his father might not survive that limit. At half-past eleven at night he had lain down for an hour's rest. He had woken up at one o'clock, and had been told by a medical friend that his father had died. He had reproached himself with not having been present at his death; and the reproach had been intensified when the nurse told him that his father had spoken his name once during the last days, and had said to her as she came up to the bed: "Is that Paul?" He had thought he noticed that his mother and sisters had been inclined to reproach themselves in a similar way; but they had never spoken about it. At first, however, the reproach had not tormented him. For a long time he had not realized the fact of his father's death. It had constantly happened that, when he heard a good joke, he would say to himself: "I must tell Father that." His imagination, too, had been occupied with his father, so that often, when there was a knock at the door, he would think: "Here comes Father," and when he walked into a room he would expect to find his father in it. And although he had never forgotten that his father was dead, the prospect of seeing a ghostly apparition of this kind had had no terrors for him; on the contrary, he had greatly desired it. It had not been until eighteen months later that the recollection of his neglect had recurred to him and begun to torment him terribly, so that he had come to treat himself as a criminal. The occasion of this happening had been the death of an aunt by marriage and of a visit of condolence that he had paid at her house. From that time forward he had extended the structure of his obsessional thoughts so as to include the next world. The immediate consequence of this development had been that he became seriously incapacitated from working.[13] He told me that the only thing that had kept him going at that time had been the consolation given him by his friend, who had always brushed his self-reproaches aside on the ground that they were grossly exaggerated. Hearing this, I took the opportunity of giving him a first glance at the underlying principles of psychoanalytic therapy. When there is a *mésalliance,* I began, between an affect and its ideational content (in this instance, between the intensity of the self-reproach and the occasion for it), a layman will say that the affect is too great for the occasion—that it is exaggerated—and that consequently the inference following from the self-reproach (the inference, that is, that the patient is a criminal) is false. On the contrary, the physician says: "No. The affect is justified. The sense of guilt cannot in itself be further criticized. But it belongs to another content, which is unknown (*unconscious*), and which requires to be looked for. The known ideational content has only got into its actual position owing to a mistaken association. We are not used to feeling strong affects without their having any ideational content, and therefore, if the content is missing, we seize as a substitute upon another content which is in some way or other suitable, much as our police, when they cannot catch the right murderer, arrest a wrong one instead. Moreover, this fact of there being a mistaken association is the only way of accounting for the powerlessness of logical processes in combating the tormenting idea." I concluded by admitting that this new way of looking at the matter gave immediate rise to some hard problems; for how could he admit that his self-reproach of being a criminal towards his

[13] A more detailed description of the event, which the patient gave me later on, made it possible to understand the effect that it produced on him. His uncle, lamenting the loss of his wife, had exclaimed: "Other men allow themselves every possible indulgence, but I lived for this woman alone!" The patient had assumed that his uncle was alluding to his father and was casting doubts upon his conjugal fidelity; and although his uncle had denied this construction of his words most positively, it was no longer possible to counteract their effect.

father was justified, when he must know that as a matter of fact he had never committed any crime against him?

At the next sitting the patient showed great interest in what I had said, but ventured, so he told me, to bring forward a few doubts.—How, he asked, could the information that the self-reproach, the sense of guilt, was justified have a therapeutic effect?—I explained that it was not the information that had this effect, but the discovery of the unknown content to which the self-reproach was really attached.—Yes, he said, that was the precise point to which his question had been directed.—I then made some short observations upon *the psychological differences between the conscious and the unconscious,* and upon the fact that everything conscious was subject to a process of wearing-away, while what was unconscious was relatively unchangeable; and I illustrated my remarks by pointing to the antiques standing about in my room. They were, in fact, I said, only objects found in a tomb, and their burial had been their preservation: the destruction of Pompeii was only beginning now that it had been dug up.— Was there any guarantee, he next inquired, of what one's attitude would be towards what was discovered? One man, he thought, would no doubt behave in such a way as to get the better of his self-reproach, but another would not.—No, I said, it followed from the nature of the circumstances that in every case the affect would for the most part be overcome during the progress of the work itself. Every effort was made to preserve Pompeii, whereas people were anxious to be rid of tormenting ideas like his.—He had said to himself, he went on, that a self-reproach could only arise from a breach of a person's own inner moral principles and not from that of any external ones.—I agreed, and said that the man who merely breaks an external law often regards himself as a hero.—Such an occurrence, he continued, was thus only possible where a *disintegration of the personality* was already present. Was there a possibility of his effecting a re-integration of his personality? If this could be done, he thought he would be able to make a success of his life, perhaps a better one than most people.—I replied that I was in complete agreement with this notion of a splitting of his personality. He had only to assimilate this new contrast, between a moral self and an evil one, with the contrast I had already mentioned, between the conscious and the unconscious. The moral self was the conscious, the evil self was the unconscious.[14]—He then said that, though he considered himself a moral person, he could quite definitely remember having done things in his *childhood* which came from his other self.—I remarked that here he had incidentally hit upon one of the chief characteristics of the unconscious, namely, its relation to the *infantile*. The unconscious, I explained, *was* the infantile; it was that part of the self which had become separated off from it in infancy, which had not shared the later stages of its development, and which had in consequence become *repressed*. It was the derivatives of this repressed unconscious that were responsible for the involuntary thoughts which constituted his illness. He might now, I added, discover yet another characteristic of the unconscious; it was a discovery which I should be glad to let him make for himself.—He found nothing more to say in this immediate connection, but instead he expressed a doubt whether it was possible to undo modifications of such long standing. What, in particular, could be done against his idea about the next world, for it could not be refuted by logic?— I told him I did not dispute the gravity of his case nor the significance of his pathological constructions; but at the same time his youth was very much in his favour as well as the intactness of his personality. In this connection I said a word or two upon the good opinion I had formed of him, and this gave him visible pleasure.

At the next sitting he began by saying that he must tell me an event in his childhood. From the age of seven, as he had already told me, he had had a fear that his parents guessed his thoughts, and this fear had in fact persisted all through his life. When he was twelve years old he had been in love with a little girl, the sister of a friend of his. (In answer to a

[14] All of this is of course only true in the roughest way, but it serves as a first introduction to the subject.

question he said that his love had not been sensual; he had not wanted to see her naked for she was too small.) But she had not shown him as much affection as he had desired. And thereupon the idea had come to him that she would be kind to him if some misfortune were to befall him; and as an instance of such a misfortune his father's death had forced itself upon his mind. He had at once rejected the idea with energy. And even now he could not admit the possibility that what had arisen in this way could have been a "wish"; it had clearly been no more than a "connection of thought."[15]—By way of objection I asked him why, if it had not been a wish, he had repudiated it.—Merely, he replied, on account of the content of the idea, the notion that his father might die.—I remarked that he was treating the phrase as though it were one that involved *lèse-majesté*; it was well known, of course, that it was equally punishable to say "The Emperor is an ass" or to disguise the forbidden words by saying "If any one says, etc., . . . then he will have me to reckon with." I added that I could easily insert the idea which he had so energetically repudiated into a context which would exclude the possibility of any such repudiation: for instance, "If my father dies, I shall kill myself upon his grave."—He was shaken, but did not abandon his objection. I therefore broke off the argument with the remark that I felt sure this had not been the first occurrence of his idea of his father's dying; it had evidently originated at an earlier date, and some day we should have to trace back its history.—He then proceeded to tell me that a precisely similar thought had flashed through his mind a second time, six months before his father's death. At that time[16] he had already been in love with his lady, but financial obstacles made it impossible to think of an alliance with her. The idea had then occurred to him that *his father's death might make him rich enough to marry her*. In defending himself against this idea he had gone to the length of wishing that his father might leave him nothing at all, so that he

---

[15] Obsessional neurotics are not the only people who are satisfied with euphemisms of this kind.

[16] That is, ten years ago.

might have no compensation for his terrible loss. The same idea, though in a much milder form, had come to him for a third time, on the day before his father's death. He had then thought: "Now I may be going to lose what I love most"; and then had come the contradiction: "No, there is some one else whose loss would be even more painful to you."[17] These thoughts surprised him very much, for he was quite certain that his father's death could never have been an object of his desire but only of his fear.—After his forcible enunciation of these words I thought it advisable to bring a fresh piece of theory to his notice. According to psychoanalytical theory, I told him, every fear corresponded to a former wish which was now repressed; we were therefore obliged to believe the exact contrary of what he had asserted. This would also fit in with another theoretical requirement, namely, that the unconscious must be the precise contrary of the conscious.—He was much agitated at this and very incredulous. He wondered how he could possibly have had such a wish, considering that he loved his father more than any one else in the world; there could be no doubt that he would have renounced all his own prospects of happiness if by so doing he could have saved his father's life.—I answered that it was precisely such intense love as his that was the condition of the repressed hatred. In the case of people to whom he felt indifferent he would certainly have no difficulty in maintaining side by side inclinations to a moderate liking and to an equally moderate dislike: supposing, for instance, that he were an official, he might think that his chief was agreeable as a superior, but at the same time pettifogging as a lawyer and inhuman as a judge. Shakespeare makes Brutus speak in a similar way of Julius Caesar: "As Caesar loved me, I weep for him; as he was fortunate, I rejoice at it; as he was valiant, I honour him; but as he was ambitious, I slew him." But these words already strike us as rather strange, and for the very reason that we had imagined Brutus's feeling for Caesar as something deeper.

[17] There is here an unmistakable indication of an opposition between the two objects of his love, his father and the "lady."

In the case of some one who was closer to him, of his wife for instance, he would wish his feelings to be unmixed, and consequently, as was only human, he would overlook her faults, since they might make him dislike her—he would ignore them as though he were blind to them. So it was precisely the intensity of his love that would not allow his hatred—though to give it such a name was to caricature the feeling—to remain conscious. To be sure, the hatred must have a source, and to discover that source was certainly a problem; his own statements pointed to the time when he was afraid that his parents guessed his thoughts. On the other hand, too, it might be asked why this intense love of his had not succeeded in extinguishing his hatred, as usually happened where there were two opposing impulses. We could only presume that the hatred must flow from some source, must be connected with some particular cause, which made it indestructible. On the one hand, then, some connection of this sort must be keeping his hatred for his father alive, while on the other hand, his intense love prevented it from becoming conscious. Therefore nothing remained for it but to exist in the unconscious, though it was able from time to time to flash out for a moment into consciousness.

He admitted that all of this sounded quite plausible, but he was naturally not in the very least convinced by it.[18] He would venture to ask, he said, how it was that an idea of this kind could have remissions, how it could appear for a moment when he was twelve years old, and again when he was twenty, and then once more two years later, this time for good. He could not believe that his hostility had been extinguished in the intervals, and yet during them there had been

---

[18] It is never the aim of discussions like this to create conviction. They are only intended to bring the repressed complexes into conciousness, to set the conflict going in the field of conscious mental activity, and to facilitate the emergence of fresh material from the unconscious. A sense of conviction is only attained after the patient has himself worked over the reclaimed material, and so long as he is not fully convinced the material must be considered as unexhausted.

no sign of self-reproaches.—To this I replied that whenever any one asked a question like that, he was already prepared with an answer; he needed only to be encouraged to go on talking.—He then proceeded, somewhat disconnectedly as it seemed, to say that he had been his father's best friend, and that his father had been his. Except on a few subjects, upon which fathers and sons usually hold aloof from one another— (What could he mean by that?)—there had been a greater intimacy between them than there now was between him and his best friend. As regards the lady on whose account he had slighted his father in that idea of his, it was true that he had loved her very much, but he had never felt really sensual wishes towards her, such as he had constantly had in his childhood. Altogether, in his childhood his sensual impulses had been much stronger than during his puberty.—At this I told him I thought he had now produced the answer we were waiting for, and had at the same time discovered the third great characteristic of the unconscious. The source from which his hostility to his father derived its indestructibility was evidently something in the nature of *sensual desires,* and in that connection he must have felt his father as in some way or other an *interference.* A conflict of this kind, I added, between sensuality and childish love was entirely typical. The remissions he had spoken of had occurred because the premature explosion of his sensual feelings had had as its immediate consequence a considerable diminution of their violence. It was not until he was once more seized with intense erotic desires that his hostility reappeared again owing to the revival of the old situation. I then got him to agree that I had not led him on to the subject either of childhood or of sex, but that he had raised them both of his own free will.—He then went on to ask why he had not simply come to a decision, at the time he was in love with the lady, that his father's interference with that love could not for a moment weigh against his love of his father.—I replied that it was scarcely possible to destroy a person *in absentia.* Such a decision would only have been possible if the wish that he took objection to had made its first appearance on that occasion; whereas, as a matter of fact, it was *a long-repressed wish,* towards which he could not behave otherwise than he had formerly done, and which was consequently immune from destruction. This wish (to get rid of his father as being an interference) must have originated at a time when circumstances had been very different—at a time, perhaps, when he had not loved his father more than the person whom he desired sensually, or when he was incapable of making a clear decision. It must have been in his very early childhood, therefore, before he had reached the age of six, and before the date at which his memory became continuous; and things must have remained in the same state ever since.— With this piece of construction our discussion was broken off for the time being.

At the next sitting, which was the seventh, he took up the same subject once more. He could not believe, he said, that he had ever entertained such a wish against his father. He remembered a story of Sudermann's, he went on, that had made a deep impression upon him. In this story there was a woman who, as she sat by her sister's sick-bed, felt a wish that her sister should die so that she herself might marry her husband. The woman thereupon committed suicide, thinking she was not fit to live after being guilty of such baseness. He could understand this, he said, and it would be only right if his thoughts were the death of him, for he deserved nothing less.[19]—I remarked that it was well known to us that patients derived a certain satisfaction from their sufferings, so that in reality they all resisted their own recovery to some extent. He must never lose sight of the fact that a treatment like ours proceeded to the accompaniment of a *constant resistance*; I should be repeatedly reminding him of this fact.

He then went on to say that he would like to speak of a

[19] This sense of guilt involves the most glaring contradiction of his opening denial that he had ever entertained such an evil wish against his father. This is a common type of reaction to repressed material which has become conscious: the "No" with which the fact is first denied is immediately followed by a confirmation of it, though, to begin with, only an indirect one.

criminal act, in the author of which he did not recognize himself, though he quite clearly recollected doing it. He quoted a saying of Nietzsche's:[20] "'I did this,' says my Memory, 'I cannot have done this,' says my Pride and remains inexorable. In the end—Memory yields." "Well," he continued, "my memory has *not* yielded on this point."—"That is because you derive pleasure from your reproaches as being a means of self-punishment."—"My younger brother—I am really very fond of him now, and he is causing me a great deal of worry just at present, for he wants to make what I consider a preposterous match; I have thought before now of going and killing the person so as to prevent his marrying her—well, my younger brother and I used to fight a lot when we were children. We were very fond of one another at the same time, and were inseparable; but I was plainly filled with jealousy, as he was the stronger and better-looking of the two and consequently the favourite."—"Yes. You have already given me a description of a scene of jealousy in connection with Fräulein Lina."—"Very well then, on some such occasion (it was certainly before I was eight years old, for I was not going to school yet, which I began to do when I was eight)—on some such occasion, this is what I did. We both had toy guns of the usual make. I loaded mine with the ramrod and told him that if he looked up the barrel he would see something. Then, while he was looking in, I pulled the trigger. He was hit on the forehead and not hurt; but I had meant to hurt him very much indeed. Afterwards I was quite beside myself, and threw myself on the ground and asked myself how ever I could have done such a thing. But I *did* do it."—I took the opportunity of urging my case. If he had preserved the recollection of an action so foreign to' him as this, he could not, I maintained, deny the possibility of something similar, which he had now forgotten entirely, having happened at a still earlier age in relation to his father.—He then told me he was aware of having felt other vindictive impulses, this time towards the lady he admired so much, of

[20] *Jenseits von Gut und Böse,* iv., 68.

whose character he painted a glowing picture. It might be true, he said, that she could not love easily; but she was reserving her whole self for the one man to whom she would some day belong. She did not love him. When he had become certain of that, a conscious phantasy had taken shape in his mind of how he should grow very rich and marry some one else, and should then take her to call on the lady in order to hurt her feelings. But at that point the phantasy had broken down, for he had been obliged to own to himself that the other woman, his wife, was completely indifferent to him; then his thoughts had become confused, till finally it had been clearly borne in upon him that this other woman would have to die. In this phantasy, just as in his attempt upon his brother, he recognized the quality of *cowardice* which was so particularly horrible to him.[21]—In the further course of our conversation I pointed out to him that he ought logically to consider himself as in no way responsible for any of these traits in his character; for all of these reprehensible impulses originated from his infancy, and were only derivatives of his infantile character surviving in his unconscious; and he must know that moral responsibility could not be applied to children. It was only by a process of development, I added, that a man, with his moral responsibility, grew up out of the sum of his infantile predispositions.[22] He expressed a doubt, however, whether all his evil impulses had originated from that source. But I promised to prove it to him in the course of the treatment.

He went on to adduce the fact of his illness having become so enormously intensified since his father's death; and I said I agreed with him in so far as I regarded his sorrow at his father's death as the chief source of the *intensity* of his illness. His sorrow had found, as it were, a pathological expression in his illness. Whereas, I told him, a normal period of mourning

---

[21] This quality of his will find an explanation later on.

[22] I only produced these arguments so as once more to demonstrate to myself their inefficacy. I cannot understand how other psychotherapists can assert that they successfully combat neuroses with such weapons as these.

would last from one to two years, a pathological one like his would last indefinitely.

This is as much of the present case history as I am able to report in a detailed and consecutive manner. It coincides roughly with the expository portion of the treatment; this lasted in all for more than eleven months.

(e) SOME OBSESSIONAL IDEAS AND THEIR EXPLANATION

Obsessional ideas, as is well known, have an appearance of being either without motive or without meaning, just as dreams do. The first problem is how to give them a sense and a status in the mental life of the individual, so as to make them comprehensible and even obvious. The problem of translating them may seem insoluble; but we must never let ourselves be misled by that illusion. The wildest and most eccentric obsessional or compulsive ideas can be cleared up if they are investigated deeply enough. The solution is effected by bringing the obsessional ideas into temporal relationship with the patient's experiences, that is to say, by inquiring when a particular obsessional idea made its first appearance and in what external circumstances it is apt to recur. When, as so often happens, an obsessional idea has not succeeded in establishing itself permanently, the task of cleaning it up is correspondingly simplified. We can easily convince ourselves that, when once the interconnections between an obsessional idea and the patient's experiences have been discovered, there will be no difficulty in obtaining access to whatever else may be puzzling or worth knowing in the pathological structure we are dealing with—its meaning, the mechanism of its origin, and its derivation from the preponderant motive forces of the patient's mind.

As a particularly clear example I will begin with one of the *suicidal impulses* which appeared so frequently in our patient. This instance almost analysed itself in the telling. He had once, he told me, lost some weeks of study owing to his lady's absence: she had gone away to nurse her grandmother, who was seriously ill. Just as he was in the middle of a very hard piece of work the idea had occurred to him: "If you received a command to take your examination this term at the first possible opportunity, you might manage to obey it. But if you were commanded to cut your throat with a razor, what then?" He had at once become aware that this command had already been given, and was hurrying to the cupboard to fetch his razor when he thought: "No, it's not so simple as that. You must[23] go and kill the old woman." Upon that, he had fallen to the ground, beside himself with horror.

In this instance the connection between the compulsive idea and the patient's life is contained in the opening words of his story. His lady was absent, while he was working very hard for an examination so as to bring the possibility of an alliance with her nearer. While he was working he was overcome by a longing for his absent lady, and he thought of the cause of her absence. And now there came over him something which, if he had been a normal man, would probably have been some kind of feeling of annoyance against her grandmother: "Why must the old woman get ill just at the very moment when I'm longing for *her* so frightfully?" We must suppose that something similar but far more intense passed through our patient's mind—an unconscious fit of rage which could combine with his longing and find expression in the exclamation: "Oh, I should like to go and kill that old woman for robbing me of my love!" Thereupon followed the command: "Kill yourself, as a punishment for these savage and murderous passions!" The whole process then passed into the obsessional patient's consciousness accompanied by the most violent affect and *in a reverse order*—the punitive command coming first, and the mention of the guilty outburst afterwards. I cannot think that this attempt at an explanation will seem forced or that it involves many hypothetical elements.

Another impulse, which might be described as indirectly suicidal and which was of longer duration, was not so easily explicable. For its relation to the patient's experiences succeeded in concealing itself behind one of those purely ex-

[23] The sense requires that the word "first" should be interpolated here.

ternal associations which are so repellent to our consciousness. One day while he was away on his summer holidays the idea suddenly occurred to him that he was too fat [German *"dick"*] and that he must *make himself thinner*. So he began getting up from table before the pudding came round and tearing along the road without a hat in the blazing heat of an August sun. Then he would dash up a mountain at the double, till, dripping with perspiration, he was forced to come to a stop. On one occasion his suicidal intentions actually emerged without any disguise from behind this mania for getting thinner: as he was standing on the edge of a steep precipice he suddenly received a command to jump over, which would have been certain death. Our patient could think of no explanation of this senseless obsessional behaviour until it suddenly occurred to him that at that time his lady had also been stopping at the same resort; but she had been in the company of an English cousin, who was very attentive to her and of whom the patient had been very jealous. This cousin's name was Richard, and, according to the usual practice in England, he was known as *Dick*. Our patient, then, had wanted to kill this Dick; he had been far more jealous of him and enraged with him than he could admit to himself, and that was why he had imposed on himself this course of banting by way of a punishment. This obsessional impulse may seem very different from the directly suicidal command which was discussed above, but they have nevertheless one important feature in common. For they both arose as reactions to a tremendous feeling of rage, which was inaccessible to the patient's consciousness and was directed against some one who had cropped up as an interference with the course of his love.[24]

Some other of the patient's obsessions, however, though

[24] Names and words are not nearly so frequently or so recklessly employed in obsessional neuroses as in hysteria for the purpose of establishing a connection between unconscious thoughts (whether they are impulses or phantasies) and symptoms. I happen, however, to recollect another instance in which the very same name, Richard, was similarly used by a patient whom I analysed a long

they too were centred upon his lady, exhibited a different mechanism and owed their origin to a different instinct. Besides his banting mania he produced a whole series of other obsessional activities at the period during which the lady was stopping at his summer resort; and, in part at least, these directly related to her. One day, when he was out with her in a boat and there was a stiff breeze blowing, he was obliged to make her put on his cap, because a command had been formulated in his mind that *nothing must happen to her.*[25] This was a kind of *obsession for protecting,* and it bore other fruit besides this. Another time, as they were sitting together during a thunderstorm, he was obsessed, he could not tell why, with the necessity *for counting* up to forty or fifty between each flash of lightning and its accompanying thunder-clap. On the day of her departure he knocked his foot against a stone lying in the road, and was *obliged* to put it out of the way by the side of the road, because the idea struck him that her carriage would be driving along the same road in a few hours' time and might come to grief against this stone. But a few minutes later it occurred to him that this was absurd, and he was *obliged* to go back and replace the stone in its original position in the middle of the road. After her departure he became a prey to an *obsession for understanding,* which made him a curse to all his companions. He forced himself to understand the precise meaning of every syllable that was addressed to him, as though he might otherwise be missing some priceless treasure. Accordingly he kept asking: "What was it you said just then?" And after it had been repeated to him he could not help thinking it had sounded different the first time, so he remained dissatisfied.

All of these products of his illness depended upon a certain

---

time since. After a quarrel with his brother he began brooding over the best means of getting rid of his fortune, and declaring that he did not want to have anything more to do with money, and so on. His brother was called Richard, and *"richard"* is the French for "a rich man."

[25] The words "for which he might be to blame" must be added to complete the sense.

circumstance which at that time dominated his relations to his lady. When he had been taking leave of her in Vienna before the summer holidays, she had said something which he had construed into a desire on her part to disown him before the rest of the company; and this had made him very unhappy. During her stay at the holiday resort there had been an opportunity for discussing the question, and the lady had been able to prove to him that these words of hers which he had misunderstood had on the contrary been intended to save him from being laughed at. This made him very happy again. The clearest allusion to this incident was contained in the obsession for understanding. It was constructed as though he were saying to himself: "After such an experience you must never misunderstand any one again, if you want to spare yourself unnecessary pain." This resolution was not merely a generalization from a single occasion, but it was also displaced—perhaps on account of the lady's absence—from a single highly valued individual on to all the remaining inferior ones. And the obsession cannot have arisen solely from his satisfaction at the explanation she had given him; it must have expressed something else besides, for it ended in an unsatisfying doubt as to whether what he had heard had been correctly repeated.

The other compulsive commands that had been mentioned put us upon the track of this other element. His obsession for protecting can only have been a reaction—as an expression of remorse and penitence—to a contrary, that is a hostile, impulse which he must have felt towards his lady before they had their *éclaircissement*. His obsession for counting during the thunderstorm can be interpreted, with the help of some material which he produced, as having been a defensive measure against fears that some one was in danger of death. The analysis of the obsessions which we first considered has already warned us to regard our patient's hostile impulses as particularly violent and as being in the nature of senseless rage; and now we find that even after their reconciliation his rage against the lady continued to play a part in the formation of his obsessions. His doubting mania as to whether he had heard correctly was an expression of the doubt still lurking in his mind as to whether he had really understood his lady correctly this time and as to whether he had been justified in taking her words as a proof of her affection for him. The doubt implied in his obsession for understanding was a doubt of her love. A battle between love and hate was raging in the lover's breast, and the object of both these feelings was one and the same person. The battle was represented in a plastic form by his compulsive and symbolic act of removing the stone from the road along which she was to drive, and then of undoing this deed of love by replacing the stone where it had lain, so that her carriage might come to grief against it and she herself be hurt. We shall not be forming a correct judgement of this second part of the compulsive act if we take it at its face value as having merely been a critical repudiation of a pathological action. The fact that it was accompanied by a sense of compulsion betrays it as having itself been a part of the pathological action, though a part which was determined by a motive contrary to that which produced the first part.

Compulsive acts like this, in two successive stages, of which the second neutralizes the first, are a typical occurrence in obsessional neuroses. The patient's consciousness naturally misunderstands them and puts forward a set of secondary motives to account for them—*rationalizes* them, in short.[26] But their true significance lies in their being a representation of a conflict between two opposing impulses of approximately equal strength: and hitherto I have invariably found that this opposition has been one between love and hate. Compulsive acts of this sort are theoretically of special interest, for they show us a new type of symptom-formation. What regularly occurs in hysteria is that a compromise is arrived at which enables both the opposing tendencies to find expression simultaneously—which kills two birds with one stone;[27] whereas

[26] Cf. Ernest Jones, "Rationalization in Every-day Life" (1908).
[27] Cf. "Hysterical Phantasies and their Relation to Bisexuality," *Dora—An Analysis of a Case of Hysteria,* Collier Books edition AS 581V.

here each of the two opposing tendencies finds satisfaction singly, first one and then the other, though naturally an attempt is made to establish some sort of logical connection (often in defiance of all logic) between the antagonists.[28]

The conflict between love and hatred showed itself in our patient by other signs as well. At the time of the revival of his piety he used to make up prayers for himself, which took up more and more time and eventually lasted for an hour and a half. The reason for this was that he found, like an inverted Balaam, that something always inserted itself into his pious phrases and turned them into their opposite. For instance, if he said, "May God protect him," an evil spirit would hurriedly insinuate a "not."[29] On one such occasion the idea occurred to him of cursing instead, for in that case, he thought, the contrary words would be sure to creep in. His original intention, which had been repressed by his praying, was forcing its way through in this last idea of his. In the end he found his way out of his embarrassment by giving up the prayers and replacing them by a short formula concocted out of the initial letters or syllables of various prayers. He then recited this formula so quickly that nothing could slip into it.

---

[28] Another obsessional patient once told me the following story. He was walking one day in the park at Schönbrunn [the imperial palace on the outskirts of Vienna] when he kicked his foot against a branch that was lying on the ground. He picked it up and flung it into the hedge that bordered the path. On his way home he was suddenly seized with uneasiness that the branch in its new position might perhaps be projecting a little from the hedge and might cause an injury to some one passing by the same place after him. He was obliged to jump off his tram, hurry back to the park, find the place again, and put the branch back in its former position— although any one else but the patient would have seen that, on the contrary, it was bound to be more dangerous to passers-by in its original position than where he had put it in the hedge. The second and hostile act, which he carried out under compulsion, had clothed itself to his conscious view with the motives that really belonged to the first and philanthropic one.

[29] Compare the similar mechanism in the familiar case of sacrilegious thoughts entering the minds of devout persons.

He once brought me a dream which represented the same conflict in relation to his transference on to the physician. He dreamed that my mother was dead; he was anxious to offer me his condolences, but was afraid that in doing so he might break into *an impertinent laugh,* as he had repeatedly done on similar occasions in the past. He preferred, therefore, to leave a card on me with "p. c." written on it; but as he was writing them the letters turned into "p. f."[30]

The mutual antagonism between his feelings for his lady was too marked to have escaped his conscious perception entirely, although we may conclude from the obsessions in which it was manifested that he did not rightly appreciate the depth of his negative impulses. The lady had refused his first proposal, ten years earlier. Since then he had to his own knowledge passed through alternating periods, in which he either believed that he loved her intensely, or felt indifferent to her. Whenever in the course of the treatment he was faced by the necessity of taking some step which would bring him nearer the successful end of his courtship, his resistance usually began by taking the form of a conviction that after all he did not very much care for her—though this resistance, it is true, used soon to break down. Once when she was lying seriously ill in bed and he was most deeply concerned about her, there crossed his mind as he looked at her a wish that she might lie like that for ever. He explained this idea by an ingenious piece of sophistry: maintaining that he had only wished her to be permanently ill so that he might be relieved of his intolerable fear that she would have a repeated succession of attacks![31] Now and then he used to occupy his imagination with day-dreams, which he himself recognized as

---

[30] [The customary abbreviations for *"pour condoler"* and *"pour féliciter"* respectively.] This dream provides the explanation of the compulsive laughter which so often occurs on mournful occasions and which is regarded as such an unaccountable phenomenon.

[31] It cannot be doubted that another contributory motive to this compulsive idea was a wish to know that she was powerless against his designs.

"phantasies of revenge" and felt ashamed of. Believing, for instance, that the lady set great store by the social standing of a suitor, he made up a phantasy in which she was married to a man of that kind, who was in some government office. He himself then entered the same department, and rose much more rapidly than her husband, who eventually became his subordinate. One day, his phantasy proceeded, this man committed some act of dishonesty. The lady threw herself at his feet and implored him to save her husband. He promised to do so; but at the same time informed her that it had only been for love of her that he had entered the service, because he had foreseen that such a movement would occur; and now that her husband was saved, his own mission was fulfilled and he would resign his post.

He produced other phantasies in which he did the lady some great service without her knowing that it was he who was doing it. In these he only recognized his affection, without sufficiently appreciating the origin and aim of his magnanimity, which was designed to repress his thirst for revenge, after the manner of Dumas' Count of Monte-Cristo. Moreover he admitted that occasionally he was overcome by quite distinct impulses to do some mischief to the lady he admired. These impulses were mostly in abeyance when she was there, and only appeared in her absence.

(f) THE EXCITING CAUSE OF THE ILLNESS

One day the patient mentioned quite casually an event which I could not fail to recognize as the exciting cause of his illness, or at least as the immediate occasion of the attack which had begun some six years previously and had persisted to that day. He himself had no notion that he had brought forward anything of importance; he could not remember that he had ever attached any importance to the event; and moreover he had never forgotten it. Such an attitude on his part calls for some theoretical consideration.

In hysteria it is the rule that the exciting causes of the

illness are overtaken by amnesia no less than the infantile experiences by whose help the exciting causes are able to transform their affective energy into symptoms. And where the amnesia cannot be complete, it nevertheless subjects the recent traumatic exciting cause to a process of erosion and robs it at least of its most important components. In this amnesia we see the evidence of the repression which has taken place. The case is different in obsessional neuroses. The infantile preconditions of the neurosis may be overtaken by amnesia, though this is often an incomplete one; but the immediate occasions of the illness are, on the contrary, retained in the memory. Repression makes use of another, and in reality a simpler, mechanism. The trauma, instead of being forgotten, is deprived of its affective cathexis;[32] so that what remains in consciousness is nothing but its ideational content, which is perfectly colourless and is judged to be unimportant. The distinction between what occurs in hysteria and in an obsessional neurosis lies in the psychological processes which we can reconstruct behind the phenomena; the *result* is almost always the same, for the colourless mnemonic content is rarely reproduced and plays no part in the patient's mental activity. In order to differentiate between the two kinds of repression we have on the surface nothing to rely upon but the patient's assurance that he has a feeling in the one case of having always known the thing and in the other of having long ago forgotten it.[33]

---

[32] [German *"Besetzung,"* used on the analogy of an electric charge.—*Trans.*]

[33] It must therefore be admitted that in an obsessional neurosis there are two kinds of knowledge, and it is just as reasonable to hold that the patient "knows" his traumas as that he does *not* "know" them. For he knows them in that he has not forgotten them, and he does not know them in that he is unaware of their significance. It is often the same in ordinary life. The waiters who used to serve Schopenhauer at his regular restaurant "knew" him in a certain sense, at a time when, apart from that, he was not known either in Frankfort or outside it; but they did not "know" him in the sense in which we speak to-day of "knowing" Schopenhauer.

For this reason it not uncommonly happens that obsessional neurotics, who are troubled with self-reproaches but have connected their affects with the wrong causes, will also tell the physician the true causes, without any suspicion that their self-reproaches have simply become detached from them. In relating such an incident they will sometimes add with astonishment or even with an air of pride: "But I think nothing of that." This happened in the first case of obsessional neurosis which gave me an insight many years ago into the nature of the malady. The patient, who was a government official, was troubled by innumerable scruples. He was the man whose compulsive act in connection with the branch in the park at Schönbrunn I have already described. I was struck by the fact that the florin notes with which he paid his consultation fees were invariably clean and smooth. (This was before we had a silver coinage in Austria.) I once remarked to him that one could always tell a government official by the brand-new florins that he drew from the State treasury, and he then informed me that his florins were by no means new, but that he had them ironed out at home. It was a matter of conscience with him, he explained, not to hand any one dirty paper florins; for they harboured all sorts of dangerous bacteria and might do some harm to the recipient. At that time I already had a vague suspicion of the connection between neuroses and sexual life, so on another occasion I ventured to ask the patient how he stood in regard to that matter. "Oh, that's quite all right," he answered airily, "I'm not at all badly off in that respect. I play the part of a dear old uncle in a number of respectable families, and now and then I make use of my position to invite some young girl to go out with me for a day's excursion in the country. Then I arrange that we shall miss the train home and be obliged to spend the night out of town. I always engage two rooms— I do things most handsomely; but when the girl has gone to bed I go in to her and masturbate her with my fingers."— "But aren't you afraid of doing her some harm, fiddling about in her genitals with your dirty hand?"—At this he flared up: "Harm? Why, what harm should it do her? It hasn't done a single one of them any harm yet, and they've all of them enjoyed it. Some of them are married now, and it hasn't done them any harm at all."—He took my remonstrance in very bad part, and never appeared again. But I could only account for the contrast between his fastidiousness with the paper florins and his unscrupulousness in abusing the girls entrusted to him by supposing that the self-reproachful affect had become *displaced*. The aim of this displacement was obvious enough: if his self-reproaches had been allowed to remain where they belonged he would have had to abandon a form of sexual gratification to which he was probably impelled by some powerful infantile determinants. The displacement therefore ensured his deriving a considerable advantage from his illness [*paranosic gain*].

But I must now return to a more detailed examination of the exciting cause of our patient's illness. His mother had been brought up in a wealthy family with which she was distantly connected. This family carried on a large industrial concern. His father, at the time of his marriage, had been taken into the business, and had thus by his marriage made himself a fairly comfortable position. The patient had learnt from some chaff exchanged between his parents (whose marriage was an extremely happy one) that his father, some time before making his mother's acquaintance, had made advances to a pretty but penniless girl of humble birth. So much by way of introduction. After his father's death the patient's mother told him one day that she had been discussing his future with her rich relations, and that one of her cousins had declared himself ready to let him marry one of his daughters when his education was completed; a business connection with the firm would offer him a brilliant opening in his profession. This family plan stirred up in him a conflict as to whether he should remain faithful to the lady he loved in spite of her poverty, or whether he should follow in his father's footsteps and marry the lovely, rich, and well-connected girl who had been assigned to him. And he resolved this conflict, which was in fact one between his love and the persisting influence of his father's wishes, by falling ill; or, to put it more correctly, by falling ill he avoided the task of resolving it in real life.[34]

The proof that this view was correct lies in the fact that the chief result of his illness was an obstinate incapacity for work, which allowed him to postpone the completion of his education for years. But the results of such an illness are never unintentional; what appears to be the consequence of the illness is in reality the cause or motive of falling ill.

As was to be expected, the patient did not, to begin with, accept my elucidation of the matter. He could not imagine, he said, that the plan of marriage could have had any such affects: it had not made the slightest impression on him at the time. But in the further course of treatment he was forcibly brought to believe in the truth of my suspicion, and in a most singular manner. With the help of a transference phantasy, he experienced, as though it were new and belonged to the present, the very episode from the past which he had forgotten, or which had only passed through his mind unconsciously. There came an obscure and difficult period in the treatment; eventually it turned out that he had once met a young girl on the stairs in my house and had on the spot promoted her into being my daughter. She had pleased him, and he pictured to himself that the only reason I was so kind and incredibly patient with him was that I wanted to have him for a son-in-law. At the same time he raised the wealth and position of my family to a level which agreed with the model he had in mind. But his undying love for his lady fought against the temptation. After we had gone through a series of the severest resistances and bitterest vituperations on his part, he could no longer remain blind to the overwhelming effect of the perfect analogy between the transference phantasy and the actual state of affairs in the past. I will repeat one of the dreams which he had at this period, so as to give an example of his manner of treating the subject. He dreamed that *he*

[34] It is worth emphasizing that his flight into disease was made possible by his identifying himself with his father. The identification enabled his affects to regress on to the residues of his childhood.

saw my daughter in front of him with two patches of dung instead of eyes. No one who understands the language of dreams will find much difficulty in translating this one: it declared that *he was marrying my daughter not for her "beaux yeux" but for her money.*

(g) THE FATHER COMPLEX AND THE SOLUTION OF THE RAT IDEA

From the exciting cause of the patient's illness in his adult years there was a thread leading back to his childhood. He had found himself in a situation similar to that in which, as he knew or suspected, his father had been before *his* marriage; and he had thus been able to identify himself with his father. But his dead father was involved in his recent attack in yet another way. The conflict at the root of his illness was in essentials a struggle between the persisting influence of his father's wishes and his own amatory predilections. If we take into consideration what the patient reported in the course of the first hours of his treatment, we shall not be able to avoid a suspicion that this struggle was a very ancient one and had arisen as far back as in his childhood.

By all accounts our patient's father was a most excellent man. Before his marriage he had been a non-commissioned officer, and, as relics of that period of his life, he had retained a straightforward soldierly manner and a *penchant* for using downright language. Apart from those virtues which are celebrated upon every tombstone, he was distinguished by a hearty sense of humour and a kindly tolerance towards his fellow-men. That he could be hasty and violent was certainly not inconsistent with his other qualities, but was rather a necessary complement to them; but it occasionally brought down the most severe castigations upon the children, while they were young and naughty. When they grew up, however, he differed from other fathers in not attempting to exalt himself into a sacrosanct authority, but in sharing with them a knowledge of the little failures and misfortunes of his life with good-natured candour. His son was certainly not exaggerating when he declared that they had lived together like the best of friends, except upon a single point (see p. 41). And it must no doubt have been in connection with that very point that thoughts about his father's death had occupied his mind when he was a small boy with unusual and undue intensity (see p. 23), and that those thoughts made their appearance in the wording of the obsessional ideas of his childhood; and it can only have been in that same connection that he was able to wish for his father's death, in order that a certain little girl's sympathy might be aroused and that she might become kinder towards him (see p. 37).

There can be no question that there was something in the sphere of sexuality that stood between the father and son, and that the father had come into some sort of opposition to the son's prematurely developed erotic life. Several years after his father's death, the first time he experienced the pleasurable sensations of copulation, an idea sprang into his mind: "This is glorious! One might murder one's father for this!" This was at once an echo and an elucidation of the obsessional ideas of his childhood. Moreover, his father, shortly before his death, had directly opposed what later became our patient's dominating passion. He had noticed that his son was always in the lady's company, and had advised him to keep away from her, saying that it was imprudent of him and that he would only make a fool of himself.

To this unimpeachable body of evidence we shall be able to add fresh material, if we turn to the history of the onanistic side of our patient's sexual activities. There is a conflict between the opinions of doctors and patients on this subject which has not hitherto been properly appreciated. The patients are unanimous in their belief that onanism, by which they mean masturbation during puberty, is the root and origin of all their troubles. The doctors are, upon the whole, unable to decide what line to take; but, influenced by the knowledge that not only neurotics but most normal persons pass through a period of onanism during their puberty, the majority of them are inclined to dismiss the patients' assertions as gross exaggerations. In my opinion the patients are once again nearer to a correct view than the doctors; for the patients have some glimmering notion of the truth, while the doctors are in danger of overlooking an essential point. The thesis propounded by the patients certainly does not correspond to the facts in the sense in which they themselves construe it, namely, that onanism during puberty (which may almost be described as a typical occurrence) is responsible for all neurotic disturbances. Their thesis requires interpretation. The onanism of puberty is in fact no more than a revival of the onanism of infancy, a subject which has hitherto invariably been neglected. Infantile onanism reaches a kind of climax, as a rule, between the ages of three and four or five; and it is the clearest expression of a child's sexual constitution, in which the aetiology of subsequent neuroses must be sought. In this disguised way, therefore, the patients are putting the blame for their illnesses upon their infantile sexuality; and they are perfectly right in doing so. On the other hand, the problem of onanism becomes insoluble if we attempt to treat it as a clinical unit, and forget that it can represent the discharge of every variety of sexual component and of every sort of phantasy to which such components can give rise. The injurious effects of onanism are only in a very small degree autonomous—that is to say, determined by its own nature. They are in substance merely part and parcel of the pathogenic significance of the sexual life as a whole. The fact that so many people can tolerate onanism—that is, a certain amount of it—without injury merely shows that their sexual constitution and the course of development of their sexual life have been such as to allow them to exercise the sexual function within the limits of what is culturally permissible;[35] whereas other people, because their sexual constitution has been less favourable or their development has been disturbed, fall ill as a result of their sexuality,—they cannot, that is, achieve the necessary suppression or sublimation of their sexual components without having recourse to inhibitions or substitute-formations.

[35] Cf. Freud, *Drei Abhandlungen zur Sexualtheorie*, 1905.

Our present patient's behaviour in the matter of onanism was most remarkable. He did not indulge in it during puberty to an extent worth mentioning, and therefore, according to one set of views, he might have expected to be exempt from neurosis. On the other hand, an impulsion towards onanistic practices came over him in his twenty-first year, *shortly after his father's death*. He felt very much ashamed of himself each time he gave way to this kind of gratification, and soon foreswore the habit. From that time onwards it reappeared only upon rare and extraordinary occasions. It was provoked, he told me, when he experienced especially fine moments or when he read especially fine passages. It occurred once, for instance, on a lovely summer's afternoon when, in the middle of Vienna, he heard a postilion blowing his horn in the most wonderful way, until a policeman stopped him, because blowing horns is not allowed in the centre of the town. And another time it happened, when he read in *Dichtung und Wahrheit* how the young Goethe had freed himself in a burst of tenderness from the effects of a curse which a jealous mistress had pronounced upon the next woman who should kiss his lips after her; he had long, almost superstitiously, suffered the curse to hold him back, but now he broke his bonds and kissed his love joyfully again and again.

It seemed to the patient not a little strange that he should be impelled to masturbate precisely upon such beautiful and uplifting occasions as these. But I could not help pointing out that these two occasions had something in common—a prohibition, and the defiance of a command.

We must also consider in the same connection his curious behaviour at a time when he was working for an examination and toying with his favourite phantasy that his father was still alive and might any any moment reappear. He used to arrange that his working hours should be as late as possible in the night. Between twelve and one o'clock at night he would interrupt his work, and open the front door of the flat as though his father were standing outside it; then, coming back into the hall, he would take out his penis and look at it in the looking-glass. This crazy conduct becomes intelligible if we suppose that he was acting as though he expected a visit from his father at the hour when ghosts are abroad. He had on the whole been idle at his work during his father's lifetime, and this had often been a cause of annoyance to his father. And now that he was returning as a ghost, he was to be delighted at finding his son hard at work. But it was impossible that his father should be delighted at the other part of his behaviour; in this therefore he must be defying him. Thus, in a single unintelligible obsessional act, he gave expression to the two sides of his relation with his father, just as he did subsequently with regard to his lady by means of his obsessional act with the stone.

Starting from these indications and from other data of a similar kind, I ventured to put forward a construction to the effect that when he was a child of under six he had been guilty of some sexual misdemeanour connected with onanism and had been soundly castigated for it by his father. This punishment, according to my hypothesis, had, it was true, put an end to his onanism, but on the other hand it had left behind it an ineradicable grudge against his father and had established him for all time in his rôle of an interferer with the patient's sexual enjoyment.[36] To my great astonishment the patient then informed me that his mother had repeatedly described to him an occurrence of this kind which dated from his earliest childhood and had evidently escaped being forgotten by her on account of its remarkable consequences. He himself, however, had no recollection of it whatever. The tale was as follows. When he was very small—it became possible to establish the date more exactly owing to its having coincided with the fatal illness of an elder sister—he had done something naughty, for which his father had given him a beating. The little boy had flown into a terrible rage and had hurled abuse at his father even while he was under his blows. But as he knew no bad language, he had called him all the names of common objects that he could think of,

---

[36] Compare my suspicions to a similar effect in one of the first sittings (p. 25).

and had screamed: "You lamp! You towel! You plate!" and so on. His father, shaken by such an outburst of elemental fury, had stopped beating him, and had declared: "The child will be either a great man or a great criminal!"[37] The patient believed that the scene made a permanent impression upon himself as well as upon his father. His father, he said, never beat him again; and he also attributed to this experience a part of the change which came over his own character. From that time forward he was a coward—out of fear of the violence of his own rage. His whole life long, moreover, he was terribly afraid of blows, and used to creep away and hide, filled with terror and indignation, when one of his brothers or sisters was beaten.

The patient subsequently questioned his mother again. She confirmed the story, adding that at the time he had been between three and four years old and that he had been given the punishment because he had *bitten* some one. She could remember no further details, except for a very uncertain idea that the person the little boy had hurt might have been his nurse. In her account there was no suggestion of his misdeed having been of a sexual nature.[38]

---

[37] These alternatives did not exhaust the possibilities. His father had overlooked the commonest outcome of such premature passions—a neurosis.

[38] In psychoanalyses we frequently come across occurrences of this kind, dating back to the earliest years of the patient's childhood, in which his infantile sexual activity appears to reach its climax and often comes to a catastrophic end owing to some misfortune or punishment. Such occurrences are apt to appear in a shadowy way in dreams. Often they will become so clear that the analyst thinks he has a firm hold of them, and will nevertheless evade any final elucidation; and unless he proceeds with the greatest skill and caution he may be compelled to leave it undecided whether the scene in question actually took place or not. It will help to put us upon the right track in interpreting it, if we recognize that more than one version of the scene (each often differing greatly from the other) may be detected in the patient's unconscious phantasies. If we do not wish to go astray in our judgement of their historical reality, we must above all bear in mind that people's "childhood memories" are only consolidated at a later period, usually at the age of puberty; and that this involves

A discussion of this childhood scene will be found in a footnote, and here I will only remark that its emergence shook the patient for the first time in his refusal to believe that at some prehistoric period in his childhood he had been seized with fury (which had subsequently become latent) against the father whom he loved so much. I must confess that I had expected it to have a greater effect, for the incident had been described to him so often—even by his father himself—that there could be no doubt of its objective reality. But, with that capacity for being illogical which never fails to bewilder one in such highly intelligent people as obsessional neurotics, he kept urging against the evidential value of the story the fact that he himself could not remember the scene. And so it was only along the painful road of transference that he was able to reach a conviction that his relation to

---

a complicated process of remodelling, analogous in every way to the process by which a nation constructs legends about its early history. It at once becomes evident that in his phantasies about his infancy the individual as he grows up *endeavours to efface the recollection of his auto-erotic activities*; and this he does by exalting their memory-traces to the level of object-love, just as a real historian will view the past in the light of the present. This explains why these phantasies abound in seductions and assaults, where the facts will have been confined to auto-erotic activities and the caresses or punishments that stimulated them. Furthermore, it becomes clear that in constructing phantasies about his childhood the individual *sexualizes his memories*; that is, he brings common-place experiences into relation with his sexual activity, and extends his sexual interest to them—though in doing this he is probably following upon the traces of a really existing connection. No one who remembers my "Analysis of a Phobia in a Five-year-old Boy" [*The Sexual Enlightenment of Children*, Collier Books edition BS 190V] will need to be told that it is not my intention in these remarks to detract from the importance which I have hitherto attached to infantile sexuality by reducing it to nothing more than sexual interest at the age of puberty. I merely wish to give some technical advice that may help to clear up a class of phantasy which is calculated to falsify the picture of infantile sexual activity.

It is seldom that we are in the fortunate position of being able, as in the present instance, to establish the facts upon which these tales of the individual's prehistoric past are based, by recourse to

his father really necessitated the postulation of this unconscious complement. Things soon reached a point at which, in his dreams, his waking phantasies, and his associations, he began heaping the grossest and filthiest abuse upon me and my family, though in his deliberate actions he never treated me with anything but the greatest respect. His demeanour as he repeated these insults to me was that of a man in despair. "How can a gentleman like you, sir," he used to ask, "let yourself be abused in this way by a low, good-for-nothing wretch like me? You ought to turn me out: that's all I deserve." While he talked like this, he would get up from the sofa and roam about the room,—a habit which he explained at first as being due to delicacy of feeling: he could not bring himself, he said, to utter such horrible things while he was lying there so comfortably. But soon he himself found a more cogent explanation, namely, that he was avoiding my proximity for fear of my giving him a beating. If he stayed on the sofa he behaved like some one in desperate terror trying to save himself from castigations of boundless dimensions;

---

the unimpeachable testimony of a grown-up person. Even so, the statement made by our patient's mother leaves the way open to various possibilities. That she did not proclaim the sexual character of the offence for which the child was punished may have been due to the activity of her own censorship; for with all parents it is precisely this sexual element in their children's past that their own censorship is most anxious to eliminate. But it is just as possible that the child was reproved by his nurse or by his mother herself for some commonplace piece of naughtiness of a non-sexual nature, and that his reaction was so violent that he was castigated by his father. In phantasies of this kind nurses and servants are regularly replaced by the superior figure of the mother. A deeper interpretation of the patient's dreams in relation to this episode revealed the clearest traces of the presence in his mind of an imaginative production of a positively epic character. In this his sexual desires for his mother and sister and his sister's premature death were linked up with the young hero's chastisement at his father's hands. It was impossible to unravel this tissue of phantasy thread by thread; the therapeutic success of the treatment was precisely what stood in the way of this. The patient recovered, and his ordinary life began to assert its claims: there were many tasks before him, which he had already neglected far too long, and which were incompatible with a continuation of the

he would bury his head in his hands, cover his face with his arm, jump up suddenly and rush away, his features distorted with pain, and so on. He recalled that his father had had a passionate temper, and sometimes in his violence had not known where to stop. Thus, little by little, in this school of suffering, the patient won the sense of conviction which he had lacked—though to any disinterested mind the truth would have been almost self-evident. And now the path was clear to the solution of his rat idea. The treatment had reached its turning-point, and a quantity of material information which had hitherto been withheld became available, and so made possible a reconstruction of the whole concatenation of events.

In my description I shall, as I have already said, content myself with the briefest possible summary of the circumstances. Obviously the first problem to be solved was why the two speeches of the Czech captain—his rat story, and his request to the patient that he should pay back the money to Lieutenant A.—should have had such an agitating effect on him

---

treatment. I am not to be blamed, therefore, for this gap in the analysis. The scientific results of psychoanalysis are at present only a by-product of its therapeutic aims, and for that reason it is often just in those cases where treatment fails that most discoveries are made.

The content of the sexual life of infancy consists in auto-erotic activity on the part of the dominant sexual components, in traces of object-love, and in the formation of that complex which deserves to be called *the nuclear complex of the neuroses*. It is the complex which comprises the child's earliest impulses, alike tender and hostile, towards its parents and brothers and sisters, after its curiosity has been awakened—usually by the arrival of a new baby brother or sister. The uniformity of the content of the sexual life of children, together with the unvarying character of the modifying tendencies which are later brought to bear upon it, will easily account for the constant sameness which as a rule characterizes the phantasies that are constructed around the period of childhood, irrespective of how greatly or how little real experiences have contributed towards them. It is entirely characteristic of the nuclear complex of infancy that the child's father should be assigned the part of a sexual opponent and of an interferer with auto-erotic sexual activities; and real events are usually to a large extent responsible for bringing this about.

and should have provoked such violently pathological re-actions. The presumption was that it was a question of "complexive sensitiveness," and that the speeches had jarred upon certain hyperaesthetic spots in his unconscious. And so it proved to be. As always happened with the patient in connection with military matters, he had been in a state of unconscious identification with his father, who had seen many years' service and had been full of stories of his soldiering days. Now it happened by chance—for chance may play a part in the formation of a symptom, just as the wording may help in the making of a joke—that one of his father's little adventures had an important element in common with the captain's request. His father, in his capacity as non-commissioned officer, had control over a small sum of money and had on one occasion lost it at cards. (Thus he had been a *"Spielratte"*[39]). He would have found himself in a serious position if one of his comrades had not advanced him the amount. After he had left the army and become well-off, he had tried to find this friend in need so as to pay him back the money, but had not managed to trace him. The patient was uncertain whether he had ever succeeded in returning the money. The recollection of this sin of his father's youth was painful to him, for, in spite of appearances, his unconscious was filled with hostile strictures upon his father's character. The captain's words, "You must pay back the 3.80 crowns to Lieutenant A.," had sounded to his ears like an allusion to this unpaid debt of his father's.

But the information that the young lady at the post office at Z—— had herself paid the charges due upon the packet, with a complimentary remark about himself,[40] had intensified his identification with his father in quite another direction. At

---

[39] [Literally, "play-rat." Colloquial German for "gambler."—Trans.]

[40] It must not be forgotten that he had learnt this *before* the captain, owing to a misapprehension, requested him to pay back the money to Lieutenant A. This circumstance was the vital point of the story, and by suppressing it the patient reduced himself to a state of the most hopeless muddle and for some time prevented me from getting any idea of the meaning of it all.

this stage in the analysis he brought out some new information, to the effect that the landlord of the inn at the little place where the post office was had had a pretty daughter. She had been decidedly encouraging to the smart young officer, so that he had thought of returning there after the manoeuvres were over and of trying his luck with her. Now, however, she had a rival in the shape of the young lady at the post office. Like his father in the tale of his marriage, he could afford now to hesitate upon which of the two he should bestow his favours when he had finished his military service. We can see at once that his singular indecision whether he should travel to Vienna or go back to the place where the post office was, and the constant temptation he felt to turn back while he was on the journey (see p. 31), were not so senseless as they seemed to us at first. To his conscious mind, the attraction exercised upon him by Z——, the place where the post office was, was explained by the necessity for seeing Lieutenant A. and fulfilling the vow with his assistance. But in reality what was attracting him was the young lady at the post office, and the lieutenant was merely a good substitute for her, since he lived at the same place and had himself been in charge of the military postal service. And when subsequently he heard that it was not Lieutenant A. but another officer, B., who had been on duty at the post office that day, he drew him into his combination as well; and he was then able to reproduce in his deliria[41] in connection with the two officers the hesitation he felt between the two girls who were so kindly disposed towards him.[42]

In elucidating the effects produced by the captain's rat story we must follow the course of the analysis more closely.

[41] [See below, p. 78.]

[42] (*Additional Note*, 1923).—My patient did his very best to throw confusion over the little episode of the repayment of the charges for his pince-nez, so that perhaps my own account of it may also have failed to clear it up entirely. I therefore reproduce here a little map (Fig. 1), by means of which Mr. and Mrs. Strachey have endeavoured to make the situation at the end of the manœuvres plainer. My translators have justly observed that the patient's behaviour remains unintelligible so long as a further cir-

The patient began by producing an enormous mass of associative material, which at first, however, threw no light upon the circumstances in which the formation of his obsession had taken place. The idea of the punishment carried out by means of rats had acted as a stimulus to a number of his instincts and had called up a whole quantity of recollections; so that, in the short interval between the captain's story and his request to him to pay back the money, rats had acquired a series of symbolical meanings, to which, during the period which followed, fresh ones were continually being added. I must confess that I can only give a very incomplete account of the whole business. What the rat punishment stirred up more than anything else was his *anal erotism*, which had played an important part in his childhood and had been kept in activity for many years by a constant irritation

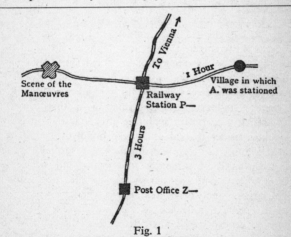

Fig. 1

cumstance is not expressly stated, namely, that Lieutenant A. had formerly lived at the place Z—— where the post office was situated and had been in charge of the military post office there, but that during the last few days he had handed over this billet to Lieutenant B. and had been transferred to another village. The "cruel" captain had been in ignorance of this transfer, and this was the explanation of his mistake in supposing that the charges had to be paid back to Lieutenant A.

due to worms. In this way rats came to have the meaning of *"money."*[43] The patient gave an indication of this connection by reacting to the word *"Ratten"* ["rats"] with the association *"Raten"* ["instalments"]. In his obsessional deliria he had coined himself a regular rat currency. When, for instance, in reply to a question, I told him the amount of my fee for an hour's treatment, he said to himself (as I learned six months later), "So many florins, so many rats." Little by little he translated into this language the whole complex of money interests which centred round his father's legacy to him; that is to say, all his ideas connected with that subject were, by way of the verbal bridge *"Raten—Ratten,"* carried over into his obsessional life and became subjected to his unconscious. Moreover, the captain's request to him to pay back the charges due upon the packet served to strengthen the money significance of rats, by way of another verbal bridge *"Spiel-ratte,"* which led back to his father's gambling debt.

But the patient was also familiar with the fact that rats are carriers of dangerous infectious diseases; he could therefore employ them as symbols of his dread (justifiable enough in the army) of *syphilitic infection.* This dread concealed all sorts of doubts as to the kind of life his father had led during his term of military service. Again, in another sense, the *penis* itself is a carrier of syphilitic infection; and in this way he could consider the rat as a male organ of sex. It had a further title to be so regarded; for a penis (especially a child's penis) can easily be compared to a *worm,* and the captain's story had been about rats burrowing in some one's anus, just as the large round-worms had in his when he was a child. Thus the penis significance of rats was based, once more, upon anal erotism. And apart from this, the rat is a dirty animal, feeding upon excrement and living in sewers.[44] It is

---

[43] See "Character and Anal Erotism," *Character and Culture,* Collier Books edition BS 193V.

[44] If the reader feels tempted to shake his head at the possibility of such leaps of imagination in the neurotic mind, I may remind him that artists have sometimes indulged in similar freaks of fancy. Such, for instance, are Le Poitevin's *Diableries érotiques.*

perhaps unnecessary to point out how great an extension of the rat delirium became possible owing to this new meaning. For instance, "So many rats, so many florins," could serve as an excellent characterization of a certain female profession which he particularly detested. On the other hand, it is certainly not a matter of indifference that the substitution of a penis for a rat in the captain's story resulted in a situation of intercourse *per anum,* which could not fail to be especially revolting to him when brought into connection with his father and the woman he loved. And when we consider that the same situation was reproduced in the compulsive threat which had formed in his mind after the captain had made his request, we shall be forcibly reminded of certain curses in use among the Southern Slavs.[45] Moreover, all of this material, and more besides, was woven into the fabric of the rat discussions behind the screen-association *"heiraten"* ["to marry"].

The story of the rat punishment, as was shown by the patient's own account of the matter and by his facial expression as he repeated the story to me, had fanned into a flame all of his prematurely suppressed impulses of cruelty, egoistic and sexual alike. Yet, in spite of all this wealth of material, no light was thrown upon the meaning of his obsessional idea until one day the Rat-Wife in Ibsen's *Little Eyolf* came up in the analysis, and it became impossible to escape the inference that in many of the shapes assumed by his obsessional deliria rats had another meaning still—namely, that of *children.*[46] Inquiry into the origin of this new meaning at once brought me up against some of the earliest and most important roots. Once when the patient was visiting his father's grave he had

[45] The exact terms of these curses will be found in the periodical *Anthropophyteia,* edited by F. S. Krauss.

[46] Ibsen's Rat-Wife must certainly be derived from the legendary Pied Piper of Hamelin, who first enticed away the rats into the water, and then, by the same means, lured the children out of the town, never to return. So too, Little Eyolf threw himself into the water under the spell of the Rat-Wife. In legends generally the rat appears not so much as a disgusting creature but as something uncanny—as a chthonic animal, one might almost say; and it is used to represent the souls of the dead.

seen a big beast, which he had taken to be a rat, gliding along over the grave.[47] He assumed that it had actually come out of his father's grave, and had just been having a meal off his corpse. The notion of a rat is inseparably bound up with the fact that it has sharp teeth with which it gnaws and bites.[48] But rats cannot be sharp-toothed, greedy and dirty with impunity: they are cruelly persecuted and mercilessly put to death by man, as the patient had often observed with horror. He had often pitied the poor creatures. But he himself had been just such a nasty, dirty little wretch, who was apt to bite people when he was in a rage, and had been fearfully punished for doing so (see p. 63). He could truly be said to find "a living likeness of himself" in the rat.[49] It was almost as though Fate, when the captain told him his story, had been putting him through an association test: she had called out a "complex stimulus-word," and he had reacted to it with his obsessional idea.

According, then, to his earliest and most momentous experiences, rats were children. And at this point he brought out a piece of information which he had kept away from its context long enough, but which now fully explained the interest

[47] It was no doubt a weasel, of which there are great numbers in the Zentralfriedhof [the principal cemetery] in Vienna.

[48] Compare the words of Mephistopheles [when he wishes to make his way through a door that is guarded by a magic pentagram]:

> "Doch dieser Schwelle Zauber zu zerspalten
> Bedarf ich eines Rattenzahns.
>
> Noch einen Biss, so ist's geschehn!"

["But to break through the magic of this threshold
I need a rat's tooth. (*He conjures up a rat.*)

Another bite, and it is done!"

GOETHE, *Faust*, Part I.]

[49]
> "Er sieht in der geschwollnen Ratte
> Sein ganz natürlich Ebenbild."

["For in the bloated rat he sees
A living likeness of himself."

Faust, Part I., Scene in Auerbach's Cellar.]

he was bound to feel in children. The lady, whose admirer he had been for so many years, but whom he had nevertheless not been able to make up his mind to marry, was condemned to childlessness by reason of a gynaecological operation which had involved the removal of both ovaries. This indeed—for he was extraordinarily fond of children—had been the chief reason for his hesitation.

It was only then that it became possible to understand the inexplicable process by which his obsessional idea had been formed. With the assistance of our knowledge of infantile sexual theories and of symbolism (as learnt from the interpretation of dreams) the whole thing could be translated and given a meaning. When, during the afternoon halt (upon which he had lost his pince-nez), the captain had told him about the rat punishment, the patient had only been struck at first by the combined cruelty and lasciviousness of the situation depicted. But immediately afterwards a connection had been set up with the scene from his childhood in which he himself had bitten some one. The captain—a man who could defend such punishments—had been substituted by him for his father, and had thus drawn down upon himself a part of the reviving exasperation which had burst out, upon the original occasion, against his cruel father. The idea which came into his consciousness for a moment, to the effect that something of the sort might happen to some one he was fond of, is probably to be translated into a wish such as "You ought to have the same thing done to you!" aimed at the teller of the story, but through him at his father. A day and a half later,[50] when the captain had handed him the packet upon which the charges were due and had requested him to pay back the 3.80 crowns to Lieutenant A., he had already been aware that his "cruel

[50] Not that evening, as he first told me. It is quite impossible that that pince-nez he had ordered can have arrived the same day. The patient shortened the interval of time retrospectively, because it was the period during which the decisive mental connections had been set up, and during which the repressed episode had taken place—the episode of his interview with the officer who told him of the friendly conduct of the young lady at the post office.

superior" was making a mistake, and that the only person he owed anything to was the young lady at the post office. It might easily, therefore, have occurred to him to think of some derisive reply, such as, "Will I, though?" or "Pay your grandmother!" or "Yes! You bet I'll pay him back the money!"—answers which would have been subject to no compulsive force. But instead, out of the stirrings of his father-complex and out of his memory of the scene from his childhood, there formed in his mind some such answer as: "Yes! I'll pay back the money to A. when my father or the lady have children!" or "As sure as my father or the lady can have children, I'll pay him back the money!" In short, a derisive asseveration coupled with an absurd condition which could never be fulfilled.[51]

But now the crime had been committed; he had insulted the two persons who were dearest to him—his father and his lady. The deed had called for punishment, and the penalty had consisted in his binding himself by a vow which it was impossible for him to fulfil and which entailed literal obedience to his superior's ill-founded request. The vow ran as follows: *"Now you must really pay back the money to A."* In his convulsive obedience he had repressed his better knowledge that the captain's request had been based upon erroneous premises: "Yes, you must pay back the money to A., as your father's surrogate has required. Your father cannot be mistaken." So too the king cannot be mistaken; if he addresses one of his subjects by a title which is not his, the subject bears that title ever afterwards.

Only vague intelligence of these events reached the patient's consciousness. But his revolt against the captain's order and the sudden transformation of that revolt into its opposite were both represented there. First had come the idea that he was *not* to pay back the money, or it (that is, the rat punishment) would happen; and then had come the transformation of this

---

[51] Thus absurdity signifies derision in the language of obsessional thought, just as it does in dreams. See Freud, *Die Traumdeutung* (1900), Seventh Edition, p. 295.

idea into a vow to the opposite effect, as a punishment for his revolt.

Let us, further, picture to ourselves the general conditions under which the formation of the patient's great obsessional idea occurred. His libido had been increased by a long period of abstinence coupled with the friendly welcome which a young officer can always reckon upon receiving when he goes among women. Moreover, at the time when he had started for the manœuvres, there had been a certain coolness between himself and his lady. This intensification of his libido had inclined him to a renewal of his ancient struggle against his father's authority, and he had dared to think of having sexual intercourse with other women. His loyalty to his father's memory had grown weaker, his doubts as to his lady's merits had increased; and in that frame of mind he let himself be dragged into insulting the two of them, and had then punished himself for it. In doing so he had copied an old model. And when at the end of the manœuvres he had hesitated so long whether he should travel to Vienna or whether he should stop and fulfil his vow, he had represented in a single picture the two conflicts by which he had from the very first been torn— whether or no he should remain obedient to his father and whether or no he should remain faithful to his beloved.[52]

I may add a word upon *the interpretation of the "sanction"* which, it will be remembered, was to the effect that "otherwise the rat punishment will be carried out on both of them." It was based upon the influence of two infantile sexual theories, which I have discussed elsewhere.[53] The first of these theories is that babies come out of the anus; and the second,

---

[52] It is perhaps not uninteresting to observe that once again obedience to his father coincided with abandoning the lady. If he had stopped and paid back the money to A., he would have made atonement to his father, and at the same time he would have deserted his lady in favour of some one else more attractive. In this conflict the lady had been victorious—with the assistance, to be sure, of the patient's own normal good sense.

[53] "On the Sexual Theories of Children," *The Sexual Enlightenment of Children*, Collier Books edition BS 190V.

which follows logically from the first, is that men can have babies just as well as women. According to the technical rules for interpreting dreams, the notion of coming out of the rectum can be represented by the opposite notion of creeping into the rectum (as in the rat punishment), and *vice versa*.

We should not be justified in expecting such severe obsessional ideas as were present in this case to be cleared up in any simpler manner or by any other means. When we reached the solution that has been described above, the patient's rat delirium disappeared.

II

Theoretical

(a) SOME GENERAL CHARACTERISTICS OF OBSESSIONAL FORMATIONS[1]

IN THE YEAR 1896 I defined obsessional or compulsive ideas as "reproaches re-emerging in a transmuted form from under repression—reproaches which invariably relate to a sexual deed performed with pleasure in childhood."[2] This definition now seems to me to be open to criticism upon formal grounds, though its component elements are unobjectionable. It was aiming too much at unification, and took as its model the practice of obsessional neurotics themselves, when, with their characteristic liking for indeterminateness, they heap together under the name of "obsessional ideas" the most heterogene-

---

[1] Several of the points dealt with in this and the following section have already been mentioned in the literature of obsessional neuroses, as may be gathered from Löwenfeld's exhaustive study, *Die psychischen Zwangserscheinungen*, 1904, which is the standard work upon this form of disease.

[2] "Further Remarks on the Defence Neuro-Psychoses," *Early Psychoanalytic Writings*, Collier Books edition BS 188V.

ous psychological formations.[3] In point of fact, it would be more correct to speak of "obsessive thinking," and to make it clear that obsessional structures can correspond to every sort of mental act. They can be distinctively classed as wishes, temptations, impulses, reflections, doubts, commands, or prohibitions. Patients endeavour in general to tone down such distinctions and to regard what remains of these mental acts after they have been deprived of their affective index simply as "obsessional ideas." Our present patient gave an example of this type of behaviour in one of his first sittings, when he attempted to reduce a wish to the level of a mere "connection of thought" (see p. 38).

It must be confessed, moreover, that even the phenomenology of obsessional thinking has not yet had sufficient attention paid to it. During the secondary defensive struggle, which the patient carries on against the "obsessional ideas" that have forced their way into his consciousness, psychological formations make their appearance which deserve to be given a special name. (Such, for example, were the sequences of thoughts that occupied our patient's mind on his journey back from the manœuvres.) They are not purely reasonable considerations which arise in opposition to the obsessional thoughts, but, as it were, hybrids between the two species of thinking; they accept certain of the premises of the obsession they are combating, and thus, while using the weapons of reason, are established upon a basis of pathological thought. I think such formations as these deserve to be given the name of *"deliria."* To make the distinction clear, I will give an instance, which should be inserted into its proper

---

[3] This fault in my definition is to some extent corrected in the paper itself. The following passage will be found in *ibid.*, p. 158: "The reanimated memories and the self-reproach which is built up on them, however, never appear in consciousness unchanged. The obsessional idea and the obsessive affects which appear in consciousness and take the place of the pathogenic memory in conscious life are *compromise-formations* between the repressed and the repressing ideas." In the definition, that is to say, especial stress is to be laid upon the words "in a transmuted form."

context in the patient's case history. I have already described the crazy conduct to which he gave way at one time when he was preparing for an examination—how, after working till far into the night, he used to go and open the front door to his father's ghost, and then look at his genitals in the looking-glass (see p. 61). He tried to bring himself to his senses by asking himself what his father would say to it all if he were really still alive. But the argument had no effect so long as it was put forward in this rational shape. The spectre was not laid until he had transformed the same idea into a "delirious" threat to the effect that if he ever went through this nonsense again some evil would befall his father in the next world.

The distinction between a primary and a secondary defensive struggle is no doubt well founded, but we find its value unexpectedly diminished when we discover that *the patients themselves do not know the wording of their own obsessional ideas*. This may sound paradoxical, but it is perfectly good sense. During the progress of a psychoanalysis it is not only the patient who plucks up courage, but his disease as well; it grows bold enough to speak more plainly than before. To drop the metaphor, what happens is that the patient, who has hitherto turned his eyes away in terror from his own pathological productions, begins to attend to them and obtains a clearer and more detailed view of them.[4]

There are, besides, two particular ways in which a more precise knowledge of obsessional formations can be gained. In the first place, experience shows that an obsessional command (or whatever it may be), which in waking life is known only in a truncated and distorted form, like a mutilated telegraph message, may have its actual text brought to light in a dream. Such texts appear in dreams in the shape of speeches, and are thus an exception to the rule that speeches in dreams are derived from speeches in real life.[5] Secondly, in the course

---

[4] Many patients carry the diversion of their attention to such lengths that they are totally unable to give the content of an obsessional idea or to describe an obsessional act though they have performed it over and over again.

[5] Cf. Freud, *Die Traumdeutung* (1900), Seventh Edition, p. 283.

of the analytic examination of a case history, one becomes convinced that if a number of obsessions succeed one another they are often—even though their wording is not identical—ultimately one and the same. The obsession may have been successfully shaken off on its first appearance, but it comes back a second time in a distorted form and without being recognized, and may then perhaps be able to hold its own in the defensive struggle more effectively, precisely because of its distortion. But the original form is the correct one, and it often displays its meaning quite openly. When we have at great pains elucidated an unintelligible obsessional idea, it often happens that the patient informs us that just such a notion, wish, or temptation as the one we have constructed did in fact make its appearance on one occasion before the obsessional idea had arisen, but that it did not persist. It would unfortunately involve us in too lengthy a digression if we were to give instances of this from the history of our present patient.

What is officially described as an "obsessional idea" exhibits, therefore, in its distortion from its original wording, traces of the primary defensive struggle. Its distortion enables it to persist, since conscious thought is thus compelled to misapprehend it, just as though it were a dream; for dreams also are a product of compromise and distortion, and are also misapprehended by waking thought.

This misapprehension on the part of consciousness can be seen at work not only in reference to the obsessional ideas themselves, but also in reference to the products of the secondary defensive struggle, such, for instance, as the protective formulas. I can produce two good examples of this. Our patient used to employ as a defensive formula a rapidly pronounced *"aber"* ["but"] accompanied by a gesture of repudiation. He told me on one occasion that this formula had become altered recently; he now no longer said *"áber"* but *"abér."* When he was asked to give the reason for this new departure, he declared that the mute *"e"* of the second syllable gave him no sense of security against the intrusion, which he so much dreaded, of some foreign and contradictory ele-

ment, and that he had therefore decided to accent the *"e."*
This explanation (an excellent sample of the obsessional
neurotic style) was, however, clearly inadequate; the most
that it could claim to be was a rationalization. The truth was
that *"abér"* was an approximation towards the similar-sound-
ing *"Abwéhr"* ["defence"], a term which he had learnt in the
course of our theoretical discussions of psychoanalysis. He
had thus put the treatment to an illegitimate and "delirious"
use in order to strengthen a defensive formula. Another time
he told me about his principal magic word, which was an
apotropaic against every evil; he had put it together out of
the initial letters of the most powerfully beneficent of his
prayers and had clapped on an "amen" at the end of it. I
cannot reproduce the word itself, for reasons which will
become apparent immediately. For, when he told it to me,
I could not help noticing that the word was in fact an ana-
gram upon the name of his lady. Her name contained an "s,"
and this he had put last, that is, immediately before the
"amen" at the end. We may say, therefore, that by this process he had brought his *"Samen"* ["semen"] into contact with
the woman he loved; in imagination, that is to say, he had
masturbated with her. He himself, however, had never noticed
this very obvious connection; his defensive forces had allowed
themselves to be fooled by the repressed ones. This is also a
good example of the rule that in time the thing which is meant
to be warded off invariably finds its way into the very means
which is being used for warding it off.

I have already asserted that obsessional thoughts have
undergone a distortion similar to that undergone by dream
thoughts before they become the manifest content of a dream.
The technique of this distortion may therefore be of interest
to us, and there should be nothing to prevent our exhibiting
its various modes by means of a series of obsessions which
have been translated and made clear. But here again the
conditions governing the publication of this case make it
impossible for me to give more than a few specimens. Not
all of the patient's obsessions were so complicated in their
structure and so difficult to solve as the great rat idea. In

some of the others a very simple technique was employed—namely, that of distortion by omission or ellipsis. This technique is pre-eminently applicable to jokes, but in our present case it also did useful work as a means of protecting things from being understood.

For instance, one of the patient's oldest and favourite obsessions (which corresponded to an admonition or warning) ran as follows: *"If I marry the lady, some misfortune will befall my father* (in the next world)." If we insert the intermediate steps, which had been skipped but were known to us from the analysis, we get the following train of thought: "If my father were alive, he would be as furious over my design of marrying the lady as he was in the scene in my childhood; so that I should fly into a rage with him once more and wish him every possible evil; and thanks to the omnipotence of my wishes[6] these evils would be bound to come upon him."

Here is another instance in which a solution can be reached by filling out an ellipsis. It is once more in the nature of a warning or an ascetic prohibition. The patient had a charming little niece of whom he was very fond. One day this idea came into his head: *"If you indulge in a coitus, something will happen to Ella"* (*i.e.* she will die). When the omissions have been made good, we have: "Everytime you copulate, even with a stranger, you will not be able to avoid the reflection that in your married life sexual intercourse can never bring you a child (on account of the lady's sterility). This will grieve you so much that you will become envious of your sister on account of little Ella, and you will grudge her the child. These envious impulses will inevitably lead to the child's death."[7]

---

[6] This omnipotence is discussed further on.

[7] An example from another of my works, *Der Witz* (1905), Fourth Edition, p. 63, will recall to the reader the manner in which this elliptical technique is employed in making jokes: "There is a witty and pugnacious journalist in Vienna, whose biting invective has repeatedly led to his being physically maltreated by the subjects of his attacks. On one occasion, when a fresh misdeed on

The technique of distortion by ellipsis seems to be typical of obsessional neuroses; I have come across it in the obsessional thoughts of other patients as well. One example, a particularly transparent one, is of especial interest on account of a certain structural similarity with the rat idea. It was a case of doubting, and occurred in a lady who suffered principally from obsessional acts. This lady was going for a walk with her husband in Nuremburg, and made him take her into a shop, where she purchased various objects for her child and amongst them a comb. Her husband, finding that the shopping was too long a business for his taste, said that he had noticed some coins in an old curiosity shop on the way which he was anxious to secure, adding that after he had made his purchase he would come and fetch her in the shop in which they at present were. But he stayed away, as she thought, far too long. When he came back she accordingly asked him where he had been. "Why," he replied, "at the old curiosity shop I told you about." At the same instant she was seized by a tormenting doubt whether she had not as a matter of fact always possessed the comb which she had just bought for her child. She was naturally quite unable to discover the simple mental link that was involved. There is nothing for it but to regard the doubt as having become displaced, and to reconstruct the complete chain of unconscious thoughts as follows: "If it is true that you were only at the old curiosity shop, if I am really to believe that, then I may just as well believe that this comb that I bought a moment ago has been in my possession for years." Here, therefore, the lady was drawing a derisive and ironical parallel, just as when our patient thought: "Oh yes, as sure as those two" (his father and the lady) "will have children, I shall pay back the money

---

the part of one of his habitual opponents was being discussed, somebody exclaimed: 'If X. hears of this, he'll get his ears boxed again.' . . . The apparent absurdity of this remark disappears if between the two clauses we insert the words: 'he'll write such a scathing article upon the man, that, etc.' "—This elliptical joke, we may note, is similar in its content, as well as in its form, to the first example quoted in the text.

to A." In the lady's case the doubt was dependent upon her unconscious jealousy, which led her to suppose that her husband had spent the interval of his absence in paying a visit of gallantry.

I shall not in the present paper attempt any discussion of the psychological significance of obsessional thinking. Such a discussion would be of extraordinary value in its results, and would do more to clarify our ideas upon the nature of the conscious and the unconscious than any study of hysteria or the phenomena of hypnosis. It would be a most desirable thing if the philosophers and psychologists who develop brilliant theoretical views on the unconscious upon a basis of hearsay knowledge or from their own conventional definitions would first submit to the convincing impressions which may be gained from a first-hand study of the phenomena of obsessional thinking. We might almost go to the length of requiring it of them, if the task were not so far more laborious than the methods of work to which they are accustomed. I will only add here that in obsessional neuroses the unconscious mental processes occasionally break through into consciousness in their pure and undistorted form, that such incursions may take place at every possible stage of the unconscious process of thought, and that at the moment of the incursion the obsessional ideas can, for the most part, be recognized as formations of very long standing. This accounts for the striking circumstance that, when the analyst tries, with the patient's help, to discover the date of the first occurrence of an obsessional idea, the patient is obliged to place it further and further back as the analysis proceeds, and is constantly finding fresh "first" occasions for the appearance of the obsession.

(b) SOME PSYCHOLOGICAL PECULIARITIES OF OBSESSIONAL NEUROTICS: THEIR ATTITUDE TOWARDS REALITY, SUPERSTITION AND DEATH

In this section I intend to deal with a few mental characteristics of obsessional neurotics which, though they do not seem important in themselves, nevertheless lie upon the road to a comprehension of more important things. They were strongly marked in our present patient; but I know that they are not attributable to his individual character, but to his disorder, and that they are to be met with quite typically in other obsessional patients.

Our patient was to a high degree superstitious, and this although he was a highly educated and enlightened man of considerable acumen, and although he was able at times to assure me that he did not believe a word of all this rubbish. Thus he was at once superstitious and not superstitious; and there was a clear distinction between his attitude and the superstition of uneducated people who feel themselves at one with their belief. He seemed to understand that his superstitition was dependent upon his obsessional thinking, although at times he gave way to it completely. The meaning of this inconsistent and vacillating behaviour can be most easily grasped if it is regarded in the light of a hypothesis which I shall now proceed to mention. I did not hesitate to assume that the truth was not that the patient still had an open mind upon this subject, but that he had two separate and contradictory convictions upon it. His oscillation between these two views quite obviously depended upon his momentary attitude towards his obsessional disorder. As soon as he had got the better of one of these obsessions, he used to smile in a superior way at his own credulity, and no events occurred that were calculated to shake his firmness; but the moment he came under the sway of another obsession which had not been cleared up—or, what amounts to the same thing, of a resistance—the strangest coincidences would happen to support him in his credulous belief.

His superstitition was nevertheless that of an educated man, and he avoided such vulgar prejudices as being afraid of Friday or of the number thirteen, and so on. But he believed in premonitions and in prophetic dreams; he would constantly meet the very person of whom, for some inexplicable reason, he had just been thinking; or he would receive a letter from some one who had suddenly come into his mind after being forgotten for many years. At the same time he was honest enough—or rather, he was loyal enough to his official conviction—not to have forgotten instances in which the strangest forebodings had come to nothing. On one occasion, for instance, when he went away for his summer holidays, he had felt morally certain that he would never return to Vienna alive. He also admitted that the great majority of his premonitions related to things which had no special personal importance to him, and that, when he met an acquaintance of whom, until a few moments previously, he had not thought for a very long time, nothing further took place between himself and the miraculous apparition. And he naturally could not deny that all the important events of his life had occurred without his having had any premonition of them, and that, for instance, his father's death had taken him entirely by surprise. But arguments such as these had no effect upon the discrepancy in his convictions. They merely served to prove the obsessional nature of his superstitions, and that could already be inferred from the way in which they came and went with the increase and decrease of his resistance.

I was not in a position, of course, to give a rational explanation of all the miraculous stories of his remoter past. But as regards the similar things that happened during the time of his treatment, I was able to prove to him that he himself invariably had a hand in the manufacture of these miracles, and I was able to point out to him the methods that he employed. He worked by means of indirect vision and reading, forgetting, and, above all, errors of memory. In the end he used himself to help me in discovering the little sleight-of-hand tricks by which these wonders were performed. I may mention one interesting infantile root of his belief that forebodings and premonitions came true. It was brought to light by his recollection that very often, when a date was being fixed for something, his mother used to say: "I sha'n't be able to on such-and-such a day. I shall have to stop in bed then." And in fact when the day in question arrived she had invariably stayed in bed!

There can be no doubt that the patient felt a need for

finding experiences of this kind to act as props for his superstition, and that it was for that reason that he occupied himself so much with the inexplicable coincidences of everyday
life with which we are all familiar, and helped out their short-
comings with unconscious activity of his own. I have come
across a similar need in many other obsessional patients and
have suspected its presence in many more besides. It seems
to me easily explicable in view of the psychological characteristics of the obsessional neurosis. In this disorder, as I have
already explained (see p. 54), repression is effected not by
means of amnesia but by a severance of causal connections
brought about by a withdrawal of affect. These repressed connections appear to persist in some kind of shadowy form
(which I have elsewhere compared to an entoptic perception),[8] and they are thus transferred, by a process of projection, into the external world, where they bear witness to what
has been effaced from consciousness.

Another mental need, which is also shared by obsessional
neurotics and which is in some respects related to the one
just mentioned, is the need for *uncertainty* in their life, or
for *doubt*. An inquiry into this characteristic leads deep into
the investigation of instinct. The creation of uncertainty is
one of the methods employed by the neurosis for drawing the
patient away from *reality* and isolating him from the world
—which is among the objects of every psychoneurotic disorder. Again, it is only too obvious what efforts are made by
the patients themselves in order to be able to avoid certainty
and remain in doubt. Some of them, indeed, give a vivid
expression to this tendency in a dislike of—clocks and
watches (for they at least make the time of day certain), and
in the unconscious artifices which they employ in order to
render these doubt-removing instruments innocuous. Our
present patient had developed a peculiar talent for avoiding
a knowledge of any facts which would have helped him in
deciding his conflict. Thus he was in ignorance upon those

8 *Zur Psychopathologie des Alltagslebens* (1905), Tenth Edition,
p. 287.

matters relating to his lady which were the most relevant to the question of his marriage: he was ostensibly unable to say who had operated upon her and whether the operation had been unilateral or bilateral. He had to be forced into remembering what he had forgotten and into finding out what he had overlooked.

The predilection felt by obsessional neurotics for uncertainty and doubt leads them to turn their thoughts by preference to those subjects upon which all mankind are uncertain and upon which our knowledge and judgements must necessarily remain open to doubt. The chief subjects of this kind are paternity, length of life, life after death, and memory—in the last of which we are all in the habit of believing, without having the slightest guarantee of its trustworthiness.[9]

In obsessional neuroses the uncertainty of memory is used to the fullest extent as a help in the formation of symptoms; and we shall learn directly the part played in the actual content of the patients' thoughts by the questions of length of life and life after death. But as an appropriate transition I will first consider one particular superstitious trait in our patient to which I have already alluded (see p. 82) and which will no doubt have puzzled more than one of my readers.

I refer to the *omnipotence* which he ascribed to his thoughts and feelings, and to his wishes, whether good or evil. It is, I must admit, decidedly tempting to declare that this idea was a delusion and that it over-steps the limits of

---

[9] As Lichtenberg says, "An astronomer knows whether the moon is inhabited or not with about as much certainty as he knows who was his father, but not with so much certainty as he knows who was his mother." A great advance was made in civilization when men decided to put their inferences upon a level with the testimony of their senses and to make the step from matriarchy to patriarchy.—The prehistoric figures which show a smaller person sitting upon the head of a larger one are representations of patrilineal descent; Athena had no mother, but sprang from the head of Zeus. A witness who testifies to something before a court of law is still called *"Zeuge"* [literally, "begetter"] in German, after the part played by the male in the act of procreation; so too in hieroglyphics a "witness" is represented pictorially by the male genitals.

obsessional neurosis. I have, however, come across the same conviction in another obsessional patient; and he was long ago restored to health and is leading a normal life. Indeed, all obsessional neurotics behave as though they shared this conviction. It will be our business to throw some light upon these patients' over-estimation of their powers. Assuming, without more ado, that this belief is a frank acknowledgement of a relic of the old megalomania of infancy, we will proceed to ask the patient for the grounds of his conviction. In reply, he adduces two experiences. When he returned for a second visit to the hydropathic establishment at which his disorder had been relieved for the first and only time, he asked to be given his old room, for its position had facilitated his relations with one of the nurses. He was told that the room was already taken and that it was occupied by an old professor. This piece of news considerably diminished his prospects of successful treatment, and he reacted to it with the unamiable thought: "I wish he may be struck dead for it!" A fortnight later he was woken up from his sleep by the disturbing idea of a corpse; and in the morning he heard that the professor had really had a stroke, and that he had been carried up into his room at about the time he himself had woken up. The second experience related to an unmarried woman, no longer young, though with a great desire to be loved, who had paid him a great deal of attention and had once asked him point-blank whether he could not love her. He had given her an evasive answer. A few days afterwards he heard that she had thrown herself out of window. He then began to reproach himself, and said to himself that it would have been in his power to save her life by giving her his love. In this way he became convinced of the omnipotence of his love and of his hatred. Without denying the omnipotence of love we may point out that both of these instances were concerned with death, and we may adopt the obvious explanation that, like other obsessional neurotics, our patient was compelled to overestimate the effects of his hostile feelings upon the external world, because a large part of their internal, mental effects escaped his conscious knowledge. His love—or rather his hatred—was in truth over-powering; it was precisely they that created the obsessional thoughts, of which he could not understand the origin and against which he strove in vain to defend himself.[10]

Our patient had a quite peculiar attitude towards the question of death. He showed the deepest sympathy whenever any one died, and religiously attended the funeral; so that among his brothers and sisters he earned the nickname of "bird of ill omen."[11] In his imagination, too, he was constantly making away with people so as to show his heartfelt sympathy for their bereaved relatives. The death of an elder sister, which took place when he was between three and four years old, played a great part in his phantasies, and was brought into intimate connection with his childish misdemeanours during the same period. We know, moreover, at what an early age thoughts about his father's death had occupied his mind, and we may regard his illness itself as a reaction to that event, for which he had felt an obsessional wish fifteen years earlier. The strange extension of his obsessional fears to the "next world" was nothing else than a compensation for these death-wishes which he had felt against his father. It was introduced eighteen months after his father had died, at a time when there had been a revival of his sorrow at the loss, and it was designed—in defiance of reality, and in deference to the wish which had previously been showing itself in phantasies of every kind—to undo the fact of his father's death. We have had occasion in several places (see pp. 79, 82) to translate the phrase "in the next world" by the words "if my father were still alive."

But the behaviour of other obsessional neurotics does not differ greatly from that of our present patient, even though it has not been their fate to come face to face with the phe-

---

[10] (*Additional Note,* 1923.)—The omnipotence of thoughts, or, more accurately speaking, of wishes, has since been recognized as an essential element in the mental life of primitive people. (See *Totem und Tabu.*)

[11] [In the original *"Leichenvogel,"* literally "corpse-bird."—*Trans.*]

nomenon of death at such an early age. Their thoughts are unceasingly occupied with other people's length of life and possibility of death; their superstitious propensities have, to begin with, had no other content and have perhaps no other source whatever. But these neurotics need the help of the possibility of death chiefly in order that it may act as a solution of conflicts they have left unsolved. Their essential characteristic is that they are incapable of coming to a decision, especially in matters of love; they endeavour to postpone every decision, and, in their doubt which person they shall decide for or what measures they shall take against a person, they are obliged to choose as their model the old German courts of justice, in which the suits were usually brought to an end, before judgement had been given, by the death of the parties to the dispute. Thus in every conflict which enters their lives they are on the look out for the death of some one who is of importance to them, usually of some one they love—such as one of their parents, or a rival, or one of the objects of their love between which their inclinations are wavering. But at this point our discussion of the death-complex in obsessional neuroses touches upon the problem of the instinctual life of obsessional neurotics. And to this problem we must now turn.

(c) The Instinctual Life of Obsessional Neurotics, and the Origins of Compulsion and Doubt

If we wish to obtain a grasp of the psychical forces whose interplay built up this neurosis, we must turn back to what we have learnt from the patient on the subject of the exciting causes of his falling ill as a grown-up man and as a child. He fell ill when he was in his twenties on being faced with a temptation to marry another woman instead of the one whom he had loved so long; and he avoided a decision of this conflict by postponing all the necessary preliminary actions. The means for doing this was given him by his neurosis. His hesitation between the lady he loved and the other girl can be reduced to a conflict between his father's influence and his

love for his lady, or, in other words, to a conflicting choice
between his father and his sexual object, such as had already
subsisted (judging from his recollections and obsessional
ideas) in his remote childhood. All through his life, moreover,
he was unmistakably victim to a conflict between love and
hatred, in regard both to his lady and to his father. His
phantasies of revenge and such obsessional phenomena as his
obsession for understanding and his exploit with the stone
in the road bore witness to his discordant feelings; and they
were to a certain degree comprehensible and normal, for the
lady by her original refusal and subsequently by her coolness
had given him some excuse for hostility. But his relations with
his father were dominated by a similar discordance of feeling,
as we have seen from our translation of his obsessional
thoughts; and his father too must have given him an excuse
for hostility in his childhood, as indeed we have been able to
establish almost beyond question. His attitude towards the
lady—a compound of tenderness and hostility—came to a
great extent within the scope of his conscious knowledge; at
most he deceived himself over the degree and strength of his
negative feelings. But his hostility towards his father, on the
contrary, though he had once been acutely conscious of it,
had long since vanished from his ken, and it was only in the
teeth of the most violent resistance that it could be brought
back into his consciousness. We may regard the repression of
his infantile hatred of his father as the event which brought
his whole subsequent career under the dominion of the
neurosis.

The conflicts of feeling in our patient which we have here
enumerated separately were not independent of each other, but
were bound together in pairs. His hatred of his lady was inevitably coupled with his attachment to his father, and in-
versely his hatred of his father with his attachment to his
lady. But the two conflicts of feeling which result from this
simplification—namely, the opposition between his relation to
his father and to his lady, and the contradiction between his
love and his hatred within each of these relations—had no

connection whatever with each other, either in their content or in their origin. The first of these two conflicts corresponds to the normal vacillation between male and female which characterizes every one's choice of a love-object. It is first brought to the child's notice by the time-honoured question: "Which do you love most, Papa or Mamma?" and it accompanies him through his whole life, whatever may be the relative intensity of his feelings to the two sexes or whatever may be the sexual aim upon which he finally becomes fixed. But normally this opposition soon loses the character of a hard-and-fast contradiction, of an inexorable "either"—"or." Room is found for satisfying the unequal demands of both sides, although even in a normal person the higher estimation of one sex is always thrown into relief by a depreciation of the other.

The other conflict, that between love and hatred, strikes us more strangely. We know that incipient love is often perceived as hatred, and that love, if it is denied satisfaction, may easily be partly converted into hatred, and poets tell us that in the more tempestuous stages of love the two opposed feelings may subsist side by side for a while as though in rivalry with each other. But the chronic coexistence of love and hatred, both directed towards the same person and both of the highest degree of intensity, cannot fail to astonish us. We should have expected that the passionate love would long ago have conquered the hatred or been devoured by it. And in fact such a protracted survival of two opposites is only possible under quite peculiar psychological conditions and with the co-operation of the state of affairs in the unconscious. The love has not succeeded in extinguishing the hatred but only in driving it down into the unconscious; and in the unconscious the hatred, safe from the danger of being destroyed by the operations of consciousness, is able to persist and even to grow. In such circumstances the conscious love attains as a rule, by way of reaction, an especially high degree of intensity, so as to be strong enough for the perpetual task of keeping its opponent under repression. The necessary condition for the occurrence of such a strange state of affairs in a person's erotic life appears to be that at a very early age, somewhere in the pre-historic period of his infancy, the two opposites should have been split apart and one of them, usually the hatred, have been repressed.[12]

If we consider a number of analyses of obsessional neu-rotics we shall find it impossible to escape the impression that a relation between love and hatred such as we have found in our present patient is among the most frequent, the most marked, and probably, therefore, the most important char-acteristics of the obsessional neurosis. But however tempting it may be to bring the problem of the "choice of neurosis" into relation with the instinctual life, there are reasons enough for avoiding such a course. For we must remember that in every neurosis we come upon the same suppressed instincts behind the symptoms. After all, hatred, kept suppressed in the uncon-scious by love, plays a great part in the pathogenesis of hys-teria and paranoia. We know too little of the nature of love to be able to arrive at any definite conclusion here; and, in par-ticular, the relation between the *negative* factor[13] in love and the sadistic components of the libido remains completely obscure. What follows is therefore to be regarded as no more than a provisional explanation. We may suppose, then, that in the cases of unconscious hatred with which we are concerned the sadistic components of love have, from constitutional causes, been exceptionally strongly developed, and have con-sequently undergone a premature and all too thorough sup-pression, and that the neurotic phenomena we have observed arise on the one hand from conscious feelings of affection

[12] Compare the discussion on this point during one of the first sittings (p. 39).—(*Additional Note,* 1923.) Bleuler subsequently introduced the appropriate term "ambivalence" to describe this emotional constellation. See also a further development of this line of thought in my paper "The Predisposition to Obsessional Neu-rosis" (1913), *Sexuality and the Psychology of Love,* Collier Books edition BS 192V.

[13] Alcibiades says of Socrates in the *Symposium:* "Many a time have I wished that he were dead, and yet I know that I should be much more sorry than glad if he were to die: so that I am at my wits' end" [Jowett's Translation].

which have become exaggerated as a reaction, and on the other hand from sadism persisting in the unconscious in the form of hatred.

But in whatever way this remarkable relation of love and hatred is to be explained, its occurrence is established beyond any possibility of doubt by the observations made in the present case; and it is gratifying to find how easily we can now follow the puzzling processes of an obsessional neurosis by bringing them into relation with this one factor. If an intense love is opposed by an almost equally powerful hatred, and is at the same time inseparably bound up with it, the immediate consequence is certain to be a partial paralysis of the will and an incapacity for coming to a decision upon any of those actions for which love ought to provide the motive power. But this indecision will not confine itself for long to a single group of actions. For, in the first place, what actions of a lover are not brought into relation with his one principal motive? And secondly, a man's attitude in sexual things has the force of a model to which the rest of his reactions tend to conform. And thirdly, it is an inherent characteristic in the psychology of an obsessional neurotic to make the fullest possible use of the mechanism of *displacement*. So the paralysis of his powers of decision gradually extends itself over the entire field of the patient's behaviour.

And here we have the domination of *compulsion* and *doubt* such as we meet with in the mental life of obsessional neurotics. The doubt corresponds to the patient's internal perception of his own indecision, which, in consequence of the inhibition of his love by his hatred, takes possession of him in the face of every intended action. The doubt is in reality a doubt of his own love—which ought to be the most certain thing in his whole mind; and it becomes diffused over everything else, and is especially apt to become displaced on to what is most insignificant and trivial.[14] A man who doubts his

[14] Compare the use of "representation by a triviality" as a technique in making jokes. Freud, *Der Witz* (1905), Fourth Edition, p. 65.

own love may, or rather *must,* doubt every lesser thing.[15]

It is this same doubt that leads the patient to uncertainty about his protective measures, and to his continual repetition of them in order to banish that uncertainty; and it is this doubt, too, that eventually brings it about that the patient's protective acts themselves become as impossible to carry out as his original inhibited decision in connection with his love. At the beginning of my investigations I was led to assume another and more general origin for the uncertainty of obsessional neurotics and one which seemed to be nearer the normal. If, for instance, while I am writing a letter some one interrupts me with questions, I afterwards feel a quite justifiable uncertainty as to what I may not have written under the influence of the disturbance, and, to make sure, I am obliged to read the letter over after I have finished it. In the same way I might suppose that the uncertainty of obsessional neurotics, when they are praying, for instance, is due to unconscious phantasies constantly mingling with their prayers and disturbing them. This hypothesis is correct, but it may be easily reconciled with our earlier statement. It is true that the patient's uncertainty whether he has carried through a protective measure is due to the disturbing effect of unconscious phantasies; but the content of these phantasies is precisely the contrary impulse—which it was the very aim of the prayer to ward off. This became clearly evident in our patient on one occasion, for the disturbing element did not remain unconscious but made its appearance openly. The words he wanted to use in his prayer were, *"May God protect her,"* but a hostile *"not"* suddenly darted out of his unconscious and inserted itself into the sentence; and he understood that this was an attempt at a curse (see p. 51). If the "not" had remained mute, he would have found himself in a state of uncertainty, and would have kept on prolonging his prayers indefinitely.

[15] So in the love-verses addressed by Hamlet to Ophelia:
> "Doubt thou the stars are fire;
> Doubt that the sun doth move;
> Doubt truth to be a liar;
> But never doubt I love."

But since it became articulate he eventually gave up praying. Before doing so, however, he, like other obsessional patients, tried every kind of method for preventing the opposite feeling from insinuating itself. He shortened his prayers, for instance, or said them more rapidly. And similarly other patients will endeavour to *"isolate"* all such protective acts from other things. But none of these technical procedures are of any avail in the long run. If the impulse of love achieves any success by displacing itself on to some trivial act, the impulse of hostility will very soon follow it on to its new ground and once more proceed to undo all that it has done.

And when the obsessional patient lays his finger on the weak spot in the security of our mental life—on the untrustworthiness of our memory—the discovery enables him to extend his doubt over everything, even over actions which have already been performed and which have so far had no connection with the love-hatred complex, and over the entire past. I may recall the instance of the woman who had just bought a comb for her little daughter in a shop, and, becoming suspicious of her husband, began to doubt whether she had not as a matter of fact been in possession of the comb for a long time. Was not this woman saying point-blank: "If I can doubt your love" (and this was only a projection of her doubt of her own love for him), "then I can doubt this too, then I can doubt everything"—thus revealing to us the hidden meaning of neurotic doubt?

The *compulsion* on the other hand is an attempt at a compensation for the doubt and at a correction of the intolerable conditions of inhibition to which the doubt bears witness. If the patient, by the help of displacement, succeeds at last in bringing one of his inhibited intentions to a decision, then the intention *must* be carried out. It is true that this intention is not his original one, but the energy dammed up in the latter cannot let slip the opportunity of finding an outlet for its discharge in the substitutive act. Thus this energy makes itself felt now in commands and now in prohibitions, according as the affectionate impulse or the hostile one snatches control of the pathway leading to discharge. If it happens that a com-

pulsive command cannot be obeyed, the tension becomes intolerable and is perceived by the patient in the form of
extreme anxiety. But the pathway leading to a substitutive act,
even where the displacement has been on to a triviality, is so
hotly contested, that such an act can as a rule be carried out
only in the shape of a protective measure intimately associated
with the very impulse which it is designed to ward off.

Furthermore, by a sort of *regression*, preparatory acts become substituted for the final decision, thinking replaces acting, and, instead of the substitutive act, some thought
preliminary to it asserts itself with all the force of compulsion.
According as this regression from acting to thinking is more
or less marked, a case of obsessional neurosis will exhibit the
characteristics of obsessive thinking (that is, of obsessional
ideas) or of obsessive acting in the narrower sense of the
word. True obsessional acts such as these, however, are only
made possible because they constitute a kind of reconciliation,
in the shape of a compromise formation, between the two
antagonistic impulses. For obsessional acts tend to approxi-
mate more and more—and the longer the disorder lasts the
more evident does this become—to infantile sexual acts of an
onanistic character. Thus in this form of the neurosis acts of
love are carried out in spite of everything, but only by the aid
of a new kind of regression; for such acts no longer relate
to another person, the object of love and hatred, but are
auto-erotic acts such as occur in infancy.

The first kind of regression, that from acting to thinking, is
facilitated by another factor concerned in the production of
the neurosis. The histories of obsessional patients almost invariably reveal an early development and premature repression of the sexual instinct of looking and knowing (the
scoptophilic and epistemophilic instinct); and, as we know, a
part of the infantile sexual activity of our present patient was
governed by that instinct.[16]

We have already mentioned the important part played by

[16] The very high average of intellectual capacity among obsessional patients is probably also connected with this fact.

the sadistic instinctual components in the genesis of obsessional neuroses. Where the epistemophilic instinct is a preponderating feature in the constitution of an obsessional patient, brooding becomes the principal symptom of the neurosis. The thought process itself becomes sexualized, for the sexual pleasure which is normally attached to the content of thought becomes shifted on to the act of thinking itself, and the gratification derived from reaching the conclusion of a line of thought is experienced as a *sexual* gratification. In the various forms of obsessional neurosis in which the epistemophilic instinct plays a part, its relation to thought processes makes it particularly well adapted to attract the energy which is vainly endeavouring to make its way forward into action, and divert it into the sphere of thought, where there is a possibility of its obtaining pleasurable gratification of another sort. In this way, with the help of the epistemophilic instinct, the substitutive act may in its turn be replaced by preparatory acts of thought. But procrastination in action is soon replaced by dilatoriness in thought, and eventually the whole process, together with all its peculiarities, is transferred into the new sphere, just as in America an entire house will sometimes be moved from one site to another.

I may now venture, upon the basis of the preceding discussion, to determine the psychological characteristic, so long sought after, which lends to the products of an obsessional neurosis their "obsessive" or compulsive quality. A thought process is obsessive or compulsive when, in consequence of an inhibition (due to a conflict of opposing impulses) at the motor end of the psychical system, it is undertaken with an expenditure of energy which (as regards both quality and quantity) is normally reserved for actions alone; or, in other words, *an obsessive or compulsive thought is one whose function it is to represent an act regressively*. No one, I think, will question my assumption that processes of thought are ordinarily conducted (on grounds of economy) with smaller displacements of energy, probably at a higher level, than are acts intended to discharge an affect or to modify the external world.

The obsessive thought which has forced its way into consciousness with such excessive violence has next to be secured against the efforts made by conscious thought to resolve it. As we already know, this protection is afforded by the *distortion* which the obsessive thought has undergone before becoming conscious. But this is not the only means employed. In addition, each separate obsessional idea is almost invariably removed from the situation in which it originated and in which, in spite of its distortion, it would be most easily comprehensible. With this end in view, in the first place *an interval of time is inserted* between the pathogenic situation and the obsession that arises from it, so as to lead astray any conscious investigation of its causal connections; and in the second place the content of the obsession is taken out of its particular setting by being *generalized*. Our patient's "obsession for understanding" is an example of this (see p. 48). But perhaps a better one is afforded by another patient. This was a woman who prohibited herself from wearing any sort of personal adornment, though the exciting cause of the prohibition related only to one particular piece of jewellery: she had envied her mother the possession of it and had had hopes that one day she would inherit it. Finally, if we care to distinguish verbal distortion from distortion of content, there is yet another means by which the obsession is protected against conscious attempts at solution. And that is the choice of an indefinite or ambiguous wording. After being misunderstood, the wording may find its way into the patient's "deliria," and whatever further processes of development or substitution his obsession undergoes will then be based upon the misunderstanding and not upon the proper sense of the text. Observation will show, however, that the deliria constantly tend to form new connections with that part of the matter and wording of the obsession which is not present in consciousness.

I should like to go back once more to the instinctual life of obsessional neurotics and add one more remark upon it. It turned out that our patient, besides all his other characteristics, was a *renifleur* (or osphresiolagniac). By his own account, when he was a child he had recognized every one by their smell, like a dog; and even when he was grown up he was more susceptible to sensations of smell than most people.[17] I have met with the same characteristic in other neurotics, both in hysterical and in obsessional patients, and I have come to recognize that a tendency to osphresiolagnia, which has become extinct since childhood, may play a part in the genesis of neurosis.[18] And here I should like to raise the general question whether the atrophy of the sense of smell (which was an inevitable result of man's assumption of an erect posture) and the consequent organic repression of his osphresiolagnia may not have had a considerable share in the origin of his susceptibility to nervous disease. This would afford us some explanation of why, with the advance of civilization, it is precisely the sexual life that must fall a victim to repression. For we have long known the intimate connection in the animal organization between the sexual instinct and the function of the olfactory organ.

In bringing this paper to a close I may express a hope that, though my communication is incomplete in every sense, it may at least stimulate other workers to throw more light upon the obsessional neurosis by a deeper investigation of the subject. What is characteristic of this neurosis—what differentiates it from hysteria—is not, in my opinion, to be found in instinctual life but in psychological relations. I cannot take leave of my patient without putting on paper my impression that he had, as it were, disintegrated into three personalities: into one unconscious personality, that is to say, and into two preconscious ones between which his consciousness could oscillate. His unconscious comprised those of his impulses which had been suppressed at an early age and which might be described as passionate and evil impulses. In his normal state he was kind, cheerful, and sensible—an enlightened and superior kind of person, while in his third psychological organization he paid homage to superstition and asceticism.

[17] I may add that in his childhood he had been subject to strong coprophilic propensities. In this connection his anal erotism has already been noticed (see p. 69).

[18] For instance, in certain forms of fetishism.

Thus he was able to have two different creeds and two different outlooks upon life. This second preconscious personality comprised chiefly the reaction-formations against his repressed wishes, and it was easy to foresee that it would have swallowed up the normal personality if the illness had lasted much longer. I have at present an opportunity of studying a lady suffering severely from obsessional acts. She has become similarly disintegrated into an easy-going and lively personality and into an exceedingly gloomy and ascetic one. She puts forward the first of them as her official ego, while in fact she is dominated by the second. Both of these psychical organizations have access to her consciousness, but behind her ascetic personality may be discerned the unconscious part of her being—quite unknown to her and composed of ancient and long-repressed conative impulses.[19]

[19] (*Additional Note*, 1923.)—The patient's mental health was restored to him by the analysis which I have reported upon in these pages. Like so many other young men of value and promise, he perished in the Great War.

PSYCHOANALYTIC NOTES UPON AN AUTOBIOGRAPHICAL ACCOUNT OF A CASE OF PARANOIA (DEMENTIA PARANOIDES)[1] (1911)

THE ANALYTIC INVESTIGATION of paranoia presents difficulties of a peculiar nature to physicians who, like myself, are not attached to public institutions. We cannot accept patients suffering from this complaint, or, at all events, we cannot keep them for long, since we cannot offer treatment unless there is some prospect of therapeutic success. It is only in exceptional circumstances, therefore, that I succeed in getting more than a superficial view of the structure of paranoia—when, for instance, the diagnosis (which is not always an easy matter) is uncertain enough to justify an attempt at influencing the patient, or when, in spite of an assured diagnosis, I yield to the entreaties of the patient's relatives and undertake to treat him for a time. Apart from this, of course, I see plenty of cases of paranoia and of dementia praecox, and I learn as much about them as other psychiatrists do about their

---

[1] [First published in *Jahrbuch für psychoanalytische und psychopathologische Forschungen*, Bd. iii., 1911. Reprinted in Freud, *Sammlung kleiner Schriften*, iii., 1913.]

cases; but that is not enough, as a rule, to lead to any analytic conclusions.

The psychoanalytic investigation of paranoia would be altogether impossible if the patients themselves did not possess the peculiarity of betraying (in a distorted form, it is true) precisely those things which other neurotics keep hidden as a secret. Since paranoiacs cannot be compelled to overcome their internal resistances, and since in any case they only say what they choose to say, it follows that this is precisely a disorder in which a written report or a printed case history can take the place of personal acquaintance with the patient. For this reason I think it is legitimate to base analytic interpretations upon the case history of a patient suffering from paranoia (or, more precisely, from dementia paranoides) whom I have never seen, but who has written his own case history and brought it before the public in print.

I refer to Dr. jur. Daniel Paul Schreber, formerly Senatspräsident in Dresden,[2] whose book, *Denkwürdigkeiten eines Nervenkranken* [*Memoirs of a Neurotic*], was published in 1903, and, if I am not mistaken, aroused considerable interest among psychiatrists. It is possible that Dr. Schreber may still be living to-day and that he may have dissociated himself so far from the delusional system which he put forward in 1903 as to be pained by these notes upon his book. In so far, however, as he still retains his identity with his former personality, I can rely upon the arguments with which he himself—"a man of superior mental gifts and endowed with an unusual keenness alike of intellect and of observation"[3]—countered the efforts that were made to restrain him from publishing his memoirs: "I have been at no pains," he writes, "to close my eyes to the difficulties that would appear to lie in the path of publication, and in particular to the problem of paying due regard to the susceptibilities of certain persons still living. On the other hand, I am of opinion that

[2] [A Senatspräsident in an Oberlandesgericht is the Judge presiding over a Division of an Appeal Court.—*Trans.*]

[3] This piece of self-portraiture, which is very far from being unjustified, will be found on p. 35 of his book.

it might well be to the advantage both of science and of the recognition of religious truths if, during my lifetime, qualified authorities were enabled to undertake some examination of my body and to hold some inquiry into my personal experiences. To this consideration all feelings of a personal character must yield."[4] He declares in another passage that he has decided to keep to his intention of publishing the book, even if the consequence were to be that his physician, Geheimrat Dr. Flechsig of Leipsic, brought an action against him. He urges upon Dr. Flechsig, however, the same considerations that I am now urging upon him. "I trust," he says, "that even in the case of Geheimrat Prof. Dr. Flechsig any personal susceptibilities that he may feel will be outweighed by a scientific interest in the subject-matter of my memoirs" (p. 446).

Though all the passages from the *Denkwürdigkeiten* upon which my interpretations are based will be quoted verbatim in the following pages, I would ask my readers to make themselves acquainted with the book by reading it through at least once beforehand.

---

[4] Preface, p. iii. [All page references in this paper relate, unless the contrary is stated, to Schreber's *Denkwürdigkeiten.—Trans.*]

I

Case History

"I HAVE SUFFERED twice from nervous disorders," writes Dr. Schreber, "and each time as a result of mental overstrain. This was due on the first occasion to my standing as a candidate for election to the Reichstag while I was Landgerichtsdirektor[1] at Chemnitz, and on the second occasion to the very heavy burden of work that fell upon my shoulders when I entered on my new duties as Senatspräsident in the Oberlandesgericht in Dresden" (p. 34).

Dr. Schreber's first illness began in the autumn of 1884, and by the end of 1885 he had completely recovered. During this period he spent six months in Flechsig's clinic, and the latter, in a formal report which he drew up at a later date, described the disorder as an attack of severe hypochondria (p. 379). Dr. Schreber assures us that this illness ran its course "without the occurrence of any incidents bordering upon the sphere of the supernatural" (p. 35).

Neither the patient's own account, nor the reports of the physicians which are reprinted at the end of his book, tell us enough about his previous history or his personal circumstances. They do not even give the patient's age at the time of his illness, though the high judicial position which he had

[1] [Judge presiding over an inferior Court.—*Trans.*]

attained before his second illness establishes some sort of lower limit. We learn that Dr. Schreber had been married long before the time of his "hypochondria." "The gratitude of my wife," he writes, "was perhaps even more heartfelt; for she revered Professor Flechsig as the man who had restored her husband to her, and hence it was that for years she kept his portrait standing upon her writing-table" (p. 36). And in the same place: "After my recovery from my first illness I spent eight years with my wife—years, upon the whole, of great happiness, rich in outward honours, and only clouded from time to time by the oft-repeated disappointment of our hope that we might be blessed with children."

In June 1893 he was notified of his prospective appointment as Senatspräsident, and he took up his duties on the first of October of the same year. Between these two dates[2] he had some dreams, though it was not until later that he came to attach any importance to them. He dreamed two or three times that his old nervous disorder had come back; and this made him as miserable in the dream as the discovery that it was only a dream made him happy when he woke up. One morning, moreover, while he was in a state between sleeping and waking, the idea occurred to him "that after all it really must be very nice to be a woman submitting to the act of copulation" (p. 36). This idea was one which he would have rejected with the greatest indignation if he had been fully conscious.

The second illness set in at the end of October 1893 with a torturing bout of sleeplessness. This forced him to return to Prof. Flechsig's clinic, where, however, his condition grew rapidly worse. The further course of the illness is described in a report drawn up subsequently by the director of the Sonnenstein Sanatorium: "At the commencement of his residence there[3] he was chiefly troubled by hypochondriacal ideas, complained that he had softening of the brain, that he would

[2] And therefore before he could have been affected by the over-work caused by his new post, which he himself blames for his illness.

[3] In Prof. Flechsig's clinic at Leipsic.

soon be dead, etc. But ideas of persecution were already finding their way into the clinical picture, based upon sensorial illusions which, however, seemed only to appear sporadically at first, while simultaneously a high degree of hyperaesthesia was observable—great sensitiveness to light and noise. Later, the visual and auditory illusions became much more frequent, and, in conjunction with coenaesthesic disturbances, dominated the whole of his feeling and thought. He believed that he was dead and decomposing, that he was suffering from the plague; he asserted that his body was being handled in all kinds of revolting ways; and, as he himself declares to this day, he went through worse horrors than any one could have imagined, and all on behalf of a sacred cause. The patient was so much occupied with these pathological phenomena that he was inaccessible to any other impression and would sit perfectly rigid and motionless for hours (hallucinatory stupor). On the other hand, they tortured him to such a degree that he longed for death. He made repeated attempts at drowning himself in his bath, and asked to be given the 'cyanide of potassium that was intended for him.' His delusional ideas gradually assumed a mystical and religious character; he was in direct communication with God, he was the plaything of devils, he saw 'miraculous apparitions,' he heard 'holy music,' and in the end he even came to believe that he was living in another world" (p. 380).

It may be added that there were certain people by whom he thought he was being persecuted and injured, and upon whom he poured abuse. The most prominent of these was his former physician, Flechsig, whom he called a "soul-murderer"; and he used to call out over and over again: *"Little* Flechsig!" putting a sharp stress upon the first word (p. 383). He was moved from Leipsic, and, after a short interval spent in another institution, was brought in June 1894 to the Sonnenstein Sanatorium, near Pirna, where he remained until his disorder assumed its final shape. In the course of the next few years the clinical picture altered in a manner which can best be described in the words of Dr. Weber, the director of the sanatorium.

"I need not enter any further into the details of the course of the disease. I must, however, draw attention to the manner in which, as time went on, the paranoic clinical picture that we have before us to-day developed more and more clearly (one might almost say crystallized out) from the initial acute psychosis, which had directly involved the patient's entire mental life and deserved the name of 'hallucinatory insanity'" (p. 385). The fact was that, on the one hand, he had developed an ingenious delusional structure, in which we have every reason to be interested, while, on the other hand, his personality had been reconstructed and now showed itself, except for a few isolated disturbances, capable of meeting the demands of everyday life.

Dr. Weber, in the report drawn up by him in 1899, makes the following remarks: "It thus appears that at the present time, apart from certain psychomotor symptoms which cannot fail to strike even the most superficial observer as being obviously pathological, Herr Senatspräsident Dr. Schreber shows no signs of confusion or of physical inhibition, nor is his intelligence noticeably impaired. His mind is collected, his memory is excellent, he has at his disposal a very considerable store of knowledge (not merely upon legal questions, but in many other fields), and he is able to reproduce it in a connected train of thought. He takes an interest in following events in the world of politics, of science, and of art, and is constantly occupied with such matters . . . and an observer who was uninstructed upon his general condition would scarcely notice anything peculiar in this direction. In spite of all this, however, the patient is full of ideas of pathological origin, which have formed themselves into a complete system; they are now more or less fixed, and seem to be inaccessible to correction by means of any objective valuation of the actual external facts" (p. 386).

Thus the patient's condition had undergone a great change, and he now considered himself capable of carrying on an independent existence. He accordingly took the necessary steps with a view to regaining control over his own affairs and to securing his discharge from the sanatorium. Dr. Weber set himself to prevent the fulfillment of these intentions and drew up reports in a contrary sense. Nevertheless, in his report dated 1900, he felt obliged to give this appreciative account of the patient's character and conduct: "Since for the last nine months Herr Präsident Schreber has taken his meals daily at my family board, I have had the most ample opportunities of conversing with him upon every imaginable topic. Whatever the subject was that came up for discussion (apart, of course, from his delusional ideas), whether it concerned events in the field of administration and law, or of politics, or of art, or of literature, or of social life—in short, whatever the topic, Dr. Schreber gave evidence of a lively interest, a well-informed mind, a good memory, and a sound judgement; his ethical outlook, moreover, was one which it was impossible not to endorse. So, too, in his lighter talk with the ladies of the party, he was both courteous and affable, and if he touched upon matters in a more humorous vein he invariably displayed tact and decorum. Never once, during these innocent talks round the dining-table, did he introduce subjects which should more properly have been raised at a medical consultation" (p. 397). Indeed, on one occasion during this period, when a business question arose which involved the interests of his whole family, he entered into it in a manner which showed both his technical knowledge and his common sense (pp. 401 and 510).

In the numerous applications to the courts, by which Dr. Schreber endeavoured to regain his liberty, he did not in the least disavow his delusion or make any secret of his intention of publishing the *Denkwürdigkeiten*. On the contrary, he dwelt upon the importance of his ideas to religious thought, and upon their invulnerability to the attacks of modern science; but at the same time he laid stress upon the absolute harmlessness of the actions which, as he was aware, his delusions obliged him to perform (p. 430). Such, indeed, were his acumen and the cogency of his logic that finally, and in spite of his being an acknowledged paranoiac, his efforts were crowned with success. In July 1902 Dr. Schreber's civil rights were restored, and in the following year his *Denkwürdigkeiten eines Nervenkranken* were issued, though in a censored form and with many valuable portions omitted.

In the judgement that gave Dr. Schreber back his liberty will be found a few sentences which summarize his delusional system: "He believed that he had a mission to redeem the world and to restore it to its lost state of bliss. This, however, he could only bring about if he were first transformed from a man into a woman" (p. 475).

For a more detailed account of his delusions as they appeared in their final shape we may turn to the report drawn up in 1899 by Dr. Weber, the physician in charge of the sanatorium: "The culminating point of the patient's delusional system is his belief that he has a mission to redeem the world, and to restore mankind to their lost state of bliss. He was called to this task, so he asserts, by direct inspiration from God, just as we are taught that the Prophets were; for nerves in a condition of great excitement, as his were for a long time, have precisely the property of exerting an attraction upon God—though this is touching upon matters which human speech is scarcely, if at all, capable of expressing, since they lie entirely outside the scope of human experience and, indeed, have been revealed to him alone. The most essential feature of his mission of redemption is that it must be preceded by his *transformation into a woman*. It is not to be supposed that he *wishes* to be transformed into a woman; it is rather a question of a 'must' based upon the order of things, which there is no possibility of his evading, much as he would personally prefer to remain in his own honourable and masculine station in life. But neither he nor the rest of mankind can win back their immortality except by his being transformed into a woman (a process which may occupy many years or even decades) by means of divine miracles. He himself, of this he is convinced, is the only object upon which divine miracles are worked, and he is thus the most remarkable man who has ever lived upon earth. Every hour and every minute for years he has experienced these miracles in his body, and he has had them confirmed by the voices that have conversed with him. During the first years of his illness certain of his bodily organs suffered such destructive injuries as would inevitably have led to the death of any other man: he lived for a long time without a stomach, without intestines, almost without lungs, with a torn oesophagus, without a bladder, and with shattered ribs, he used sometimes to swallow part of his own larynx with his food, etc. But divine miracles ('rays') always restored what had been destroyed, and therefore, as long as he remains a man, he is not in any way mortal. These alarming phenomena have ceased long ago, and his 'femaleness' has become prominent instead. This involves a process of development which will probably require decades, if not centuries, for its completion, and it is unlikely that any one now living will survive to see the end of it. He has a feeling that great numbers of 'female nerves' have already passed over into his body, and out of them a new race of men will proceed, through a process of direct impregnation by God. Not until then, it seems, will he be able to die a natural death, and, like the rest of mankind, have regained a state of bliss. In the meantime not only the sun, but trees and birds, which are in the nature of 'bemiracled relics of former human souls,' speak to him in human accents, and miraculous things happen everywhere around him" (p. 386).

The interest felt by the practical psychiatrist in such delusional formations as these is, as a rule, exhausted when once he has ascertained the character of the products of the delusion and has formed an estimate of their influence upon the patient's general behaviour: in his case astonishment is not the birth of comprehension. The psychoanalyst, in the light of his knowledge of the psychoneuroses, approaches the subject with a suspicion that even mental structures so extraordinary as these and so remote from our common modes of thought are nevertheless derived from the most general and comprehensible of human impulses; and he would be glad to discover the motives of such a transformation as well as the manner in which it has been accomplished. With this aim in view, he will be eager to go more deeply into the details of the delusion and into the history of its development.

(a) The medical report laid stress upon two points as being

of chief importance: the patient's *assumption of the rôle of Redeemer,* and *his transformation into a woman.* The Redeemer delusion is a phantasy that is familiar to us through the frequency with which it forms the nucleus of religious paranoia. The additional factor, which makes the redemption dependent upon the patient's being previously transformed into a woman, is unusual and in itself bewildering, since it shows such a wide divergence from the historical myth which the patient's phantasy is setting out to reproduce. It is natural to follow the medical report in assuming that the motive force of this delusional complex was the patient's ambition to play the part of Redeemer, and that his *emasculation* was only entitled to be regarded as a means for achieving that end. Although this may be true of his delusion in its final form, a study of the *Denkwürdigkeiten* compels us to take a very different view of the matter. For we learn that the idea of being transformed into a woman (that is, of being emasculated) was the primary delusion, that he began by regarding that act as a piece of persecution and a serious injury, and that it only became related to his playing the part of Redeemer in a secondary way. There can be no doubt, moreover, that originally he believed that the emasculation was to be effected for the purpose of sexual abuse and not so as to serve some higher design. To express the matter in more formal language, a sexual delusion of persecution was later on converted, in the patient's mind, into a religious delusion of grandeur. The part of persecutor was at first assigned to Prof. Flechsig, the physician in whose charge he was; subsequently, however, the place was occupied by God himself.

I will quote the relevant passages from the *Denkwürdigkeiten* in full: "In this way a conspiracy against me was brought to a head (in about March or April 1894). Its object was to contrive that, when once my nervous complaint had been recognized as incurable or assumed to be so, I should be handed over to a certain person in a particular manner. Thus my soul was to be delivered up to him, but my body— owing to a misapprehension of what I have described above as a purpose underlying the order of things—was to be transformed into a female body, and as such surrendered to the person in question[4] with a view to sexual abuse, and was then simply to be 'left where it was'—that is to say, no doubt, abandoned to corruption" (p. 56).

"It was, moreover, perfectly natural that from the human standpoint (which was the one by which at that time I was still chiefly governed) I should regard Professor Flechsig or his soul as my only true enemy—at a later date there was also the von W. soul, about which I shall have more to say presently—and that I should look upon God Almighty as my ally. I merely fancied that he was in great straits as regards Professor Flechsig, and consequently felt myself bound to support him by every conceivable means, even to the length of sacrificing myself. It was not until very much later that the idea forced itself upon my mind that God himself had played the part of accomplice, if not of instigator, in the plot whereby my soul was to be murdered and my body used like a strumpet. I may say, in fact, that this idea has in part become clearly conscious to me only in the course of my writing the present work" (p. 59).

"Every attempt at murdering my soul, or at emasculating me for purposes *contrary to the order of things*[34] (that is, for the gratification of the sexual appetites of a human individual), or later at destroying my understanding—every such attempt has come to nothing. From this apparently unequal struggle between one weak man and God himself, I have emerged triumphant—though not without undergoing much bitter suffering and privation—because the order of things stands upon my side" (p. 61).

In footnote 34, referring to the above passage, the author foreshadows the subsequent transformation in his delusion of emasculation and in his relation to God: "I shall show later on that emasculation for quite another purpose—a purpose *in consonance with the order of things*—is within the bounds of

---

[4] It appears from the context in this and other passages that "the person in question," who was to practise this abuse, was none other than Flechsig. (See below.)

possibility, and, indeed, that it may quite probably afford a solution of the conflict."

These statements are of decisive importance in determining the view we are to take of the delusion of emasculation and in thus giving us a general understanding of the case. It may be added that the "voices" which the patient heard never treated his transformation into a woman as anything but a sexual disgrace, which gave them an excuse for jeering at him. "Rays of God[5] not infrequently thought themselves entitled to mock at me by calling me 'Miss[6] Schreber,' in allusion to the emasculation which, it was alleged, I was about to undergo" (p. 127). Or they would say: "So *this* sets up to have been a Senatspräsident, this person who lets himself be f——d!"[7] (p. 177). Or again: "Don't you feel ashamed in front of your wife?" (p. 177).

That the emasculation phantasy was of a primary nature and originally independent of the Redeemer idea becomes still more probable when we recollect the "idea" which, as I mentioned on an earlier page, occurred to him while he was half-asleep, to the effect that it must be nice to be a woman submitting to the act of copulation (p. 36). This phantasy appeared during the incubation period of his illness, and before he had begun to feel the effects of being overworked in Dresden.

Schreber himself gives the month of November 1895 as the date at which the connection was established between the emasculation phantasy and the Redeemer idea and the way thus paved for his becoming reconciled to the former. "Now, however," he writes, "I became clearly aware that the order of things imperatively demanded my emasculation, whether I personally liked it or no, and that no *reasonable* course lay

---

[5] The "rays of God," as we shall see, are identical with the voices which talked the "root-language."

[6] [In English in the original.—*Trans.*]

[7] The omission is copied from the *Denkwürdigkeiten,* like every other peculiarity in their author's style. I myself should have found no reason for being so shame-faced over a serious matter.

open to me but to reconcile myself to the thought of being transformed into a woman. The further consequence of my emasculation could, of course, only be my impregnation by divine rays to the end that a new race of men might be created" (p. 177).

The idea of being transformed into a woman was the salient feature and the earliest germ of his delusional system. It also proved to be the one part of it that survived his recovery and was afterwards able to retain a place in his practical life. "The *only thing* which could appear unreasonable in the eyes of other people is the fact, already touched upon in the expert's report, that I am sometimes to be found, standing before the mirror or elsewhere, with the upper portion of my body partly bared, and wearing sundry feminine adornments, such as ribbons, trumpery necklaces, and the like. This only occurs, I may add, when I am *by myself*, and never, at least so far as I am able to avoid it, in the presence of other people" (p. 429). The Herr Senatspräsident confesses to this frivolity at a date (July 1901) at which he was already in a position to express very aptly the completeness of his recovery in the region of practical life: "I have now long been aware that the persons I see about me are not 'cursory contraptions' but real people, and that I must therefore behave towards them as a reasonable man is used to behave towards his fellows" (p. 409). In contrast to the way in which he put his emasculation phantasy into action, the patient never took any steps towards inducing people to recognize his mission as Redeemer, beyond the publication of his *Denkwürdigkeiten*.

(*b*) The attitude of our patient towards *God* is so singular and so full of internal contradictions that it requires more than a little faith to persist in the belief that there is nevertheless "method" in his "madness." With the help of what Dr. Schreber tells us in the *Denkwürdigkeiten*, we must now endeavour to arrive at a more exact view of his theologico-psychological system, and we must expound his opinions concerning *nerves, the state of bliss, the divine hierarchy,* and *the attributes of God,* as they occur in his delusional system. At every point in his theory we shall be struck by the astonishing mixture of the platitudinous and the clever, of what has been borrowed and what is original.

The human soul is contained in the *nerves* of the body. These are to be conceived of as structures of extraordinary fineness, comparable to the finest thread. Some of these nerves are designed only for the reception of sensory impressions, while others (*the nerves of understanding*) carry out all the functions of the mind; and in this connection it is to be noticed that *each single nerve of understanding represents a person's entire mental individuality,* and that the presence of a greater or lesser number of nerves of understanding has no influence except upon the length of time during which the mind can retain its impressions.[8]

Whereas men consist of bodies and nerves, God is from his very nature nothing but nerve. But the nerves of God are not, as is the case with human bodies, present in limited numbers, but are infinite or eternal. They possess all the properties of human nerves to an enormously intensified degree. In their creative capacity, that is their power of turning themselves into every imaginable object in the created world, they are known as *rays*. There is an intimate relation between God and the starry heaven and the sun.[9]

---

[8] The words in which Schreber states this theory are italicized by him, and he adds a footnote, in which he insists that it can be used as an explanation of heredity: "The male semen," he declares, "contains a nerve belonging to the father, and it unites with a nerve taken from the mother to form a new entity" (p. 7). Here, therefore, we find a quality properly belonging to the spermatozoon transferred on to the nerves, which makes it probable that Schreber's "nerves" are derived from the sphere of ideas connected with sexuality. It not infrequently happens in the *Denkwürdigkeiten* that an incidental note upon some piece of delusional theory gives us the desired indication of the genesis of the delusion and so of its meaning.

[9] In this connection see my discussion below upon the significance of the sun.—The comparison between (or rather the condensation of) nerves and rays may well have been based upon the linear extension which they have in common.—The ray-nerves, by the way, are no less creative than the spermatozoon-nerves.

When the work of creation was finished, God withdrew to an immense distance (pp. 11 and 252) and, in general, resigned the world to its own laws. He limited his activities to drawing up to himself the souls of the dead. It was only in exceptional instances that he would enter into relations with particular, highly gifted persons,[10] or would intervene by means of a miracle in the destinies of the world. God does not have any regular intercourse with human souls, according to the order of things, until after death.[11] When a man dies, his spiritual parts (that is, his nerves) undergo a process of purification before being finally reunited with God himself as "fore-courts of Heaven." Thus it comes about that everything moves in an eternal round, which lies at the basis of the order of things (p. 19). In creating anything, God is parting with a portion of himself, or is clothing a portion of his nerves in a new shape. The apparent loss which he thus sustains is made good when, after hundreds and thousands of years, the nerves of dead men, that have entered the state of bliss, once more accrue to him as "fore-courts of Heaven."

Souls that have passed through the process of purification enter into the enjoyment of a *state of bliss*.[12] In the meantime they have lost some of their individual consciousness, and have become fused together with other souls into higher unities. Important souls, such as those of men like Goethe, Bismarck, etc., may have to retain their sense of identity for hundreds of years to come, before they too can become resolved into higher soul-complexes, such as "Jehovah rays" in the case of ancient Jewry, or "Zoroaster rays" in the case of ancient Persia. In the course of their purification souls learn the language which is spoken by God himself, the so-called "root-language." This is "a vigorous though somewhat

[10] In the root-language (see below) this is described as "forming a nerve-connection with them."

[11] We shall find later that certain criticisms against God are based on this fact.

[12] This consists essentially in feelings of voluptuousness (see below).

antiquated German, which is especially characterized by its great wealth of euphemisms"[13] (p. 13).

God himself is not a simple entity. "Above the 'fore-courts of Heaven' floated God himself, who, in contradistinction to these 'anterior realms of God,' was also described as the 'posterior realms of God.' The posterior realms of God were, and still are, divided in a strange manner into two parts, so that a lower God (Ahriman) was differentiated from an upper God (Ormuzd)" (p. 19). As regards the significance of this division Schreber can tell us no more than that the lower God was more especially attached to the peoples of a dark race (the Semites) and the upper God to those of a fair race (the Aryans); nor would it be reasonable, in such sublime matters, to expect human knowledge to carry us further. Nevertheless, we are also told that "in spite of the fact that in certain respects God Almighty forms a unity, the lower and the upper God must be regarded as separate beings, each of which possesses its own particular egoism and its own particular instinct of self-preservation, *even in relation to the other,* and each of which in turn is therefore constantly endeavouring to thrust the other forward" (p. 140). Moreover, the two divine beings behaved in quite different ways towards the unlucky Schreber during the acute stage of his illness.[14]

In the days before his illness Senatspräsident Schreber had been a doubter in religious matters (pp. 29 and 64); he had never been able to persuade himself into a firm belief in the existence of a personal God. Indeed, he adduces this fact about his earlier life as an argument in favour of the objective

[13] On one single occasion during his illness the patient was vouchsafed the privilege of seeing, with his spiritual eyes, God Almighty clear and undisguised before him. On that occasion God uttered what was a very current word in the root-language, and a forcible though not an amiable one—the word "Scoundrel!" (p. 136).

[14] A footnote upon p. 20 leads us to suppose that a passage in Byron's *Manfred* may have determined Schreber's choice of the names of Persian divinities. We shall later come upon further evidence of the influence of this poem upon his mind.

reality of his delusions.[15] But any one who reads the account which follows of the characteristics of Schreber's God will have to allow that the transformation effected by the paranoic disorder was no very fundamental one, and that in the Redeemer of to-day much remains of the doubter of yesterday.

For there is a flaw in the order of things, as a result of which the existence of God himself seems to be endangered. Owing to circumstances which are incapable of further explanation, the nerves of *living* men, especially when in a condition of *intense excitement,* may exercise such a powerful attraction upon the nerves of God that he cannot get free from them again, and thus his own existence may be threatened (p. 11). This exceedingly rare occurrence took place in Schreber's case and involved him in the greatest sufferings. The instinct of self-preservation was aroused in God (p. 30), and it then became evident that God was far removed from the perfection ascribed to him by religions. Through the whole of Schreber's book there runs the bitter complaint that God, being only accustomed to intercourse with the dead, *does not understand living men.*

"In this connection, however, *a fundamental misunderstanding* prevails, which has since run through my whole life like a scarlet thread. It is based precisely upon the fact that, *in accordance with the order of things, God was not really acquainted with living men* and did not need to be; consonantly with the order of things, he needed only to have intercourse with corpses" (p. 55).—"This state of things . . . I am convinced, is once more to be ascribed to the fact that God was, if I may so express it, quite incapable of dealing

[15] "That it was simply a matter of illusions seems to me to be *in my case,* from the very nature of things, psychologically unthinkable. For illusions of holding intercourse with God or with departed souls can properly only arise in the minds of persons who, before falling into their condition of pathological nervous excitement, already have a firm belief in God and in the immortality of the soul. *This was not by any means so, however, in my case, as has been explained at the beginning of this chapter"* (p. 79).

with living men, and was only accustomed to intercourse with corpses, or at most with men as they lay asleep (that is, in their dreams)" (p. 141).—"I myself feel inclined to exclaim: *'Incredibile scriptu!'* Yet it is all literally true, however difficult it may be for other people to grasp the idea of God's complete inability to judge living men correctly, and however long I myself took to accustom myself to this idea after my innumerable observations upon the subject" (p. 246).

It was solely as a result of God's misunderstanding of living men that it was possible for him himself to become the instigator of the plot against Schreber, to take him for a dement, and to subject him to such exhausting ordeals (p. 264). To avoid being set down as a dement, he submitted himself to an extremely burdensome system of "enforced thinking." For "every time that my intellectual activities ceased, God jumped to the conclusion that my mental faculties were extinct and that the destruction of my understanding (the dementia), for which he was hoping, had actually set in, and that a withdrawal had now become possible" (p. 206).

The behaviour of God in the matter of the "call to sh—" (the need for evacuating the bowels) rouses him to a specially high pitch of indignation. The passage is so characteristic that I will quote it in full. But to make it clear I must first explain that both the miracles and the voices proceed from God, that is, from the divine rays.

"Although it will necessitate my touching upon an unsavoury subject, I must devote a few more words to the question that I have just quoted ('Why don't you sh—?') on account of the typical character of the whole business. The need for evacuation, like all else that has to do with my body, is evoked miraculously. It is brought about by my faeces being forced forward (and sometimes back again) in my intestines; and if, owing to there having already been an evacuation, enough material is not present, then such small remains as there may still be of the contents of my intestines are smeared over my anal orifice. This occurence is a miracle performed by the upper God, and it is repeated several dozens of times at the least every day. It is associated with an idea which is utterly incomprehensible to human beings and can only be accounted for by God's complete ignorance of man as a living organism. According to this idea 'sh—ing' is in a certain sense the final act; that is to say, when once the call to sh— has been miracled up, the aim of destroying my understanding is achieved and a final withdrawal of the rays become possible. To get to the bottom of the origin of this idea, we must suppose, as it seems to me, that there is a misapprehension in connection with the symbolic meaning of the act of evacuation, a notion, in fact, that any one who has been in such a relation as I have with divine rays is to some extent entitled to sh— upon the whole world.

"But now what follows reveals the full perfidy[16] of the policy that has been pursued towards me. Almost every time the need for evacuation was miracled up in me, some other person in my vicinity was sent (by having his nerves stimulated for that purpose) to the lavatory, in order to prevent my evacuating. This is a phenomenon which I have observed for years and upon such countless occasions—thousands of them—and with such regularity, as to exclude any possibility of its being attributable to chance. And thereupon comes the question: 'Why don't you sh—?' to which this brilliant repartee is made on my behalf: 'Because I'm so stupid or something.' The pen well-nigh shrinks from recording so monumental a piece of absurdity as that God, blinded by his ignorance of human nature, can positively go to such lengths as to suppose that there can exist a man too stupid to do what every animal can do—too stupid to be able to sh—. When, upon the occasion of such a call, I actually succeed in evacuating—and as a rule, since I nearly always find the lavatory engaged, I use a pail for the purpose—the process is always accompanied by the generation of an exceedingly strong feeling of spiritual voluptuousness. For the relief from the pressure caused by the presence of the faeces in the intestines produces a sense of

---

[16] In a footnote at this point the author endeavours to mitigate the harshness of the word "perfidy" by a reference to one of his arguments in justification of God. These will be discussed presently.

intense well-being in the nerves of voluptuousness; and the same is equally true of making water. For this reason, even down to the present day, while I am passing stool or making water, all the rays are invariably and without exception united; and for this same reason, too, whenever I address myself to these natural functions, an attempt is invariably made, though as a rule in vain, to miracle back again the call to pass stool and to make water"[17] (p. 225).

Furthermore, this singular God of Schreber's is incapable of learning anything by experience: "Owing to some quality or other inherent in his nature, it seems to be impossible for God to derive any lessons for the future from the experience thus gained" (p. 186). He can therefore go on repeating the same tormenting ordeals and miracles and voices, without alteration, year after year, until he inevitably becomes a laughingstock to the victim of his persecutions.

"The consequence is that, now that the miracles have to a great extent lost the power which they formerly possessed of producing terrifying effects, God strikes me above all, in almost everything that he does in relation to me, as being ridiculous or childish. As regards my own behaviour, this often results in my being obliged in self-defence to assume the part of a scoffer at God, and even, on occasion, to mock at him aloud"[18] (p. 333).

This critical and rebellious attitude towards God is, however, opposed in Schreber's mind by an energetic counter-current, which finds expression in many places: "But here again I must most emphatically declare that this is nothing

---

[17] This confession to a pleasure in the excretory processes, which we have learnt to recognize as one of the auto-erotic components of infantile sexuality, may be compared with the remarks made by little Hans in my "Analysis of a Phobia in a Five-year-old Boy." (See *The Sexual Enlightenment of Children,* Collier Books edition BS 190V.)

[18] Even in the root-language it occasionally happened that God was not the abuser but the abused. For instance: "Deuce take it! What a thing to have to say—that God lets himself be f——d!" (p. 194).

more than an episode, which will, I hope, terminate at the latest with my decease, and that the right of scoffing at God belongs in consequence to me alone and not to other men. For them he remains the almighty creator of Heaven and earth, the first author of all things, and the rock of their salvation, to whom—notwithstanding that a few of the conventional religious ideas may require revision—worship and the deepest reverence are due" (p. 333).

Repeated attempts are therefore made to find a justification for God's behaviour to the patient. In these attempts, which display as much ingenuity as every other theodicy, the explanation is based now upon the general nature of souls, and now upon the necessity for self-preservation which was forced upon God, and upon the misleading influence of the Flechsig soul (pp. 60 *et seq.* and 160). In general, however, the illness is looked upon as a struggle between the man Schreber and God, in which victory lies with the man, weak though he is, because the order of things is on his side (p. 61).

The medical reports might easily lead us to suppose that Schreber exhibited the everyday form of Redeemer phantasy, in which the patient believes he is the son of God, destined to save the world from its misery or from the destruction that is threatening it, and so on. It is for this reason that I have been careful to present in detail the peculiarities of Schreber's relations with God. The significance of these relations for the rest of mankind is only rarely alluded to in the *Denkwürdigkeiten* and not until the last phase of his delusional formation. It consists essentially in the fact that no one who dies can enter the state of bliss so long as the greater part of the rays of God are absorbed in Schreber owing to his powers of attraction (p. 32). It is only at a very late stage, too, that his identification with Jesus Christ makes an undisguised appearance (pp. 338 and 431).

No attempt at explaining Schreber's case will have any chance of being correct which does not take into account these peculiarities in his conception of God, this mixture of reverence and rebelliousness in his attitude towards him.

I will now turn to another subject, which is closely related to God, namely, the *state of bliss*. This is also spoken of by Schreber as "the life in the next world" to which the human soul is raised after death by the process of purification. He describes it as a state of uninterrupted enjoyment, associated with the contemplation of God. This is not very original, but on the other hand it is surprising to learn that Schrieber makes a distinction between a male and a female state of bliss.[19] "The male state of bliss was superior to the female, which seems to have consisted chiefly in an uninterrupted feeling of voluptuousness" (p. 18). In other passages this coincidence between the state of bliss and voluptuousness is expressed in plainer language and without reference to sex-distinction; whereas that element of the state of bliss which consists in the contemplation of God is not further discussed. Thus, for instance: ". . . with the nature of the nerves of God, in virtue of which the state of bliss . . . is accompanied by a very intense sensation of voluptuousness, even though it does not consist exclusively of it" (p. 51). And again: "Voluptuousness may be regarded as a fragment of the state of bliss given in advance, as it were, to men and other living creatures" (p. 281). So that the state of heavenly bliss is to be understood as being in its essence an intensified continuation of sensual pleasure upon earth!

It must not be supposed that this view of the state of bliss was an element in Schreber's delusion that originated in the first stages of his illness and was later eliminated as being incompatible with the rest. So late as in the Statement of his Case, drawn up by the patient for the Appeal Court in July

---

[19] For surely the expectation that in the next world we shall at last be free from differences of sex is in complete harmony with the view that the future life is a wish-fulfilment.

> "Und jene himmlischen Gestalten
> sie fragen nicht nach Mann und Weib."
> GOETHE, *Wilhelm Meister.*

> ["And those calm shining sons of morn
> They ask not who is maid or boy."
> (Carlyle's Translation.)]

1901, he emphasizes as one of his greatest discoveries the fact "that voluptuousness stands in a close relationship (not hitherto perceptible to the rest of mankind) to the state of bliss enjoyed by departed spirits"[20] (p. 442).

We shall find, indeed, that this "close relationship" is the rock upon which the patient builds his hopes of an eventual reconciliation with God and of his sufferings being brought to an end. The rays of God abandon their hostility as soon as they are certain that in becoming absorbed into his body they will experience spiritual voluptuousness (p. 133); God himself demands that he shall be able to find voluptuousness in him (p. 283), and threatens him with the withdrawal of his rays if he neglects to cultivate voluptuousness and cannot offer God what he demands (p. 320).

This surprising sexualization of the state of heavenly bliss suggests the possibility that Schreber's concept of the state of bliss[21] is derived from a condensation of the two principal meanings of the German word *"selig"* ["blest"], namely, "dead" and "sensually happy."[22] But this instance of sexualization will also give us occasion to examine the patient's general attitude to the erotic side of life and to questions of sexual indulgence. For we psychoanalysts have hitherto supported the view that the roots of every nervous and mental disorder are chiefly to be found in the patient's sexual life; but whereas some of us have done so merely upon empirical

---

[20] The possibility of this discovery of Schreber's having a deeper meaning is discussed below.

[21] [*"Seligkeit"* in the original; literally, "blessedness."—*Trans.*]

[22] Extreme instances of the two uses of the word are to be found in the phrase *"mein seliger Vater"* ["my late father"] and in these lines from the German text of the duet in *Don Giovanni:*

> "Ja, dein zu sein auf ewig,
> wie selig werd' ich sein."
> ["Ah, to be thine for ever—
> What rapture that would be!"]

But the fact that the same word should be used in our language in two such different situations cannot be without significance.

could only regret that he was not able to devote himself to its cultivation the whole day long[24] (p. 285).

Such, then, was the result of the changes produced in Schreber by his illness, as we find them expressed in the two main features of his delusion. Before it he had been inclined to sexual asceticism and had been a doubter in regard to God; while after it he was a believer in God and a devotee to sensual pleasure. But just as his re-conquered belief in God was of a peculiar kind, so too the sexual enjoyment which he had won for himself was of a most unusual character. It was not the sexual liberty of a man, but the sexual feelings of a woman. He took up a feminine attitude towards God; he felt that he was God's wife.[25]

No other part of his delusion is treated by the patient so exhaustively, one might almost say so insistently, as his alleged transformation into a woman. The nerves absorbed by him have, so he says, assumed in his body the character of female nerves of voluptuousness, and have given to his body a more or less female stamp, and more particularly to his skin a softness peculiar to the female sex (p. 87). If he presses lightly with his fingers upon any part of his body, he can feel these nerves, under the surface of the skin, as a tissue of a

[24] The following passage shows how this fitted into his delusion: "*This attraction, however, lost its terrors for the nerves in question, if, and in so far as, upon entering my body, they encountered a feeling of spiritual voluptuousness in which they themselves shared.* For, if this happened, they found an equivalent or approximately equivalent substitute in my body for the state of heavenly bliss which they had lost, and which itself consisted in a kind of voluptuous enjoyment" (p. 179).

[25] "Something occurred in my own body similar to the conception of Jesus Christ in an immaculate virgin, that is, in a woman who had never had intercourse with a man. On two separate occasions (both while I was in Professor Flechsig's sanatorium) I have possessed female genitals, though somewhat imperfectly developed ones, and have felt a stirring in my body, such as would arise from the quickening of a human embryo. Nerves of God corresponding to male semen had, by a divine miracle, been projected into my body, and impregnation had thus taken place."

thread-like or stringy texture; they are especially present in the region of the chest, where, in a woman, her breasts would be. "By applying pressure to this tissue, I am able to evoke a sensation of voluptuousness such as women experience, and especially if I think of something feminine at the same time" (p. 277). He knows with certainty that this tissue was originally nothing else than nerves of God, which could hardly have lost the character of nerves merely through having passed over into his body (p. 279). By means of what he calls "drawing" (that is, by calling up visual images) he is able to give both himself and the rays an impression that his body is fitted out with female breasts and genitals: "It has become so much a habit with me to draw female buttocks on to my body—*honi soit qui mal y pense*—that I do it almost involuntarily every time I stoop" (p. 233). He is "bold enough to assert that any one who should happen to see me before the mirror with the upper portion of my torso bared—especially if the illusion were assisted by my wearing a little feminine finery—would receive an unmistakable impression of a *female bust*" (p. 280). He calls for a medical examination, in order to establish the fact that his whole body has nerves of voluptuousness dispersed over it from head to foot, a state of things which is only to be found, in his opinion, in the female body, whereas, in the male, to the best of his knowledge, nerves of voluptuousness exist only in the sexual organs and their immediate vicinity (p. 274). The spiritual voluptuousness which has been developed owing to this accumulation of nerves in his body is so intense that it only requires a slight effort of his imagination (especially when he is lying in bed) to procure him a feeling of sensual well-being that affords a tolerably distinct foretaste of the sexual pleasure enjoyed by a woman during copulation (p. 269).

If we now recall the dream which the patient had during the incubation period of his illness, before he had moved to Dresden, it will become clear beyond a doubt that his delusion of being transformed into a woman was nothing else than a realization of that dream. At that time he had rebelled against the dream with masculine indignation, and in the same way he began by striving against its fulfilment in his illness and looked upon his transformation into a woman as a disgrace with which he was threatened from a hostile source. But there came a time (it was in November 1895) when he began to reconcile himself to the transformation and bring it into harmony with the higher purposes of God: "Since then, and with a full consciousness of what I did, I have inscribed upon my banner the cultivation of femaleness" (pp. 177 and 178).

He then arrived at the firm conviction that it was God himself who, for his own satisfaction, was demanding femaleness from him.

"No sooner, however (if I may so express it), am I alone with God than it becomes a necessity for me to employ every imaginable device and to summon up the whole of my mental faculties, and especially my imagination, in order to bring it about that the divine rays may have the impression as continuously as possible (or, since this is beyond mortal power, at least at certain times of day) that I am a woman luxuriating in voluptuous sensations" (p. 281).

"On the other hand, God demands a *constant state of enjoyment*, such as would be in keeping with the conditions of existence imposed upon souls by the order of things; and it is my duty to provide him with this . . . in the shape of the greatest possible output of spiritual voluptuousness. And if, in this process, a little sensual pleasure falls to my share, I feel justified in accepting it as some slight compensation for the inordinate measure of suffering and privation that has been mine for so many past years . . ." (p. 283).

". . . I think I may even venture to advance the view, based upon impressions I have received, that God would never take any steps towards effecting a withdrawal—the first result of which is invariably to alter my physical condition markedly for the worse—but would quietly and permanently yield to my powers of attraction, if it were possible for me *always* to be playing the part of a woman lying in my own amorous embraces, *always* to be casting my looks upon female forms, *always* to be gazing at pictures of women, and so on" (p. 24).

In Schreber's system the two principal elements of his delusion (his transformation into a woman and his favoured relation to God) are united in his assumption of a feminine attitude towards God. It will be a necessary part of our task to show that there is an essential *genetic* relation between these two elements. Or else our attempts at elucidating Schreber's delusions will leave us in the absurd position described in Kant's famous simile in the *Critique of Pure Reason*:—we shall be like a man holding a sieve under a he-goat while some one else milks it.

grounds, others have been influenced in addition by theoretical considerations.

The samples of Schreber's delusions that have already been given enable us without more ado to dismiss the suspicion that it might precisely be this paranoid disorder which would turn out to be the "negative case" which has so long been sought for—a case in which sexuality plays only a very minor part. Schreber speaks again and again as though he himself shared our prejudices. He is constantly talking in the same breath of "neurotic states" and sexual lapses, as though the two things were inseparable.[23]

Before his illness Senatspräsident Schreber had been a man of strict morals: "Few people," he declares, and I see no reason to doubt his assertion, "can have been brought up upon such strict moral principles as I was, and few people, all through their lives, can have exercised (especially in sexual matters) a self-restraint conforming so closely to those principles as I may say of myself that I have done" (p. 281). After the severe mental struggle, of which the phenomena of his illness were the outward signs, his attitude towards the erotic side of life had altered. He had come to see that the cultivation of voluptuousness was incumbent upon him as a duty, and that it was only by discharging it that he could end the grave conflict which had broken out within him—or, as he thought, regarding him. Voluptuousness, so the voices assured him, had become "God-fearing" (p. 285), and he

[23] "When moral corruption ('voluptuous excesses') or perhaps neurotic states had taken a strong enough hold upon the whole population of a terrestrial body," then, thinks Schreber, bearing in mind the Biblical stories of Sodom and Gomorrah, the Deluge, etc., the world in question might come to a catastrophic end (p. 52).—". . . . sowed fear and terror among men, wrecked the foundations of religion, and spread abroad neurotic states and general immorality, so that devastating pestilences have descended upon mankind" (p. 91).—"Thus it seems probable that by a 'Prince of Hell' the souls meant the mysterious force that was able to develop in a sense hostile to God as a result of moral depravity among men or of a general state of nervous super-excitement following upon over-civilization" (p. 163).

II

Attempts at Interpretation

THE PROBLEM NOW LIES before us of endeavouring to pene-
trate the meaning of this history of a case of paranoia and
to lay bare in it the familiar complexes and motive forces
of mental life; and it is a task which might be approached
from two different angles. We might start either from the
patient's own delusional utterances or from the exciting causes
of his illness.

The former method cannot fail to seem enticing since the
brilliant example given us by Jung in his interpretation of a
case of dementia praecox which was far severer than this
one and which exhibited symptoms far more remote from the
normal.[1] The high level of our present patient's intelligence,
too, and his communicativeness, would seem likely to facilitate
the accomplishment of our task, if we approached it along
these lines. By no means infrequently he himself presses the
key into our hands, by adding a gloss to some delusional
proposition in an apparently incidental manner, or by making
a quotation or producing an example in connection with it,
or even by expressly denying some parallel to it that has arisen
in his own mind. For when this happens, we have only to

---

[1] Jung, *Über die Psychologie der Dementia praecox*, 1907.

follow our usual psychoanalytic technique (to strip his sentence of its negative form, to take his example as being the actual thing, or his quotation or gloss as being the original source) and we find ourselves in possession of what we are looking for—a translation of the paranoic mode of expression into the normal one. It is perhaps worth giving a more detailed illustration of the correctness of this procedure. Schreber complains of the nuisance created by the so-called "miracled birds" or "talking birds," to which he ascribes a number of very remarkable qualities (pp. 208-214). It is his belief that they are composed of relics of former "fore-courts of Heaven," that is, of human souls once in a state of bliss, and that they are charged with ptomaine[2] poison and let loose upon him. They have been brought to the condition of repeating "meaningless phrases that they have learnt by heart" and that have been "crammed into them." Each time that they have discharged their load of ptomaine poison on to him— that is, each time that they have "reeled off the phrases with which they have been crammed, as it were"— they become to some extent absorbed into his soul, with the words "What a deuced fellow!" or "Deuce take it!" which are the only words they are still capable of using to express a genuine feeling. They cannot understand the meaning of the words they speak, but they are by nature susceptible to similarity of sounds, though the similarity need not necessarily be a complete one. Thus it is immaterial to them whether one says:

"Santiago" or *"Karthago,"*

"Chinesentum" or *"Jesum Christum,"*

"Abendrot" or *"Atemnot,"*

"Ariman" or *"Ackermann,"* etc.[3] (p. 210).

As we read this description, the idea forces itself upon us that what it really refers to must be young girls. In a carping

---

[2] [German *"Leichengift,"* literally "corpse poison."—*Trans.*]

[3] ["Santiago" or "Carthage,"
   "Chinese-dom" or "Jesus Christ,"
   "Sunset" or "Breathlessness,"
   "Ahriman" or "Farmer."—*Trans.*]

mood people often compare them to geese, ungallantly accuse them of having "the brains of a bird," declare that they can say nothing but phrases learnt by rote, and that they betray their lack of education by confusing foreign words that sound alike. The phrase "What a deuced fellow!" which is the only thing that they are serious about, would in that case be an allusion to the triumph of the young man who has succeeded in impressing them. And, sure enough, a few pages later we come upon a passage in which Schreber confirms this interpretation: "For purposes of distinction, I have as a joke given girls' names to a great number of the remaining bird-souls; since by their inquisitiveness, their voluptuous bent, etc., they one and all most readily suggest a comparison with little girls. Some of these girls' names have since been adopted by the rays of God and have been retained as a designation of the bird-souls in question" (p. 214). This easy method of interpreting the "miracled birds" gives us a hint which may help us towards understanding the enigmatic "fore-courts of Heaven."

I am quite aware that a psychoanalyst needs no small amount of tact and restraint whenever in the course of his work he goes beyond the standard lines of interpretation, and that his listeners or readers will only follow him as far as their own familiarity with analytic technique will allow them. He has every reason, therefore, to guard against the risk that an increased display of acumen on his part may be accompanied by a diminution in the certainty and trustworthiness of his results. It is thus only natural that one analyst will tend too much in the direction of caution and another too much in the direction of boldness. It will not be possible to define the proper limits of justifiable interpretation until many experiments have been made and until the subject has become more familiar. In working upon the case of Schreber I have had a policy of restraint forced upon me by the circumstance that the opposition to his publishing the *Denkwürdigkeiten* was so far effective as to withhold a considerable portion of the material from our knowledge, the portion, too, which would in all probability have thrown the most important light upon the case.[4] Thus, for instance, the third chapter of the book opens with this promising announcement: "I shall now proceed to describe certain events which occurred to *other members of my family* and which may conceivably have been connected with the soul-murder which I have postulated. There is at any rate something more or less problematical about all of them, something not easily explicable upon the lines of ordinary human experience" (p. 33). But the next sentence, which is also the last of the chapter, is as follows: "The remainder of this chapter has been withheld from print as being unsuitable for publication." I shall therefore have to be satisfied if I can succeed in tracing back at any rate the nucleus of the delusional structure with some degree of certainty to familiar human motives.

With this object in view I shall now mention a further element in the case history to which sufficient weight is not given in the reports, although the patient himself has done all he can to put it in the foreground. I refer to Schreber's relations to his first physician, Geheimrat Prof. Flechsig of Leipsic.

As we already know, Schreber's case at first took the form of delusions of persecution, and did not begin to lose it until the turning-point of his illness (the time of his "reconciliation"). From that time onwards the persecutions became less and less intolerable, and the disgraceful purpose which at first

[4] "When we survey the contents of this document," writes Dr. Weber in his report, "and consider the mass of indiscretions in regard to himself and other persons which it contains, when we observe the unblushing manner in which he describes situations and events which are of the most delicate nature and indeed, in an aesthetic sense, utterly impossible, when we reflect upon his use of strong language of the most offensive kind, and so forth, we shall find it quite impossible to understand how a man, distinguished apart from this by his tact and refinement, could contemplate taking a step so compromising to himself in the public eye, unless we bear in mind the fact that . . ." etc. etc. (p. 402). Surely the last qualities that we have a right to demand from a case history which sets out to give a picture of deranged humanity and of its struggles to rehabilitate itself are "discretion" and "aesthetic" charm.

underlay his threatened emasculation began to be superseded by a purpose in consonance with the order of things. But the first author of all these acts of persecution was Flechsig, and he remains their instigator throughout the whole course of the illness.[5]

Of the actual nature of Flechsig's enormity and of the motives with which he perpetrated it the patient speaks indefinitely and unintelligibly. Such characteristic vagueness and obscurity, if it is legitimate to judge paranoia upon the model of a far more familiar mental phenomenon—the dream—, may be regarded as signs of an especially intense activity on the part of the forces engaged upon the construction of the delusion. Flechsig, according to the patient, committed, or attempted to commit, "soul-murder" upon him—an act which may perhaps be compared with the efforts made by the devil or by demons to gain possession of a soul, and which may have had its prototype in events which occurred between members of the Flechsig and Schreber families long since deceased (pp. 22 *et seq.*). We should be glad to learn more of the meaning of this "soul-murder," but at this point our sources relapse once more into a tendentious silence: "As to what constitutes the true essence of soul-murder, and as to its technique, if I may so describe it, I am able to say nothing beyond what has already been indicated. There is only this, perhaps, to be added . . . (The passage which follows is unsuitable for publication)" (p. 28). As a result of this omission we are left in the dark on the question of what is meant by "soul-murder." We shall refer later on to the only hint upon the subject which has evaded censorship.

[5] Thus Schreber writes as follows in the Open Letter to Prof. Flechsig with which he prefaces his volume: "Even now the voices that talk with me call out your name to me hundreds of times each day. They name you in certain constantly recurring connections, and especially as being the first author of the injuries I have suffered. And yet the personal relations which existed between us for a time, have, so far as I am concerned, long since faded into the background; so that I myself could have little enough reason to be for ever recalling you to my mind, and still less for doing so with any feelings of resentment" (p. viii.).

However this may be, a further development of Schreber's delusions soon took place, which affected his relations to God without altering his relations to Flechsig. Hitherto he had regarded Flechsig (or rather his soul) as his only true enemy and had looked upon God Almighty as his ally; but now he could not avoid the thought that God himself had played the part of accomplice, if not of instigator, in the plot against him (p. 59). Flechsig, however, remained the first seducer, to whose influence God had yielded (p. 60). He had succeeded in making his way up to Heaven with his whole soul or a part of it and in becoming a "captain of rays," without dying or undergoing any preliminary purification (p. 56).[6] The Flechsig soul continued to play this rôle even after the patient had been moved from the Leipsic clinic to Dr. Pierson's sanatorium. The effect of the new environment was shown by the emergence of another soul, known as the von W. soul, which was that of the chief attendant, whom the patient recognized as a person who had formerly lived in the same block of flats as himself.[7] The Flechsig soul then introduced the system of "soul-division," which assumed very considerable proportions. At one time there were as many as forty to sixty sub-divisions of the Flechsig soul; two of its larger divisions were known as the "upper Flechsig" and the "middle Flechsig" (p. 111). The von W. soul behaved in just

---

[6] According to another and very significant version, which, however, was soon rejected, Prof. Flechsig had shot himself, either at Weissenburg in Alsace or in a police cell at Leipsic. The patient saw his funeral go past, though not in the direction that was to be expected, in view of the relative positions of the University Clinic and the cemetery. On other occasions Flechsig appeared to him in the company of a policeman, or in conversation with his (Flechsig's) wife. Schreber was present at this conversation by the method of "nerve-connection," and in the course of it Prof. Flechsig called himself "God Flechsig" to his wife, so that she was half inclined to think he had gone mad (p. 82).

[7] The voices informed him that in the course of an official inquiry this von W. had made some untrue statements about him, either deliberately or out of carelessness, and in particular had accused him of onanism. As a punishment for this he was now obliged to wait upon the patient (p. 108).

the same fashion. It was sometimes most entertaining to notice the way in which these two souls, in spite of their alliance, carried on a feud with one another, the aristocratic pride of the one pitted against the professorial vanity of the other (p. 113). During his first weeks at Sonnenstein (to which he was finally moved in the summer of 1894) the soul of his new physician, Dr. Weber, came into play; and shortly afterwards the revulsion took place in the development of his delusions which we have come to know as his "reconciliation."

During the later part of his stay at Sonnenstein, when God had begun to appreciate him better, a raid was made upon the souls, which had become multiplied into a nuisance. As a result of this, the Flechsig soul survived in only one or two shapes, and the von W. soul in only a single one. The latter soon disappeared altogether. The divisions of the Flechsig soul, which slowly lost both their intelligence and their power, then came to be described as the "posterior Flechsig" and the "Ah well! Party." That the Flechsig soul retained its importance to the last, is made clear by Schreber's preface, his "Open Letter to Herr Geheimrat Prof. Dr. Flechsig."

In this remarkable document Schreber expresses his firm conviction that the physician who influenced him must have had the same visions and have received the same disclosures upon supernatural things as he himself. He protests on the very first page that the author of the *Denkwürdigkeiten* has not the remotest intention of making an attack upon the physician's honour, and the same point is earnestly and emphatically repeated in the patient's Statements of his Case (pp. 343, 445). It is evident that he is endeavouring to distinguish the "soul Flechsig" from the living man of the same name, the real Flechsig from the Flechsig of his delusions.[8]

The study of a number of cases of delusions of persecution

[8] "I am accordingly obliged *to admit as a possibility* that everything in the first chapters of my *Denkwürdigkeiten* which is connected with the name of Flechsig may only refer to the soul Flechsig as distinguished from the living man. For that his soul has a separate existence is a certain fact, though it cannot be explained upon any natural basis" (p. 342).

have led me as well as other investigators to the view that the relation between the patient and his persecutor can be reduced to quite a simple formula.[9] It appears that the person to whom the delusion ascribes so much power and influence, in whose hands all the threads of the conspiracy converge, is either, if he is definitely named, identical with some one who played an equally important part in the patient's emotional life before his illness, or else is easily recognizable as a substitute for him. The intensity of the emotion is projected outwards in the shape of external power, while its quality is changed into the opposite. The person who is now hated and feared as a persecutor was at one time loved and honoured. The main purpose of the persecution constructed by the patient's delusion is to serve as a justification for the change in his emotional attitude.

Bearing this point of view in mind, let us now examine the relations which had formerly existed between Schreber and his physician and persecutor, Flechsig. We have already heard that, in the years 1884 and 1885, Schreber suffered from a first attack of nervous disorder, which ran its course "without the occurrence of any incidents bordering upon the sphere of the supernatural" (p. 35). While he was in this condition, which was described as "hypochondria" and seems not to have overstepped the limits of a neurosis, Flechsig acted as his physician. At that time Schreber spent six months in the University Clinic at Leipsic. We learn that after his discovery he had grateful feelings towards his physician. "The main thing was that, after a fairly long period of convalescence which I spent in travelling, I was finally cured; and it was therefore impossible that I should feel anything at that time but the liveliest gratitude towards Prof. Flechsig. I gave a marked expression to this feeling both in a personal visit which I subsequently paid him and in what I deemed to be

---

[9] Cf. Abraham, "Die psychosexuellen Differenzen der Hysterie und der Dementia praecox," 1908. In the course of this paper its author, referring to a correspondence between us, scrupulously attributes to myself an influence upon the development of his views.

an appropriate honorarium" (p. 35). It is true that Schreber's encomium in the *Denkwürdigkeiten* upon this first treatment of Flechsig's is not entirely without reservations; but that can easily be understood if we consider that his attitude had in the meantime been reversed. The passage immediately following the one that has just been quoted bears witness to the original cordiality of his feelings towards the physician who had treated him so successfully: "The gratitude of my wife was perhaps even more heartfelt; for she revered Professor Flechsig as the man who had restored her husband to her, and hence it was that for years she kept his portrait standing upon her writing-table" (p. 36).

Since we cannot obtain any insight into the causes of the first illness (a knowledge of which is no doubt indispensable for properly elucidating the second and severer illness) we must now plunge at random into an unknown concatenation of circumstances. During the incubation period of his illness, as we are aware (that is, between June 1893, when he was appointed to his new post, and the following October, when he took up his duties), he repeatedly dreamed that his old nervous disorder had returned. Once, moreover, when he was half-asleep, he had a feeling that after all it must be nice to be a woman submitting to the act of copulation. The dreams and the phantasy are reported by Schreber in immediate succession; and if we also bring together their subject-matter, we shall be able to infer that, at the same time as his recollection of his illness, a recollection of his physician was also aroused in his mind, and that the feminine attitude which he assumed in the phantasy was primarily directed towards the physician. Or it may be that the dream of his illness having returned simply expressed some such longing as: "I wish I could see Flechsig again!" Our ignorance of the mental content of the first illness bars our way in this direction. Perhaps that illness had left behind in him a feeling of affectionate dependence upon his physician, which had now, for some unknown reason, become intensified to the pitch of an erotic desire. This feminine phantasy, which was still kept apart from his personality, was met at once by an indignant repudiation—a true "masculine protest," to use Adler's expression, but in a sense different from his.[10] But in the grave psychosis which broke out soon afterwards the feminine phantasy carried everything before it; and it only requires a slight correction of the characteristic paranoic indefiniteness of Schreber's mode of expression to enable us to divine the fact that the patient was in fear of sexual abuse at the hands of his physician himself. The exciting cause of his illness, then, was an outburst of homosexual libido; the object of this libido was probably from the very first his physician, Flechsig; and his struggles against this libidinal impulse produced the conflict which gave rise to the pathological phenomena.

I will pause here for a moment to meet a storm of remonstrances and objections. Any one acquainted with the present state of psychiatry must be prepared to face the worst.

"Is it not an act of irresponsible levity, an indiscretion and a calumny to charge a man of such high ethical standing as the former Senatspräsident Schreber with homosexuality?"—No. The patient has himself informed the world at large of his phantasy of being transformed into a woman, and he has allowed all personal considerations to be outweighed by interests of a higher nature. Thus he has himself given us the right to occupy ourselves with his phantasy, and by translating it into the technical terminology of medicine we have not made the slightest addition to its content.—"But he was not in his right mind when he did it. His delusion that he was being transformed into a woman was a pathological idea."—We have not forgotten that. Indeed our only concern is with the meaning and origin of this pathological idea. We will appeal to the distinction he himself draws between the man Flechsig and the "Flechsig soul." We are not making reproaches of any kind against him—whether for having had

[10] Adler, "Der psychische Hermaphroditismus im Leben und in der Neurose," 1910. According to Adler the masculine protest has a share in the production of the symptom, whereas in the present instance the patient's self is protesting against a symptom that is already fully fledged.

homosexual impulses or for having endeavoured to suppress them. Psychiatrists should take a lesson from this patient, when they see him trying, in spite of his delusions, not to confuse the world of the unconscious with the world of reality.

"But it is nowhere expressly stated that the transformation into a woman which he so much dreaded was to be carried out for the benefit of Flechsig."—That is true; and it is not difficult to understand why, in preparing his memoirs for publication, since he was anxious not to insult the "man Flechsig," he should have avoided so gross an accusation. His consideration for other people's feelings did not, however, lead him to tone down his language sufficiently to conceal the true meaning of his accusation. Indeed, it may be maintained that after all it is expressed openly in such a passage as the following: "In this way a conspiracy against me was brought to a head (in about March or April 1894). Its object was to contrive that, when once my nervous complaint had been recognized as incurable or assumed to be so, *I should be handed over to a certain person in a particular manner.* Thus, my soul was to be delivered up to him, but my body . . . was to be transformed into a female body, and *as such surrendered to the person in question* with a view to sexual abuse . . ."[11] (p. 56). It is unnecessary to remark that no other individual is ever named in the book who could be put in Flechsig's place. Towards the end of Schreber's stay in the clinic at Leipsic, a fear occurred to his mind that he "was to be thrown to the attendants" for the purpose of sexual abuse (p. 98). Any remaining doubts that we have upon the nature of the part originally attributed to the physician are dispelled when, in the later stages of his delusion, we find Schreber outspokenly admitting his feminine attitude towards God. The other accusation against Flechsig resounds noisily through the book. Flechsig, he says, tried to commit soul-murder upon him. As we already know, the patient was himself not clear upon the actual nature of that crime, but it was connected with

---

[11] The italics in this passage are mine.

matters of such a delicate character as to preclude their publication (as we see from the suppressed third chapter). From this point a single thread takes us a little way further. Schreber illustrates the nature of soul-murder by referring to the legends embodied in Goethe's *Faust,* Byron's *Manfred,* Weber's *Freischütz,* etc. (p. 22), and one of these instances is further cited in another passage. In discussing the division of God into two persons, Schreber identifies his "lower God" and "upper God" with Ahriman and Ormuzd respectively (p. 19); and a little later a casual footnote occurs: "Moreover, the name of Ahriman also appears in connection with a soul-murder in, for example, Lord Byron's *Manfred*" (p. 20). In the play which is thus referred to there is scarcely anything comparable to the bartering of Faust's soul, and I have searched it in vain for the expression "soul-murder." But the essence and the secret of the whole work lies in—an incestuous relation between a brother and a sister. And here our thread breaks off short.[12]

At a later stage in this paper I intend to return to a discussion of some further objections; but in the meantime I shall consider myself justified in maintaining the view that the

---

[12] By way of substantiating the above assertion I will quote a passage from the last scene of the play, in which Manfred says to the demon who has come to fetch him away:

> ". . . my past power
> Was purchased by no compact with thy crew."

There is thus a direct contradiction of a soul having been bartered. This mistake on Schreber's part was probably not without its purpose.—It is tempting, by the way, to connect the plot of *Manfred* with the incestuous relations which have repeatedly been asserted to exist between the poet and his half-sister. And it is not a little striking that the action of Byron's other play, his celebrated *Cain,* should be laid in the primal family, where no objections could exist to incest between brother and sister.—Finally, we cannot leave the subject of soul-murder without quoting one more passage from the *Denkwürdigkeiten*: "in this connection Flechsig used formerly to be named as the first author of the soul-murder, whereas for some time past the facts have been deliberately inverted and an attempt has been made to 'represent' me as being the perpetrator of the soul-murder . . ." (p. 23).

basis of Schreber's illness was an outburst of homosexual feeling. This hypothesis harmonizes with a noteworthy detail of the case history, which remains otherwise inexplicable. While his wife was taking a short holiday on account of her own health, the patient had a fresh "nervous collapse" which exercised a decisive effect upon the course of his illness. Up till then she had spent several hours with him every day and had taken her mid-day meal with him. But when she returned after an absence of four days, she found him most sadly altered: so much so, indeed, that he himself no longer wished to see her. "What especially determined my mental breakdown was a particular night, during which I had a quite extraordinary number of emissions—quite half a dozen, all in that one night" (p. 44). It is easy to understand that the mere presence of his wife must have acted as a protection against the attractive power of the men about him; and if we are prepared to admit that an emission cannot occur in an adult without some mental concomitant, we shall be able to supplement the patient's emissions that night by assuming that they were accompanied by homosexual phantasies which remained unconscious.

The question of why this outburst of homosexual libido overtook the patient precisely at this period (that is, between the dates of his appointment and of his move to Dresden) cannot be answered in the absence of more precise knowledge of the story of his life. Generally speaking, every human being oscillates all through his life between heterosexual and homosexual feelings, and any frustration or disappointment in the one direction is apt to drive him over into the other. We know nothing of these factors in Schreber's case, but we must not omit to draw attention to a somatic factor which may very well have been relevant. At the time of this illness Dr. Schreber was fifty-one years of age, and he had therefore reached a time of life which is of critical importance in sexual development. It is a period at which in women the sexual function, after a phase of intensified activity, enters upon a process of far-reaching involution; nor do men appear to be exempt from its influence, for men as well as women are subject to a "climacteric" and to the special susceptibility to disease which goes along with it.[13]

I can well imagine what a dubious hypothesis it must appear to be that a man's friendly feeling towards his physician can suddenly break out in an intensified form after a lapse of eight years[14] and become the occasion of such a severe mental disorder. But I do not think we should be justified in dismissing such a hypothesis merely on account of its inherent improbability, if it recommends itself to us upon other grounds; we ought rather to inquire how far we shall be helped by adopting it and following it up. For the improbability may be of a passing kind and may be due to the fact that the doubtful hypothesis has not as yet been brought into relation with any other pieces of knowledge and that it is the first hypothesis with which the problem has been approached. But for the benefit of those who are unable to hold their judgement in suspense and who regard our hypothesis as altogether untenable, it is easy to suggest a possibility which would rob it of its bewildering character. The patient's friendly feeling towards his physician may very well have been due to a process of "transference," by means of which an emotional cathexis[15] became transposed from some person who was important to him on to the physician who was in reality indifferent to him; so that the physician will have been chosen as a deputy or surrogate for some one much closer to the patient. To put the matter in a more concrete form: the patient having been reminded by the physician of his brother or of his father, having rediscovered them in him, there will be nothing to wonder at if, in certain circumstances, a longing for the surrogate figure reappears in him and operates

[13] I owe my knowledge of Schreber's age at the time of his illness to some information which was kindly given me by one of his relatives, through the agency of Dr. Stegmann of Dresden. Apart from this one fact, however, I have made use of no material in this paper that is not derived from the actual text of the *Denkwürdigkeiten.*

[14] This was the length of the interval between Schreber's first and second illnesses.

[15] [See footnote 32, p. 54.]

. with a violence that is only to be explained in the light of its origin and primary significance.

With a view to following up this attempt at an explanation, I naturally thought it worth while discovering whether the patient's father was still alive at the time of his illness, whether he had had a brother, and if so whether he was then living or among the "blest." I was delighted, therefore, when, after a prolonged search through the pages of the *Denkwürdig-keiten*, I came at last upon a passage in which the patient sets these doubts at rest: "The memory of my father and my brother . . . is as sacred to me as . . ." etc. (p. 442). So that both of them were dead at the time of his second illness (and, it may be, at the time of his first illness as well).

We shall therefore raise no further objections to the hypothesis that the exciting cause of the illness was the appearance in him of a feminine (that is, a passive homosexual) wish-phantasy, which took as its object the figure of his physician. An intense resistance to this phantasy arose on the part of Schreber's personality, and the ensuing defensive struggle, which might perhaps just as well have assumed some other shape, took on, for reasons unknown to us, that of a delusion of persecution. The person he longed for now became his persecutor, and the content of his wish-phantasy became the content of his persecution. It is to be presumed that the same schematic outline may turn out to be applicable to other cases of delusions of persecution. What distinguishes Schreber's case from others, however, is its further development and the transformation it underwent in the course of it.

One such change was the replacement of Flechsig by the superior figure of God. This seems at first as though it were a sign of aggravation of the conflict, an intensification of the unbearable persecution, but it soon becomes evident that it was preparing the way for the second change and, with it, the solution of the conflict. It was impossible for Schreber to become reconciled to playing the part of a female prostitute towards his physician; but the task of providing God himself with the voluptuous sensations that he required called up no such resistance on the part of his ego. Emasculation was now no longer a disgrace; it became "consonant with the order of things," it took its place in a great cosmic chain of events, and was instrumental in the re-creation of humanity after its extinction. "A new race of men, born from the spirit of Schreber," would, so he thought, revere as their ancestor this man who believed himself the victim of persecution. By this means an outlet was provided which would satisfy both of the contending forces. His ego found compensation in his megalomania, while his feminine wish-phantasy gained its ascendancy and became acceptable. The struggle and the illness could cease. The patient's sense of reality, however, which had in the meantime become stronger, compelled him to postpone the solution from the present to the remote future, and to content himself with what might be described as an asymptotic wish-fulfilment.[16] Some time or other, he anticipated, his transformation into a woman would come about; until then the personality of Dr. Schreber would remain indestructible.

In textbooks of psychiatry we frequently come across statements to the effect that megalomania is developed out of delusions of persecution. The process is supposed to be as follows. The patient is primarily the victim of a delusion that he is being persecuted by the most powerful influences. He then feels the need of accounting to himself for this persecution, and in that way hits upon the idea that he himself is a very exalted personage and worthy of such attentions. The development of megalomania is thus attributed by the textbooks to a process which (borrowing a useful word from Ernest Jones) we may describe as "rationalization." But to ascribe such important affective consequences to a rationalization is, as it seems to us, an entirely unpsychological proceeding; and we would consequently draw a sharp distinction between our opinion and the one which we have just quoted.

[16] "It is only," he writes towards the end of the book, "as possibilities which must be taken into account, that I mention that my emasculation may even yet be accomplished and may result in a new generation issuing from my womb by divine impregnation" (p. 293).

We are making no claim, for the moment, to knowing the origin of the megalomania.

Turning once more to the case of Schreber, we are bound to admit that any attempt at throwing light upon the transformation in his delusion brings us up against extraordinary difficulties. In what manner and by what means was the ascent from Flechsig to God brought about? From what source did he derive the megalomania which so fortunately enabled him to become reconciled to his persecution, or, in analytical phraseology, to accept the wish-phantasy which had had to be repressed? The *Denkwürdigkeiten* give us a first clue; for they show us that in the patient's mind "Flechsig" and "God" were ideas belonging to the same class. In one of his phantasies he overheard a conversation between Flechsig and his wife, in which the former asserted that he was "God Flechsig," so that his wife thought he had gone mad (p. 82). But there is another feature in the development of Schreber's delusions which claims our attention. If we take a survey of the delusions as a whole we see that the persecutor is divided into Flechsig and God; in just the same way Flechsig himself subsequently splits up into two personalities, the "upper" and the "middle" Flechsig, and God into the "lower" and the "upper" God. In the later stages of the illness the decomposition of Flechsig goes further still (p. 193). A process of decomposition of this kind is very characteristic of paranoia. Paranoia decomposes just as hysteria condenses. Or rather, paranoia resolves once more into their elements the products of the condensations and identifications which are effected in the unconscious. The constant repetition of the decomposing process in Schreber's case would, according to Jung, be an expression of the importance which the person in question possessed for him.[17] All of this dividing up of Flechsig and

---

[17] Jung, "Ein Beitrag zur Psychologie des Gerüchtes," 1910. Jung is probably right when he goes on to say that this decomposition follows the general lines taken by schizophrenia in that it uses a process of analysis in order to produce a watering-down effect, and is thus designed to prevent the occurrence of unduly powerful impressions. When, however, one of his patients said to

God into a number of persons would have the same meaning as the splitting of the persecutor into Flechsig and God. They would all be duplications of one and the same important relationship.[18] But the interpretation of all these details may also be assisted, if we bear in mind the decomposition of the persecutor into Flechsig and God and the explanation we have already given of this decomposition as being a paranoid reaction to a previously established identification of the two figures or to the fact of their belonging to the same class. If the persecutor Flechsig was originally a person whom Schreber loved, then God must also simply be the reappearance of some one else whom he loved, and probably of some one of greater importance.

. If we pursue this train of thought, which seems to be a legitimate one, we shall be driven to the conclusion that this other person must have been his father; in which case it will become all the clearer that Flechsig must have stood for his brother—who, let us hope, may have been older than himself.[19] The feminine phantasy, which aroused such violent opposition in the patient, thus had its root in a longing, intensified to an erotic pitch, for his father and brother. This feeling, so far as it referred to his brother, passed, by a process of transference, on to his physician Flechsig; and when it was carried back on to his father a settlement of the conflict was reached.

We shall not feel that we have been justified in thus introducing Schreber's father into his delusions, until the new hypothesis has shown itself of some use to us in understanding

---

him: "Oh, are you Dr. J. too? There was some one here this morning who said he was Dr. J.," we must interpret it as being an admission to this effect: "You remind me now of a different member of the class of my transferences from the one you reminded me of when you visited me last."

[18] Otto Rank has found the same process at work in myth-formations (Rank, *Der Mythus von der Geburt des Helden,* 1909).

[19] No information upon this point is to be found in the *Denkwürdigkeiten.*

the case and in elucidating details of the delusions which are as yet unintelligible. It will be recalled that Schreber's God and his relations to him exhibited the most curious features: how they showed the strangest mixture of blasphemous criticism and mutinous insubordination on the one hand and of reverent devotion on the other. God, according to him, had succumbed to the misleading influence of Flechsig; he was incapable of learning anything by experience, and did not understand living men because he only knew how to deal with corpses; and he manifested his power in a succession of miracles which, striking though they might be, were none the less futile and silly.

Now the father of Senatspräsident Dr. Schreber was no insignificant person. He was the Dr. Daniel Gottlieb Moritz Schreber whose memory is kept green to this day by the numerous Schreber Associations which flourish especially in Saxony; and, moreover, he was a *physician*. His activities in favour of promoting the harmonious upbringing of the young, of securing co-ordination between education in the home and in the school, of introducing physical culture and manual work with a view to raising the standards of hygiene—all of these activities exerted a lasting influence upon his contemporaries.[20] His great reputation as the founder of therapeutic gymnastics in Germany is still shown by the wide circulation of his *Ärztliche Zimmergymnastik* [*Medical Indoor Gymnastics*] in medical circles and the numerous editions through which it has passed.

Such a father as this was by no means unsuitable for transfiguration into a God in the affectionate memory of the son from whom he had been so early separated by death. We

[20] I have to thank my colleague Dr. Stegmann of Dresden for his kindness in letting me see a copy of a journal entitled *Der Freund der Schreber-Vereine* [*The Friend of the Schreber Associations*]. This number (Vol. ii. No. 10) celebrates the centenary of Dr. Schreber's birth, and some biographical data are contained in it. Dr. Schreber senior was born in 1808 and died in 1861, at the age of only fifty-three. From the source which I have already mentioned I know that our patient was at that time nineteen years old.

ourselves cannot help feeling that there is an impassable gulf between the personality of God and that of any human being, however eminent he may be. But we must remember that this has not always been so. The gods of the nations of antiquity stood in a closer human relationship to them. The Romans used to deify their dead emperors as a matter of routine; and Vespasian, a sensible and competent man, exclaimed when he was first taken ill: "Alas! Methinks I am about to become a God!"[21]

We are perfectly familiar with the infantile attitude of boys towards their father; it is composed of the same mixture of reverent submission and mutinous insubordination that we have found in Schreber's relation with his God, and is the unmistakable prototype of that relation, which is faithfully copied from it. But the circumstance that Schreber's father was a physician, and a most eminent physician, and one who was no doubt highly respected by his patients, is what explains the most striking characteristics of his God and those upon which he dwells in such a critical fashion. Could more bitter scorn be shown for a physician such as this than by declaring that he understands nothing about living men and only knows how to deal with corpses? No doubt it is an attribute of God to perform miracles; but a physician performs miracles too, effects miraculous cures—or so his enthusiastic clients proclaim. So that when we see that these very miracles (the material for which was provided by the patient's hypochondria) turn out to be incredible, absurd, and to some extent positively silly, we are reminded of the assertion in my *Traumdeutung* that absurdity in dreams expresses scorn and derision.[22] Evidently, therefore, it is used for the same purposes in paranoia. As regards some of the other reproaches which he levelled against God, such, for instance, as that he learned nothing by experience, it is natural to suppose that they are examples of the same mech-

[21] Suetonius, *Lives of the Caesars,* book viii. chapter xxiii. This practice of deification began with Julius Caesar. Augustus styled himself *"Divi filius"* in his inscriptions.
[22] *Traumdeutung* (1900), Seventh Edition, p. 295.

anism as the *tu quoque* argument so often used by children,[23] who, when they receive a reproof, are inclined to fling it back unchanged upon the person who originated it. Similarly, the voices give us grounds for suspecting that the accusation of soul-murder brought against Flechsig was in the first instance a self-accusation.[24]

Emboldened by the discovery that his father's profession helps to explain the peculiarities of Schreber's God, we shall now venture upon an interpretation which may throw some light upon the remarkable structure of that Being. The heavenly world consisted, as we know, of the "anterior realms of God," which were also called the "fore-courts of Heaven" and which contained the souls of the dead, and of the "lower" and the "upper" God, who together constituted the "posterior realms of God" (p. 19). Although we must be prepared to find that there is a condensation here which we shall not be able to resolve, it is nevertheless worth while referring to a clue that is already in our hands. If the "miracled" birds, which have been shown to be girls, were originally fore-courts of Heaven, may it not be that the *anterior* realms of God and the fore-courts[25] of Heaven are to be regarded as a symbol of what is female, and the *posterior* realms of God as a symbol of what is male? If we knew for certain that Schreber's dead brother was older than himself, we might suppose that the decomposition of God into the lower and the upper God gave expression to the patient's recollection that after his father's early death his elder brother had stepped into his place.

In this connection, finally, I should like to draw attention

---

[23] It looks remarkably like a *revanche* of this sort when we find the patient writing out the following memorandum one day on the subject of God: *"All attempts at exercising an educative influence upon him must be abandoned as hopeless"* (p. 188).

[24] "Whereas for some time past the facts have been deliberately inverted and an attempt has been made to 'represent' me as being the perpetrator of the soul murder . . ." etc. (p. 23).

[25] [The German word *"Vorhof"* besides having the literal meaning of "fore-court," is used in anatomy as a synonym for the "vestibulum," a region of the female genitals.—*Trans.*]

to the subject of the *sun,* which, through its "rays," came to have so much importance in the manifestation of his delusions. Schreber has a quite peculiar relation to the sun. It speaks to him in human language, and thus reveals itself to him as a living being, or as the organ of a yet higher being lying behind it (p. 9). We learn from a medical report that at one time he "used to shout threats and abuse at it and positively bellow at it"[26] (p. 382), and used to call out to it that it must crawl away from him and hide. He himself tells us that the sun turns pale before him.[27] The manner in which it is bound up with his fate is shown by the important alterations it undergoes as soon as changes begin to occur in him, as, for instance, during his first weeks at Sonnenstein (p. 135). Schreber makes it easy for us to interpret this solar myth of his. He identifies the sun directly with God, sometimes with the lower God (Ahriman),[28] and sometimes with the upper.[29] It is therefore no more than consistent of him to treat it in the same way as he treats God himself.

The sun, therefore, is nothing but another sublimated symbol for the father; and in pointing this out I must disclaim all responsibility for the monotony of the solutions provided by psychoanalysis. In this instance symbolism overrides grammatical gender—at least so far as German goes, for in most other languages the sun is masculine. The other parent is represented in this picture by the complementary conception

---

[26] "The sun is a whore," he used to exclaim (p. 384).

[27] "To some extent, moreover, even to this day the sun presents a different picture to my eyes from what it did before my illness. When I stand facing it and speak aloud its rays turn pale before me. I can gaze at it without any difficulty and without being more than slightly dazzled by it; whereas in my healthy days it would have been as impossible for me as for any one else to gaze at it for minutes at a time" (p. 139, footnote).

[28] "Since July 1894 the voices that talk to me have identified him [Ahriman] directly with the sun" (p. 88).

[29] "On the following day . . . I saw the upper God (Ormuzd), and this time not with my spiritual eyes but with my bodily ones. It was the sun, but not the sun in its ordinary aspect, as it is known to all men; it was . . ." etc. (p. 137).

which is found everywhere, of "Mother Earth." We frequently come upon confirmations of this assertion during the process of psychoanalysing the pathogenic phantasies of neurotics. I can make no more than the barest allusion to the light which all of this throws upon the origin of cosmic myths. One of my patients, who had lost his father at a very early age, was always seeking to rediscover him in what was grand and sublime in Nature. Since I have known this it has seemed to me probable that Nietzsche's hymn "Vor Sonnenaufgang" ["Before Sunrise"] is an expression of the same longing.[30] Another patient, who became neurotic after his father's death, was seized with his first attack of anxiety and giddiness while the sun shone upon him as he was working in the garden with a spade. He spontaneously put forward as an interpretation that he had become frightened because his father had looked at him while he was at work upon his mother with a sharp instrument. When I ventured upon a mild remonstrance he gave an air of greater plausibility to his view by telling me that even in his father's lifetime he had compared him with the sun, though then it had been in a satirical sense. Whenever he had been asked where his father was going to spend the summer he had replied in these sonorous words from the "Prologue in Heaven":

> "Und seine vorgeschrieb'ne Reise
> Vollendet er mit Donnergang."[31]

His father, acting upon medical advice, had been in the habit of paying an annual visit to Marienbad. This patient's infantile attitude towards his father took effect in two successive phases. As long as his father was alive it showed itself in unmitigated rebelliousness and open discord, but immediately after his death it took the form of a neurosis based upon abject submission to him and deferred obedience.

Thus in the case of Schreber we find ourselves once again

[30] *Also Sprach Zarathustra,* Part III. Nietzsche too only knew his father as a child.

[31] [Literally: "And with a tread of thunder he accomplishes his prescribed journey." Goethe, *Faust,* Part I.—*Trans.*]

upon the familiar ground of the father-complex.[32] Just as to the patient his struggle with Flechsig becomes revealed as a conflict with God, so we must construe the latter as an infantile conflict with the father whom he loved; the details of that conflict (of which we know nothing) are what determined the content of his delusions. None of the material which in other cases of the sort is brought to light by analysis is absent in the present one: every element is indicated in one way or another. In infantile experiences such as this the father appears as an interferer with the gratification which the child is trying to obtain; this is usually of an auto-erotic character, though at a later date it is often replaced in phantasy by some other gratification of a less inglorious kind.[33] In the final stage of Schreber's delusion a glorious victory was scored by the infantile sexual tendencies; for voluptuousness became God-fearing, and God himself (his father) never tired of demanding it from him. His father's most dreaded threat, castration, actually provided the material for his wish-phantasy (at first resisted but later accepted) of being transformed into a woman. His allusion to an offence underlying the substitute-formation of "soul-murder" could not be more transparent. The chief attendant was discovered to be identical with his neighbour von W., who, according to the voices, had falsely accused him of onanism (p. 108). The voices said, as though giving grounds for the threat of castration: "For you are to be *represented* as being given over to voluptuous excesses"[34] (p. 127). Finally, we come to the enforced thinking (p. 47) to which the patient submitted himself because he supposed that God would believe he had become a dement and would withdraw from him if he ceased thinking for a moment. This is a reaction (with which we are also familiar

---

[32] In the same way, Schreber's "feminine wish-phantasy" is simply one of the typical forms taken by the infantile nuclear complex.

[33] See some remarks on this subject in my analysis of the "Rat Man" (p. 64 of this volume).

[34] The systems of "representing" and of "noting down" (p. 126), taken in conjunction with the "qualified souls," point back to experiences in the patient's school days.

in other connections) to the threat or fear of losing one's reason[35] as a result of indulging in sexual practices and especially in onanism. Considering the enormous number of delusional ideas of a hypochondriacal nature[36] which the patient developed, no great importance should perhaps be attached to the fact that some of them coincide word for word with the hypochondriacal fears of onanists.[37]

Any one who was more daring than I am in making interpretations, or who was in touch with Schreber's family and consequently better acquainted with the society in which he moved and the small events of his life, would find it an easy matter to trace back innumerable details of his delusions to their sources and so discover their meaning, and this in spite of the censorship to which the *Denkwürdigkeiten* have been subjected. But as it is we must necessarily content ourselves with this shadowy sketch of the infantile material which was used by the paranoic disorder in portraying the current conflict.

[35] "This was the end in view, as was quite frankly admitted at an earlier date in the phrase 'We want to destroy your reason,' which I have heard proceeding from the upper God upon countless occasions" (p. 206).

[36] I must not omit to remark at this point that I shall not consider any theory of paranoia trustworthy unless it also covers the *hypochondriacal* symptoms by which that disorder is almost invariably accompanied. It seems to me that hypochondria stands in the same relation to paranoia as anxiety neurosis does to hysteria.

[37] "For this reason attempts were made to pump out my spinal cord. This was done by means of so-called 'little men' who were placed in my feet. I shall have more to say presently on the subject of these 'little men,' who showed some resemblance to the phenomena of the same name which I have already discussed in Chapter VI. There used always as a rule to be two of them—a 'little Flechsig' and a 'little von W.'—and I used to hear their voices in my feet" (p. 154). Von W. was the man who was supposed to have accused Schreber of onanism. The "little men" are described by Schreber himself as being among the most remarkable and, in some respects, the most puzzling phenomena of his illness (p. 157). It looks as though they were the product of a condensation of children and—spermatozoa.

Perhaps I may be allowed to add a few words with a view to establishing the causes of that conflict. It broke out in relation to the feminine wish-phantasy; and, as we know, when a wish-phantasy makes its appearance, our business is to bring it into connection with some *frustration*, some privation in real life. Now Schreber admits having suffered a privation of this kind. His marriage, which he describes as being in other respects a happy one, brought him no children; and in particular it brought him no son to console him for the loss of his father and brother—to drain off his unsatisfied homosexual affections.[38] His family line threatened to die out, and it seems that he felt no little pride in his birth and lineage. "Both the Flechsigs and the Schrebers were members of 'the highest aristocracy of Heaven,' as the phrase went. The Schrebers in particular bore the title of 'Margraves of Tuscany and Tasmania'; for souls, urged by some sort of personal vanity, have a custom of adorning themselves with somewhat high-sounding titles borrowed from this world"[39] (p. 24). The great Napoleon obtained a divorce from Josephine (though only after severe internal struggles) because she could not propagate the dynasty.[40] Dr. Schreber may have formed a

[38] "After my recovery from my first illness I spent eight years with my wife—years, upon the whole, of great happiness, rich in outward honours, and only clouded from time to time by the oft-repeated disappointment of our hope that we might be blessed with children" (p. 36).

[39] He goes on from this remark (which shows, by the way, that even in his delusions he preserved the good-natured irony of his saner days) to trace back through former centuries the relations between the Flechsig and Schreber families. In just the same way a young man who is newly engaged, and cannot understand how he can have lived so many years without knowing the girl he is now in love with, will insist that he really made her acquaintance at some former time.

[40] In this connection it is worth mentioning a protest entered by the patient against some statements made in the medical report: "I have never trifled with the idea of obtaining a *divorce*, nor have I displayed any indifference to the maintenance of our marriage tie, such as might be inferred from the expression used in the report to the effect that 'I am always ready with the rejoinder that my wife can get a divorce if she likes'" (p. 436).

phantasy that if he had been a woman he would have managed the business of having children more successfully; and he may thus have found his way back into the feminine attitude towards his father which he had exhibited in the earliest years of his childhood. If that were so, then his delusion that as a result of his emasculation the world was to be peopled with "a new race of men, born from the spirit of Schreber" (p. 288)—a delusion the realization of which he was continually postponing to a more and more remote future—would be designed to offer him an escape from his childlessness. If the "little men" whom Schreber himself finds so puzzling were children, then we should have no difficulty in understanding why they were collected in such great numbers upon his head (p. 158): they were in truth the "children of his spirit."[41]

[41] Compare what I have said upon the method of representing patrilineal descent and upon the birth of Athena in my analysis of the "Rat Man" (p. 88 of this volume).

III

On the Mechanism of Paranoia

WE HAVE HITHERTO been dealing with the father complex, which was the dominant element in Schreber's case, and with the wish-phantasy round which the illness centred. But in all of this there is nothing characteristic of the form of disease known as paranoia, nothing that might not be found (and that has not in fact been found) in other kinds of neuroses. The distinctive character of paranoia (or of dementia paranoides) must be sought for elsewhere, namely, in the particular form assumed by the symptoms; and we shall expect to find that this is determined, not by the nature of the complexes themselves, but by the mechanism by which the symptoms are formed or by which repression is brought about. We should be inclined to say that what was characteristically paranoic about the illness was the fact that the patient, as a means of warding off a homosexual wish-phantasy, reacted precisely with delusions of persecution of this kind.

These considerations therefore lend an added weight to the circumstance that we are in point of fact driven by experience to attribute to the homosexual wish-phantasy an intimate (perhaps an invariable) relation to this particular form of disease. Distrusting my own experience on the subject, I have during the last few years joined with my friends C. G. Jung of Zurich and S. Ferenczi of Budapest in investigating upon this single point a number of cases of paranoid disorder which have come under observation. The patients whose histories provided the material for this inquiry included both men and women, and varied in race, occupation, and social standing. Yet we were astonished to find that in all of these cases a defence against a homosexual wish was clearly recognizable at the very centre of the conflict which underlay the disease, and that it was in an attempt to master an unconsciously reinforced current of homosexuality that they had all of them come to grief.[1] This was certainly not what we had expected. Paranoia is a disorder in which a sexual aetiology is by no means obvious; on the contrary, the strikingly prominent features in the causation of paranoia, especially among males, are social humiliations and slights. But if we go into the matter only a little more deeply, we shall be able to see that the really operative factor in these social injuries lies in the part played in them by the homosexual components of affective life. So long as the individual is functioning normally and it is consequently impossible to see into the depths of his mental life, there is justification for doubting whether his emotional relations to his neighbours in society have anything to do with sexuality, either actually or genetically. But the development of delusions never fails to unmask these relations and to trace back the social feelings to their roots in a purely sensual erotic wish. So long as he was healthy, even Dr. Schreber, whose delusions culminated in a wish-phantasy of an unmistakably homosexual nature, had, by all accounts, shown no signs of homosexuality in the ordinary sense of the word.

I shall now endeavour (and I think the attempt is neither

[1] Further confirmation is afforded by A. Maeder's analysis of a paranoid patient J. B. ("Psychologische Untersuchungen an Dementia praecox-Kranken," (1910). The present paper, I regret to say, was completed before I had an opportunity of reading Maeder's work.

unnecessary nor unjustifiable) to show that the knowledge of psychological processes which, thanks to psychoanalysis, we now possess already enables us to understand the part played by a homosexual wish in the development of paranoia. Recent investigations[2] have directed our attention to a stage in the development of the libido which it passes through on the way from auto-erotism to object-love.[3] This stage has been given the name of narcissism.[4] Its nature is as follows. There comes a time in the development of the individual at which he unifies his sexual instincts (which have hitherto been engaged in auto-erotic activities) in order to obtain a love-object; and he begins by taking himself, his own body, as his love-object, and only subsequently proceeds from this to the choice of some person other than himself as his object. This half-way phase between auto-erotism and object-love may perhaps be indispensable to the normal course of life; but it appears that many people linger unusually long in this condition, and that many of its features are carried over by them into the later stages of their development. The point of central interest in the self which is thus chosen as a love-object may already be the genitals. The line of development then leads on to the choice of an outer object with similar genitals—that is, to homosexual object-choice—and thence to heterosexuality. Persons who are manifest homosexuals in later life have, it may be presumed, never emancipated themselves from the binding condition that the object of their choice must possess genitals like their own; and in this connection the infantile sexual theories which attribute the same kind of genitals to both sexes exert a considerable influence.

[2] I. Sadger, "Ein Fall von multipler Perversion mit hysterischen Absenzen," 1910. Freud, *Eine Kindheitserinnerung des Leonardo da Vinci,* 1910.

[3] Freud, *Drei Abhandlungen zur Sexualtheorie,* Second Edition, 1910.

[4] [In the original this sentence reads: "This stage has been described as '*Narzissismus*'; I prefer to give it the name of '*Narzissmus,*' which may not be so correct, but is shorter and less cacophonous."—*Trans.*]

After the stage of heterosexual object-choice has been reached, the homosexual tendencies are not, as might be supposed, done away with or brought to a stop; they are merely deflected from their sexual aim and applied to fresh uses. They now combine with portions of the ego-instincts and, as "anaclitic" components,[5] help to constitute the social instincts, thus contributing an erotic factor to friendship and comradeship, to *esprit de corps* and to the love of mankind in general. How large a contribution is in fact derived from erotic sources (though with the sexual aim inhibited) could scarcely be guessed from the normal social relations of mankind. But it is not irrelevant to note that it is precisely manifest homosexuals, and among them again precisely those that struggle against an indulgence in sensual acts, who distinguish themselves by taking a particularly active share in the general interests of humanity—interests which have themselves sprung from a sublimation of erotic instincts.

In my *Drei Abhandlungen zur Sexualtheorie* I have expressed the opinion that each stage in the development of psychosexuality affords a possibility for the occurrence of a "fixation" and thus for the laying down of a disposition to illness in later life. Persons who have not freed themselves completely from the stage of narcissism, who, that is to say, have at that point a fixation which may operate as a disposing factor for a later illness, are exposed to the danger that some unusually intense wave of libido, finding no other outlet, may lead to a sexualization of their social instincts and so undo the work of sublimation which they had achieved in the course of their development. This result may be produced by anything that causes the libido to flow backwards (*i.e.* that causes a "regression"): whether, on the one hand, for instance, the libido becomes collaterally reinforced owing to some disappointment over a woman, or is directly dammed up owing to a mishap in social relations with other men— both of these would be instances of "frustration"; or whether,

---

[5] [That is, as libidinal components "leaning up against" or supporting themselves upon the ego-instincts.—*Trans.*]

on the other hand, there is a general intensification of the libido, so that it becomes too powerful to find an outlet along the channels which are already open to it, and consequently bursts through its banks at the weakest spot. Since our analyses show that paranoiacs *endeavour to protect themselves against any such sexualization of their social instinctual cathexes,* we are driven to suppose that the weak spot in their development is to be looked for somewhere between the stages of auto-erotism, narcissism and homosexuality, and that their disposition to illness (which may perhaps be susceptible of more precise definition) must be located in that region. A similar disposition would have to be assigned to patients suffering from Kraepelin's dementia praecox or (as Bleuler has named it) *schizophrenia*; and we shall hope later on to find clues which will enable us to trace back the differences between the two disorders (as regards both the form they take and the course they run) to corresponding differences in the patients' dispositional fixations.

We consider, then, that what lies at the core of the conflict in cases of paranoia among males is a homosexual wish-phantasy of *loving a man.* But we have not in the least forgotten that the confirmation of such an important hypothesis can only follow upon the investigation of a large number of instances of every variety of paranoic disorder. We must therefore be prepared, if need be, to limit our assertion to a single type of paranoia. Nevertheless, it is a remarkable fact that the familiar principal forms of paranoia can all be represented as contradictions of the single proposition: "*I* (a man) *love him* (a man)," and indeed that they exhaust all the possible ways in which such contradictions could be formulated.

The proposition "I (a man) love him" is contradicted by:

(*a*) Delusions of persecution; for it loudly asserts: "I do not *love* him—I *hate* him."

This contradiction, which could be expressed in no other way in the unconscious,[6] cannot, however, become conscious

---

[6] Or in the "root-language," as Schreber would say.

to a paranoiac in this form. The mechanism of symptom-formation in paranoia requires that internal perceptions, or feelings, shall be replaced by external perceptions. Consequently the proposition "I hate him" becomes transformed by *projection* into another one: *"He hates* (persecutes) *me,* which will justify me in hating him." And thus the unconscious feeling, which is in fact the motive force, makes its appearance as though it were the consequence of an external perception:

"I do not *love* him—I *hate* him, because HE PERSECUTES ME."

Observation leaves room for no doubt that the persecutor is some one who was once loved.

(*b*) Another element is chosen for contradiction in *erotomania*, which remains totally unintelligible on any other view:

"I do not love *him*—I love *her*."

And in obedience to the same need for projection, the proposition is transformed into: "I notice that *she* loves me."

"I do not love *him*—I love *her,* because SHE LOVES ME." Many cases of erotomania might give an impression that they could be satisfactorily explained as being exaggerated or distorted heterosexual fixations, if our attention were not attracted by the circumstance that these infatuations invariably begin, not with any internal perception of loving, but with an external perception of being loved. But in this form of paranoia the intermediate proposition "I love *her*" can also become conscious, because the contradiction between it and the original proposition is not such a diametrical one as that between love and hate: it is, after all, possible to love both *her* and *him.* It can thus come about that the proposition which has been substituted by projection (*"she loves me"*) may make way again for the "root-language" proposition "I love *her*."

(*c*) The third way in which the original proposition can be contradicted leads us to delusions of jealousy, which we can study in the characteristic forms in which they appear in each sex.

(*α*) Let us first consider alcoholic delusions of jealousy.

The part played by alcohol in this disorder is thoroughly intelligible. We know that drink removes inhibitions and undoes the work of sublimation. It is not infrequently disappointment over a woman that drives a man to drink—which means, as a rule, that he resorts to the public-house and to the company of men, who afford him the emotional satisfaction which he has failed to get from his wife at home. If now these men become the objects of a strong libidinal cathexis in his unconscious, he will ward it off with the third kind of contradiction:

"It is not *I* who love the man—*she* loves him," and he suspects the woman in relation to all the men whom he himself is tempted to love.

Distortion by means of projection is necessarily absent in this instance, since, with the change of the subject who loves, the whole process is anyhow thrown outside the ego. The fact that the woman loves the men is a matter of external perception to him; whereas the facts that he himself does not love but hates, or that he himself loves not this but that person, are matters of internal perception.

(β) Delusions of jealousy in women are exactly analogous. "It is not *I* who love the women—but *he* loves them." The jealous woman suspects her husband in relation to all the women by whom she is herself attracted owing to her homosexuality and the dispositional effect of her excessive narcissism. The influence of the time of life at which her fixation occurred is clearly shown by the selection of the love-objects which she imputes to her husband; they are often old and quite inappropriate for a real love relation—revivals of the nurses and servants and girl friends of her childhood, or actually of sisters who were her rivals.

Now it might be supposed that a proposition consisting of three terms, such as *"I love him,"* could only be contradicted in three different ways. The delusion of jealousy contradicts the subject, delusions of persecution contradict the verb, and erotomania contradicts the object. But in fact a fourth kind of contradiction is possible, namely, one which rejects the proposition as a whole:

"I do not love at all—I do not love any one." And since, after all, one's libido must go somewhere, this proposition seems to be the psychological equivalent of the proposition: "I love only myself." So that this kind of contradiction would give us megalomania, which we may regard as a *sexual over-estimation of the ego* and may thus set beside the over-estimation of the love-object with which we are already familiar.[7]

It is of some importance in connection with other parts of the theory of paranoia to notice that we can detect an element of megalomania in most other forms of paranoic disorder. We are justified in assuming that megalomania is essentially of an infantile nature and that, as development proceeds, it is sacrificed to social considerations. Similarly, an individual's megalomania is never so vehemently suppressed as when he is in the grip of an overpowering love:

> "Denn wo die Lieb' erwachet, stirbt
> das Ich, der finstere Despot."[8]

After this discussion of the unexpectedly important part played by homosexual wish-phantasies in paranoia, let us return to the two factors in which, from the nature of things, we originally expected to find the distinguishing marks of paranoia, namely, the mechanism *by which the symptoms are formed* and the mechanism *by which repression is brought about.*

We certainly have no right to begin by assuming that these two mechanisms are identical, and that symptom-formation follows the same path as repression, each proceeding

---

[7] *Drei Abhandlungen zur Sexualtheorie* (1905), Sixth Edition, 1925, p. 23. The same view and the same formulation will be found in the papers by Abraham and Maeder to which I have already referred.

[8] Jelaleddin Rumi, translated by Rückert.

["For when the flames of Love arise,
  Then Self, the gloomy tyrant, dies."]

along it, perhaps, in an opposite direction. Nor does there seem to be any great probability that such an identity exists. Nevertheless, we shall refrain from expressing any opinion on the subject until we have completed our investigation.

The most striking characteristic of symptom-formation in paranoia is the process which deserves the name of *projection*. An internal perception is suppressed, and, instead, its content, after undergoing a certain degree of distortion, enters consciousness in the form of an external perception. In delusions of persecution the distortion consists in a transformation of affect; what should have been felt internally as love is perceived externally as hate. We should feel tempted to regard this remarkable process as the most important element in paranoia and as being absolutely pathognomonic for it, if we were not opportunely reminded of two things. For, in the first place, projection does not play the same part in all forms of paranoia; and, in the second place, it makes its appearance not only in paranoia but under other psychological conditions as well, and in fact it has a regular share assigned to it in our attitude towards the external world. For when we refer the causes of certain sensations to the external world, instead of looking for them (as we do in the case of the others) inside ourselves, this normal proceeding also deserves to be called projection. Having thus been made aware that more general psychological problems are involved in the question of the nature of projection, let us make up our minds to postpone the investigation of it (and with it that of the mechanism of paranoic symptom-formation in general) until some other occasion; and let us now turn to consider what ideas we can collect on the subject of the mechanism of repression in paranoia. I should like to say at once, however, that this temporary renunciation will turn out to be well justified; for we shall find that the manner in which the process of repression occurs is far more intimately connected with the developmental history of the libido and with the disposition to which it gives rise than is the manner in which the symptoms are formed.

In psychoanalysis we have been accustomed to look upon

pathological phenomena as being derived in a general way from repression. If we examine what is spoken of as "repression" more closely, we shall find reason to split the process up into three phases which are easily distinguishable from one another conceptually.

(1) The first phase consists in *fixation,* which is the precursor and necessary condition of every "repression." Fixation can be described in this way. One instinct or instinctual component fails to accompany the rest along the anticipated normal path of development, and, in consequence of this inhibition in its development, it is left behind at a more infantile stage. The libidinal current in question then behaves in regard to later psychological structures as though it belonged to the system of the unconscious, as though it were repressed. We have already pointed out that these instinctual fixations constitute the basis for the disposition to subsequent illness, and we may now add that they constitute above all the basis for the determination of the outcome of the third phase of repression.

(2) The second phase of repression is that of repression proper—the phase to which most attention has hitherto been given. It emanates from the more highly developed systems of the ego—systems which are capable of being conscious— and may in fact be described as a process of "after-expulsion." It gives an impression of being an essentially active process, while fixation appears rather to be a passive lagging behind. What undergo repression may either be the psychical derivatives of the original lagging instincts, when these have become reinforced and so come into conflict with the ego (or ego-syntonic instincts), or they may be psychical trends which have for other reasons aroused strong aversion. But this aversion would not in itself lead to repression, unless some connection had been established between the unwelcome trends about to be repressed and those which have been repressed already. Where this is so, the repulsion exercised by the conscious system and the attraction exercised by the unconscious one tend in the same sense, namely, towards bringing about repression. The two possibilities which are here

treated separately may in practice, perhaps, be less sharply differentiated, and the distinction between them may merely depend upon the greater or lesser degree in which the primarily repressed instincts contribute to the result.

(3) The third phase, and the most important as regards pathological phenomena, is that of miscarriage of repression, of *irruption,* of *return of the repressed*. This irruption takes its start from the point of fixation, and it involves a regression of the libidinal development to that point.

We have already alluded to the multiplicity of the possible points of fixation; there are, in fact, as many as there are stages in the development of the libido. We must be prepared to find a similar multiplicity of the mechanisms of repression proper and of the mechanisms of irruption (or of symptom-formation), and we may already begin to suspect that it will not be possible to trace back all of these multiplicities to the developmental history of the libido alone.

It is easy to see that this discussion is beginning to trench upon the problem of "choice of neurosis," which, however, cannot be taken in hand until preliminary work of another kind has been accomplished. Let us bear in mind for the present that we have already dealt with fixation, and that we have postponed the subject of symptom-formation; and let us restrict ourselves to the question of whether the analysis of Schreber's case throws any light upon the mechanism employed in paranoia for the purpose of repression proper.

At the climax of his illness, under the influence of visions which were "partly of a terrifying character, but partly, too, of an indescribable grandeur" (p. 73), Schreber became convinced of the imminence of a great catastrophe, of the end of the world. Voices told him that the work of the past 14,000 years had now come to nothing, and that the earth's allotted span was only 212 years more (p. 71); and during the last part of his stay in Prof. Flechsig's sanatorium he believed that that period had already elapsed. He himself was "the only real man still surviving," and the few human shapes that he still saw—the physician, the attendants, the other patients— he explained as being "men miracled up, cursory contraptions." Occasionally the converse current of feeling also made itself apparent; a newspaper was put into his hands in which there was a report of his own death (p. 81), he himself existed in a second, inferior shape, and in this second shape he one day quietly passed away (p. 73). But the form of his delusion in which his ego was retained and the world sacrificed proved itself by far the more powerful. He had various theories of the cause of the catastrophe. At one time he had in mind a process of glaciation owing to the withdrawal of the sun; at another it was to be destruction by an earthquake, in the occurrence of which he, in his capacity of "seer," was to act a leading part, just as another seer was alleged to have done in the earthquake of Lisbon in 1755 (p. 91). Or again, Flechsig was the culprit, since he had sown fear and terror among men, had wrecked the foundations of religion, and spread abroad neurotic states and general immorality, so that devastating pestilences had descended upon mankind (p. 91). In any case the end of the world was the consequence of the conflict which had broken out between him and Flechsig, or, according to the aetiology adopted in the second phase of his delusion, of the indissoluble bond which had been formed between him and God; it was, in fact, the inevitable result of his illness. Years afterwards, when Dr. Schreber had returned to human society, he could find no trace in the books, the musical scores, or the other articles of daily use, which fell into his hands once more, of anything to bear out his theory that there had been a gap of vast duration in the history of mankind; he was therefore forced to admit that his view was untenable: ". . . I can no longer avoid recognizing that, *externally considered,* everything is as it used to be. *Whether, nevertheless, there may not have been a profound internal change* is a question to which I shall recur later" (p. 85). He could not bring himself to doubt that during his illness the world had come to an end and that, in spite of everything, the one that he now saw before him was a different one.

Ideas of this kind about a world-catastrophe are not infrequently reported as occurring during the agitated stage in other cases of paranoia.[9] If we take our stand upon the theory of libidinal cathexis, and if we follow the hint given by Schreber's view of other people as being "cursory contraptions," we shall not find it difficult to explain these catastrophes.[10] The patient has withdrawn from the persons in his environment and from the external world generally the libidinal cathexis which he has hitherto directed on to them. Thus all things have become indifferent and irrelevant to him, and have to be explained by means of a secondary rationalization as being "miracled up, cursory contraptions." The end of the world is the projection of this internal catastrophe; for his subjective world has come to an end since he has withdrawn his love from it.[11]

After Faust has uttered the curses which free him from the world, the Chorus of Spirits sings:

> "Weh! Weh!
> Du hast sie zerstört,
> die schöne Welt,
> mit mächtiger Faust!
> sie stürzt, sie zerfällt!
> Ein Halbgott hat sie zerschlagen!
>
> .   .   .   .
>
> Mächtiger
> der Erdensöhne,
> Prächtiger

[9] An "end of the world" based upon other motives is to be found at the climax of a lovers' ecstasy (cf. Wagner's *Tristan und Isolde*); in this case it is not the ego but the single love-object which absorbs all the cathexes directed upon the external world.

[10] Cf. Abraham, "Die psychosexuellen Differenzen der Hysterie und der Dementia praecox," 1908, and Jung, *Über die Psychologie der Dementia Praecox*, 1907. Abraham's short paper contains almost all the essential views put forward in the present study of the case of Schreber.

[11] He has perhaps withdrawn from it not only his libidinal cathexis, but his interest in general—that is the cathexes that proceed from his ego as well. This question is discussed below.

> baue sie wieder,
> in deinem Busen baue sie auf!"[12]

And the paranoiac builds it up again, not more splendid, it is true, but at least so that he can once more live in it. He builds it up by the work of his delusions. *The delusion-formation, which we take to be a pathological product, is in reality an attempt at recovery, a process of reconstruction.* Such a reconstruction after the catastrophe is more or less successful, but never wholly so; in Schreber's words, there has been a "profound internal change" in the world. But the man has recaptured a relation, and often a very intense one, to the people and things in the world, although the relation may be a hostile one now, where formerly it was sympathetic and affectionate. We may conclude, then, that the process of repression proper consists in a detachment of the libido from people—and things—that were previously loved. It happens silently; we received no intelligence of it, but can only infer it from subsequent events. What forces itself so noisily upon our attention is the process of recovery, which undoes the work of repression and brings back the libido again on to the people it had abandoned. In paranoia this process is carried out by the method of projection. It was incorrect of us to say that the perception which was suppressed internally was projected outwards; the truth is rather, as we now see,

---

[12] [Literally:

> "Woe! Woe!
> Thou hast destroyed it,
> The beautiful world,
> With mighty fist!
> It tumbles, it falls in pieces!
> A demigod has shattered it!
>
> Mighty
> Among the sons of earth,
> More splendid
> Build it again,
> Build it up in thy bosom!"
>
> GOETHE, *Faust,* Part I.]

that what was abolished internally returns from without. The thorough examination of the process of projection which we have postponed to another occasion will clear up our remaining doubts on this subject.

In the meantime, however, it is a source of some satisfaction to find that our newly acquired knowledge involves us in a number of further discussions.

(1) Our first reflection will tell us that this detachment of the libido cannot occur in paranoia only; nor, on the other hand, where it does occur elsewhere, can it have such disastrous consequences. It is quite possible that a detachment of the libido is the essential and regular mechanism of every repression. We can have no positive knowledge on that point until the other disorders that are based upon repression have been similarly examined. But it is certain that in normal mental life (and not only in periods of mourning) we are constantly detaching our libido in this way from people or from other objects without falling ill. When Faust freed himself from the world by uttering his curses, the result was not a paranoia or any other neurosis but simply a particular frame of mind. The detachment of the libido, therefore, cannot in itself be the pathogenic factor in paranoia; there must be some special characteristic which distinguishes a paranoic detachment of the libido from other kinds. And it is not difficult to suggest what that characteristic may be. What use is made of the libido after it has been set free by the process of detachment? A normal person will at once begin looking about for a substitute for the lost attachment; and until that substitute has been found the liberated libido will be kept in suspension within his mind, and will there give rise to tensions and colour all his moods. In hysteria the liberated libido becomes transformed into somatic innervations or into anxiety. But in paranoia the clinical evidence goes to show that the libido, after it has been withdrawn from the object, is put to a special use. It will be remembered that the majority of cases of paranoia exhibit traces of megalomania, and that megalomania can by itself constitute a paranoia. From this it may be concluded that in paranoia the liberated libido be-

comes fixed on to the ego, and is used for the aggrandizement of the ego. A return is thus made to the stage of narcissism (familiar to us in the development of the libido), in which a person's only sexual object is his own ego. On the basis of this clinical evidence we can suppose that paranoiacs are endowed with a *fixation at the stage of narcissism,* and we can assert that the amount of *regression* characteristic of paranoia is indicated by the length of *the step back from sublimated homosexuality to narcissism.*

(2) An equally obvious objection can be based upon Schreber's case history, as well as upon many others. For it can be urged that the delusions of persecution (which were directed against Flechsig) unquestionably made their appearance at an earlier date than the phantasy of the end of the world; so that what is supposed to have been a return of the repressed actually preceded the repression itself— which is patent nonsense. In order to meet this objection we must leave the high ground of generalization and descend to the detailed consideration of actual circumstances—which are undoubtedly very much more complicated. We must admit the possibility that a detachment of the libido such as we are discussing might just as easily be a partial one, a drawing back from some single complex, as a general one. A partial detachment should be by far the commoner of the two, and should precede a general one, since to begin with it is only for a partial detachment that the influences of life provide a motive. The process may stop at the stage of a partial detachment or it may spread to a general one, which will loudly proclaim its presence by means of the symptoms of megalomania. Thus, in spite of the objection raised above, the detachment of the libido from the figure of Flechsig may have been the primary process in the case of Schreber; it was immediately followed by the appearance of the delusion, which brought back the libido on to Flechsig again (though with a negative sign to mark the fact that repression had taken place) and thus annulled the work of repression. And now the battle of repression broke out anew, but this time with more powerful weapons. In proportion as the object of con-

tention became the most important thing in the external world, trying on the one hand to draw the whole of the libido on to itself, and on the other hand mobilizing all the resistances against itself, so the struggle raging around this single object became more and more comparable to a general engagement; till at length a victory for the forces of repression could find expression in a conviction that the world had come to an end and that the self alone survived. If we review the ingenious constructions which were raised by Schreber's delusion in the domain of religion—the hierarchy of God, the qualified souls, the fore-courts of Heaven, the lower and the upper God—we can gauge in retrospect the wealth of sublimations which were brought down in ruin by the catastrophe of the general detachment of his libido.

(3) A third consideration which arises from the views that have been developed in these pages is as follows. Are we to suppose that a general detachment of the libido from the external world would be an effective enough agent to account for the idea of the "end of the world"? Or would not the egoistic cathexes which still remained in existence have been sufficient to maintain *rapport* with the external world? To meet this difficulty we should either have to assume that what we call libidinal cathexis (that is, interest emanating from erotic sources) coincides with interest in general, or we should have to consider the possibility that a very widespread disturbance in the distribution of the libido may bring about a corresponding disturbance in the egoistic cathexes. But these are problems with which we are still quite unaccustomed to deal, and before which we stand helpless. It would be otherwise if we could start out from some well-grounded theory of instincts; but in fact we have nothing of the kind at our disposal. We regard instinct as being a term situated on the frontier-line between the somatic and the mental, and consider it as denoting the mental representative of organic forces. Further, we accept the popular distinction between egoistic instincts and a sexual instinct; for such a distinction seems to agree with the biological conception that the individual has a double orientation, aiming on the one hand at

self-preservation and on the other at the preservation of the species. But beyond this are only hypotheses, which we have taken up—and are quite ready to drop again—in order to help us to find our bearings in the chaos of the obscurer processes of the mind. What we expect from psychoanalytic investigations of pathological mental processes is precisely that they shall drive us to some conclusions on questions involving the theory of instincts. These investigations, however, are in their infancy and are only being carried out by isolated workers, so that the hopes we place in them must still remain unfulfilled. We can no more dismiss the possibility that disturbances of the libido may react upon the egoistic cathexes than we can overlook the converse possibility—namely, that a secondary or induced disturbance of the libidinal processes may result from abnormal changes in the ego. Indeed, it is probable that processes of this kind constitute the distinctive characteristic of psychoses. How much of all this may apply to paranoia it is impossible at present to say. There is one consideration, however, on which I should like to lay stress. It cannot be asserted that a paranoiac, even at the height of the repressive process, withdraws his interest from the external world so completely as must be considered to occur in certain other kinds of hallucinatory psychosis (such as Meynert's amentia). The paranoiac perceives the external world and takes into account any alterations that may happen in it, and the effect it makes upon him stimulates him to invent explanatory theories (such as Schreber's description of men as "cursory contraptions"). It therefore appears to me far more probable that the paranoiac's altered relation to the world is to be explained entirely or in the main by the loss of his libidinal interest.

(4) It is impossible to avoid asking (in view of the close connection between the two disorders) how far this conception of paranoia will affect our conception of dementia praecox. I am of opinion that Kraepelin was entirely justified in taking the step of separating off a large part of what had hitherto been called paranoia and merging it, together with catatonia and certain other varieties of disease, into a new

clinical unit—though "dementia praecox" was a particularly unhappy name to choose for it. The designation chosen by Bleuler for the same group of varieties—"schizophrenia"— is also open to the objection that the name appears appropriate only so long as we forget its literal meaning. For otherwise it prejudices the issue, since the name connotes a theoretically postulated characteristic of the disease—a characteristic, moreover, which does not belong exclusively to it, and which, in the light of other considerations, cannot be regarded as the essential one. However, it is not on the whole of very great importance what names we give to clinical pictures. What seems to me more essential is that paranoia should be maintained as an independent clinical type, however frequently the picture it presents may be complicated by the presence of schizophrenic features. For, from the standpoint of the libido theory, while it would resemble dementia praecox in so far as the repression proper would in both disorders have the same principal feature—detachment of the libido, together with its regression on to the ego—it would be distinguished from dementia praecox by having its dispositional point of fixation differently located and by having a different mechanism for the return of the repressed (that is, for the formation of symptoms). It would seem to me the most convenient plan to give dementia praecox the name of *paraphrenia*. This term has no special connotation, and it would serve to indicate a relationship with paranoia (a name which may be regarded as fixed) and would further recall hebephrenia, an entity which is now merged in dementia praecox. It is true that the name has already been proposed for other purposes; but this need not concern us, since the alternative applications have not passed into general use.

Abraham has very convincingly shown[13] that the turning away of the libido from the external world is a particularly clearly-marked feature in dementia praecox. It is from this feature that we infer the fact that the repression is effected by means of detachment of the libido. Here we may regard

[13] In the paper already quoted.

the phase of agitated hallucinations as a struggle between repression and an attempt at recovery (an endeavour to bring
the libido back again on to its objects). Jung, with extraordinary analytic acumen, has perceived that the "flight of
ideas" and motor stereotypies occurring in this disorder are
the relics of former object-cathexes, clung to with convulsive
energy. This attempt at recovery (which observers mistake
for the disease itself) does not, as in paranoia, make use of
projection, but employs a hallucinatory (hysterical) mechanism. This is one of the great distinctions between dementia
praecox and paranoia; and light can be thrown upon its
genesis from another quarter. The second distinction is
shown by the issue of the disease in those cases where the
process has become sufficiently general. The prognosis is on
the whole more unfavourable than in paranoia; the victory
lies with the forces of repression and not, as in the former,
with those of reconstruction. Regression travels back not
merely to the stage of narcissism (manifesting itself in the
shape of megalomania) but to a complete abandonment of
object-love and to a restoration of infantile auto-erotism. The
dispositional point of fixation must therefore be situated further back than in paranoia, and must lie somewhere at the
beginning of the course of development from auto-erotism to
object-love. Moreover, it is not at all likely that homosexual
impulses, which are so frequently (perhaps invariably) to be
found in paranoia, play an equally important part in the
aetiology of that far more comprehensive disorder, dementia
praecox.

Our hypotheses as to the dispositional fixations in paranoia
and paraphrenia make it easy to see that a case may begin
with paranoic symptoms and may yet develop into a dementia
praecox, and that paranoid and schizophrenic phenomena
may be combined in any proportion. And we can understand
how a clinical picture such as Schreber's can come about, and
merit the name of a paranoid dementia, from the fact that
in its production of a wish-phantasy and of hallucinations it
shows paraphrenic traits, while in its exciting cause, in its use
of the mechanism of projection, and in its final issue it ex-

hibits a paranoid character. For it is possible for several fixations to be left behind in the course of development, and each of these in succession may allow an irruption of the ousted libido—beginning, presumably, with the later acquired fixations, and then, as the illness develops, affecting the original ones that lie nearer the starting-point. We should be glad to know to what conditions the relatively favourable issue of the present case is due; for we cannot willingly attribute the whole responsibility for the outcome to anything so casual as the "improvement due to change of residence,"[14] which set in after the patient's removal from Prof. Flechsig's sanatorium. But our insufficient acquaintance with the intimate circumstances of the history of the case makes it impossible to give an answer to this interesting question. It may be suspected, however, that what enabled Schreber to reconcile himself to his homosexual phantasy, and so made it possible for his illness to terminate in something approximating to a recovery, may have been the fact that his father-complex was in the main positively toned and that in real life the later years of his relationship with an excellent father had probably been unclouded.

Since I neither fear the criticism of others nor shrink from criticizing myself, I have no motive for avoiding the mention of a similarity which may possibly damage our libido theory in the estimation of many of my readers. Schreber's "rays of God," which are made up of a condensation of the sun's rays, of nerve-fibers, and of spermatozoa, are in reality nothing else than a concrete representation and external projection of libidinal cathexes; and they thus lend his delusions a striking similarity with our theory. His belief that the world must come to an end because his ego was attracting all the rays to itself, his anxious concern at a later period, during the process of reconstruction, lest God should sever his ray-connection with him,—these and many other details of Schreber's delusional formation sound almost like endopsychic perceptions of the processes whose existence I have assumed in these

[14] Cf. Riklin, "Über Versetzungsbesserungen," 1905.

pages as the basis of our explanation of paranoia. I can never-theless call a friend and fellow-specialist to witness that I had developed my theory of paranoia before I became ac-quainted with the contents of Schreber's book. It remains for the future to decide whether there is more delusion in my theory than I should like to admit, or whether there is more truth in Schreber's delusion than other people are as yet prepared to believe.

Lastly, I cannot conclude the present work, which is once again only a fragment of a larger whole, without foreshadow-ing the two chief theses towards the establishment of which the libido theory of the neuroses and psychoses is advancing, namely, that the neuroses arise in the main from a conflict between the ego and the sexual instinct, and that the forms which the neuroses assume bear the imprint of the course of development followed by the libido—and by the ego.

Postscript[1]

IN DEALING WITH the case history of Senatspräsident Schreber I purposely restricted myself to a minimum of interpretation; and I feel confident that every reader with a knowledge of psychoanalysis will have learned from the material which I presented more than was explicitly stated by me, and that he will have found no difficulty in drawing the threads closer and in reaching conclusions at which I no more than hinted. By a happy chance the same issue of this periodical as that in which my own paper appeared showed that the attention of some other contributors had been directed to Schreber's autobiography, and made it easy to guess how much more material remains to be gathered from the symbolic content of the phantasies and delusions of the gifted paranoiac.[2]

Since I published my work upon Schreber, a chance acquisition of knowledge has put me in a position to appreciate one of his delusional beliefs more adequately, and to recognize its weath of associations with *mythology*. I mentioned

[1] [First published in the second half of the same volume of the *Jahrbuch* as that in which the main part of the paper appeared.— *Trans.*]

[2] Cf. Jung, "Wandlungen und Symbole der Libido" (1911), pp. 164 and 207; and Spielrein, "Über den psychischen Inhalt eines Falles von Schizophrenie (Dementia Praecox)" (1911), p. 350.

on p. 154 the patient's peculiar relation to the sun, and I felt obliged to explain the sun as a sublimated "father-symbol." The sun used to speak to him in human language and thus revealed itself to him as a living being. Schreber was in the habit of abusing it and shouting threats at it; he declares, moreover, that when he stood facing it and spoke aloud its rays would turn pale before him. After his "recovery" he boasts that he can gaze at it without any difficulty and without being more than slightly dazzled by it, a thing which had naturally been impossible for him formerly.[3]

It is out of this delusional privilege of being able to gaze at the sun without being dazzled that the mythological interest arises. We read in Reinach[4] that the natural historians of antiquity attributed this power only to the eagle, who, as a dweller in the highest regions of the air, was brought into especially intimate relation with the heavens, with the sun, and with lightning.[5] We learn from the same sources, moreover, that the eagle puts his young to a test before recognizing them as his legitimate offspring. Unless they can succeed in looking into the sun without blinking, they are cast out from the eyrie.

There can be no doubt about the meaning of this animal myth. It is certain that what is here ascribed to animals is nothing more than a hallowed custom among men. The procedure gone through by the eagle with his young is an *ordeal*, a test of lineage, such as is reported of the most various races of antiquity. Thus the Celts living upon the banks of the Rhine used to entrust their new-born babies to the waters of the river, in order to ascertain whether they were truly of their own blood. The clan of Psylli, who inhabited what is now Tripoli, boasted that they were descended from snakes, and used to expose their infants to contact with them; those

[3] See the footnote to p. 139 of Schreber's book.

[4] *Cultes, Mythes et Religions*, 1908, tome iii. p. 80. (Quoting Keller, *Tiere des Altertums*.)

[5] Images of eagles were set up at the highest points of temples, so as to serve as "magical" lightning-conductors. (Cf. Reinach, *loc. cit.*)

who were true-born children of the clan were either not bitten or recovered rapidly from the effects of the bite.[6] The assumption underlying these trials leads us deep into the *totemistic* habits of thought of primitive peoples. The totem—an animal, or a natural force animistically conceived, to which the tribe traces back its origin—spares the members of the tribe as its own children, just as it itself is honoured by them as their ancestor and, if need be, spared by them. We have here arrived at the consideration of matters which, as it seems to me, may make it possible to arrive at a psychoanalytic explanation of the origins of religion.

The eagle, then, who makes his young look into the sun and requires of them that they shall not be dazzled by its light, is behaving as though he were himself a descendant of the sun and were submitting his children to a test of their ancestry. And when Schreber boasts that he can look into the sun without being punished and without being dazzled, he has rediscovered the mythological method of expressing his filial relation to the sun, and has confirmed us once again in our view that the sun is a symbol of the father. It will be remembered that during his illness Schreber gave free expression to his family pride,[7] and that we discovered in the fact of his childlessness a human motive for his illness having been brought on by a feminine wish-phantasy. Thus the connection between his delusional privilege and the basis of his illness becomes evident.

This short postscript to my analysis of a paranoid patient may serve to show that Jung had excellent grounds for his assertion that the mythopoeic forces of mankind are not extinct, but that to this very day they give rise in the neuroses to the same psychological products as in the remotest past ages. I should like to take up a suggestion that I myself made

---

[6] For list of references see Reinach, *op. cit.*, tome iii. p. 80, and tome i. p. 74.

[7] "The Schrebers are members of the highest aristocracy of Heaven" (p. 24).—"Aristocracy" [*"Adel"*] forms a connection with "eagle" [*"Adler,"* lit. "noble bird"].

some time ago,[8] and add that the same holds good of the forces that work for the formation of religions. And I am of opinion that the time will soon be ripe for us to make an extension of a principle of which the truth has long been recognized by psychoanalysts, and to complete whât has hitherto had only an individual and ontogenetic application by the addition of its anthropological and phylogenetically conceived counterpart. "In dreams and in neuroses," so our principle has run, "we come once more upon the *child* and the peculiarities which characterize his modes of thought and his emotional life." "And we come upon the *savage* too," thus we may complete our proposition, "upon the *primitive* man, as he stands revealed to us in the light of the researches of archaeology and of ethnology."

[8] "Obsessive Acts and Religious Practices," (*Character and Culture*, Collier Books edition BS 193V).

FROM THE HISTORY OF AN
INFANTILE NEUROSIS[1] (1918)

I

Introductory Remarks

THE CASE UPON which I propose to report in the following
pages (once again only in a fragmentary manner) is characterized by a number of peculiarities which require to be
emphasized before I proceed to a description of the facts
themselves. It is concerned with a young man whose health
had broken down in his eighteenth year after a gonorrhoeal
infection, and who was entirely incapacitated and completely

---

[1] [First published in *Sammlung kleiner Schriften*, iv., 1918;
omitted from subsequent editions of *Sammlung*, iv., and included
in *Sammlung*, v., 1922.] This case history was written down shortly
after the termination of the treatment, in the winter of 1914–15.
At that time I was still freshly under the impression of the twisted
re-interpretations which C. G. Jung and Alfred Adler were endeavouring to give to the findings of psychoanalysis. This paper
is therefore connected with my essay "On the History of the
Psychoanalytic Movement" which was published in the *Jahrbuch
der Psychoanalyse* in 1914. [*The History of the Psychoanalytic
Movement*, Collier Books edition AS 580V.] It supplements the
polemic contained in that essay, which is in its essence of a per-

dependent upon other people when he began his psychoanalytic treatment several years later. He had lived an approximately normal life during the ten years of his boyhood that preceded the date of his illness, and got through his studies at his secondary school without much trouble. But his earlier years were dominated by a severe neurotic disturbance, which began immediately before his fourth birthday in the shape of anxiety-hysteria (animal phobia), then changed into an obsessional neurosis with a religious content, and lasted with its offshoots as far as into his tenth year.

Only this infantile neurosis will be the subject of my communication. In spite of the patient's direct request, I have abstained from writing a complete history of his illness, of his treatment, and of his recovery, because I recognized that such a task was technically impracticable and socially impermissible. This at the same time removes the possibility of demonstrating the connection between his illness in infancy and his later and permanent one. As regards the latter I can only say that on account of it the patient spent a long time in German sanatoriums, and was at that period classified in the most authoritative quarters as a case of "manic-depressive insanity." This diagnosis was certainly applicable to the patient's father, whose life, with its wealth of activity and interests, was disturbed by repeated attacks of severe depression. But in the son, I was never able, during an observation which

---

sonal character, by an objective estimation of the analytical material. It was originally intended for the next volume of the *Jahrbuch,* the appearance of which was, however, postponed indefinitely owing to the obstacles raised by the Great War. I therefore decided to add it to the present collection of papers, which was being issued by a new publisher. Meanwhile I had been obliged to deal in my *Introductory Lectures on Psychoanalysis* (which I delivered in 1916 and 1917) with many points which should have been raised for the first time in this paper. No alterations of any importance have been made in the text of the first draft; additions are indicated by means of square brackets. [There are only two such additional passages, occurring on pp. 245 and 288. Elsewhere in this paper, as in the rest of the volume, square brackets indicate additions by the translators.]

lasted several years, to detect any changes of mood which were disproportionate to the apparent psychological situation either in their intensity or in the circumstances of their appearance. I have formed the opinion that this case, like many others which clinical psychiatry has labelled with the most multifarious and shifting diagnoses, is to be regarded as a condition following upon an obsessional neurosis which has come to an end spontaneously, but has left a defect behind it after recovery.

My description will therefore deal with an infantile neurosis which was analysed not while it actually existed, but only fifteen years after its termination. This state of things has its advantages as well as its disadvantages in comparison with the alternative. An analysis which is conducted upon a neurotic child itself must, as a matter of course, appear to be more trustworthy, but it cannot be very rich in material; too many words and thoughts have to be lent to the child, and even so the deepest strata may turn out to be impenetrable to consciousness. An analysis of a childhood disorder through the medium of recollection in an intellectually mature adult is free from these limitations; but it necessitates our taking into account the distortion and refurbishing to which a person's own past is subjected when it is looked back upon from a later period. The first alternative perhaps gives the more convincing results; the second is by far the more instructive.

In any case it may be maintained that analyses of children's neuroses can claim to possess a specially high theoretical interest. They afford us, roughly speaking, as much help towards a proper understanding of the neuroses of adults as do children's dreams in respect to the dreams of adults. Not, indeed, that they are more perspicuous or poorer in elements; in fact, the difficulty of feeling one's way into the mental life of a child makes them a particularly difficult piece of work for the physician. But nevertheless, so many of the later deposits are wanting in them that the essence of the neurosis springs to the eyes with unmistakable distinctness. In the present phase of the battle which is raging round psychoanalysis the resistance to its findings has, as we know, taken on a new form. People were content formerly to dispute the reality of the facts which are asserted by analysis; and for this purpose the best technique seemed to be to avoid examining them. That procedure appears to be slowly exhausting itself; and people are now adopting another plan—of recognizing the facts, but of eliminating, by means of twisted interpretations, the consequences that follow from them, so that the critics are defended against the objectionable novelties as efficiently as ever. The study of children's neuroses exposes the complete inadequacy of these shallow or highhanded attempts at re-interpretation. It shows the predominant part that is played in the formation of neuroses by those libidinal motive forces which are so eagerly disavowed, and reveals the absence of any aspirations towards remote cultural aims, of which the child still knows nothing, and which cannot therefore be of any significance for him.

Another characteristic which makes the present analysis noteworthy is connected with the severity of the illness and the duration of the treatment. Analyses which lead to a favourable conclusion in a short time are of value in ministering to the therapeutist's self-sufficiency and substantiate the medical importance of psychoanalysis; but they remain for the most part insignificant as regards the advancement of scientific knowledge. Nothing new is learnt from them. In fact they only succeed so quickly because everything that was necessary for their accomplishment was already known. Something new can only be gained from analyses that present special difficulties, and to the overcoming of these a great deal of time has to be devoted. Only in such cases do we succeed in descending into the deepest and most primitive strata of mental development and in gaining from there solutions for the problems of the later formations. And we feel afterwards that, strictly speaking, only an analysis which has penetrated so far deserves the name. Naturally a single case does not give us all the information that we should like to have. Or, to put it more correctly, it might teach us everything, if we were only in a position to make everything out, and if we were not compelled by the inexperience of our own perception to content ourselves with a little.

As regards these fertile difficulties the case I am about to discuss left nothing to be desired. The first years of the treatment produced scarcely any change. Owing to a fortunate concatenation, all of the external circumstances nevertheless combined to make it possible to proceed with the therapeutic experiment. I can easily believe that in less favourable circumstances the treatment would have been given up after a short time. Of the physician's point of view I can only declare that in a case of this kind he must behave as "timelessly" as the unconscious itself, if he wishes to learn anything or to achieve anything. And in the end he will succeed in doing so, if he has the strength to renounce any short-sighted therapeutical ambition. It is not to be expected that the amount of patience, adaptability, insight, and confidence demanded of the patient and his relatives will be forthcoming in many other cases. But the analyst has a right to feel that the results which he has attained from such lengthy work in one case will help substantially to reduce the length of the treatment in a subsequent case of equal severity, and that by submitting on a single occasion to the timelessness of the unconscious he will be brought nearer to vanquishing it in the end.

The patient with whom I am here concerned remained for a long time unassailably intrenched behind an attitude of obliging apathy. He listened, understood, and remained unapproachable. His unimpeachable intelligence was, as it were, cut off from the instinctual forces which governed his behaviour in the few relations of life that remained to him. It required a long education to induce him to take an independent share in the work; and when as a result of this exertion he began for the first time to feel relief, he immediately knocked off the work in order to avoid any further changes, and in order to remain comfortably in the situation which had been thus established. His shrinking from an independent existence was so great as to outweigh all the vexations of his illness. Only one way was to be found of overcoming it. I was obliged to wait until his attachment to myself had become strong enough to counterbalance this shrinking, and then played off this one factor against the other. I determined—but not until trustworthy signs had led me to judge that the right moment had come—that the treatment must be brought to an end at a particular fixed date, no matter how far it had advanced. I was resolved to keep to the date; and eventually the patient came to see that I was in earnest. Under the inexorable pressure of this fixed limit his resistance and his fixation to the illness gave way, and now in a disproportionately short time the analysis produced all the material which made it possible to clear up his inhibitions and remove his symptoms. All the information, too, which enabled me to understand his infantile neurosis is derived from this last period of the work, during which resistance temporarily disappeared and the patient gave an impression of lucidity which is usually attainable only in hypnosis.

Thus the course of this treatment illustrates a maxim whose truth has long been appreciated in the technique of analysis. The length of the road over which an analysis must travel with the patient, and the quantity of material which must be mastered on the way, are of no importance in comparison with the resistance which is met with in the course of the work, and are only of importance at all in so far as they are necessarily proportional to the resistance. The situation is the same as when to-day an enemy army needs weeks and months to make its way across a stretch of country which in times of peace was traversed by an express train in a few hours and which only a short time before had been passed over by the defending army in a few days.

A third peculiarity of the analysis which is to be described in these pages has only increased my difficulty in deciding to make a report upon it. On the whole its results have coincided in the most satisfactory manner with our previous knowledge, or have been easily embodied into it. Many details, however, seemed to me myself to be so extraordinary and incredible that I felt some hesitation in asking other people to believe in them. I requested the patient to make the strictest criticism of his recollections, but he found nothing improbable in his statements and adhered closely to them. Readers may at all events rest assured that I myself am only reporting what I came upon as an independent experience, uninfluenced by my expectation. So that there was nothing left for me but to remember the wise saying that there are more things in heaven and earth than are dreamed of in our philosophy. Any one who could succeed in eliminating his pre-existing convictions even more thoroughly could no doubt discover even more such things.

General Survey of the Patient's Environment and of the History of the Case

I AM UNABLE to give either a purely historical or a purely thematic account of my patient's story; I can write a consecutive history neither of the treatment nor of the disease, but I shall find myself obliged to combine the two methods of presentation. It is well known that no means has been found of in any way introducing into the reproduction of an analysis the sense of conviction which results from the analysis itself. Exhaustive verbatim reports of the proceedings during the hours of analysis would certainly be of no help at all; and in any case the technique of the treatment makes it impossible to draw them up. So analyses such as this are not published in order to produce conviction in the minds of those whose attitude has hitherto been recusant and sceptical. The intention is only to bring forward some new facts for investigators who have already been convinced by their own clinical experiences.

I shall begin, then, by giving a picture of the child's world, and by telling as much of the story of his childhood as could be learnt without any exertion; it was not, indeed, for several years that the story became any less incomplete and obscure.

His parents had been married young, and were still leading a happy married life, upon which their ill-health was soon to throw the first shadows. His mother began to suffer from abdominal disorders, and his father from his first attacks of depression, which led to his absence from home. Naturally the patient only came to understand his father's illness very much later on, but he was aware of his mother's weak health even in his early childhood. As a consequence of it she had relatively little to do with the children. One day, not later than his fourth year, while his mother was seeing off the doctor to the station and he himself was walking beside her, holding her hand, he overheard her lamenting her condition. Her words made a deep impression upon him, and later on he applied them to himself. He was not the only child; he had a sister, about two years his elder, lively, gifted, and precociously naughty, who was to play an important part in his life.

As far back as he could remember he was looked after by a nurse, an uneducated old woman of peasant birth, with an untiring affection for him. He served her as a substitute for a son of her own who had died young. The family lived on a country estate, from which they used to move to another for the summer. The two estates were not far from a large town. There was a break in his childhood when his parents sold the estates and moved into the town. Near relatives used often to pay them long visits upon one estate or the other—brothers of his father, sisters of his mother and their children, his grandparents on his mother's side. During the summer his parents used to be away for a few weeks. In a screen-memory he saw himself with his nurse looking after the carriage which was driving off with his father, mother, and sister, and then going peaceably back into the house. He must have been very small at that time.[1] Next summer his sister was left at home, and an English governess was engaged, who became responsible for the supervision of the children.

In his later years he was told many stories about his child-

---

[1] Two and a half years old. It was possible later on to determine almost all the dates with certainty.

hood.[2] He knew a great deal himself, but it was naturally disconnected both as regards date and subject-matter. One of these traditions, which was repeated over and over again in front of him on the occasion of his later illness, introduces us to the problem with whose solution we shall be occupied. He seems at first to have been a very good-natured, tractable, and even quiet child, so that they used to say of him that he ought to have been the girl and his elder sister the boy. But once, when his parents came back from their summer holiday, they found him transformed. He had become discontented, irritable, and violent, took offense at every possible occasion, and then flew into a rage and screamed like a savage; so that, when this state of things continued, his parents expressed their misgivings as to whether it would be possible to send him to school later on. This happened during the summer while the English governess was with them. She turned out to be an eccentric and quarrelsome person, and, moreover, to be addicted to drink. The boy's mother was therefore inclined to ascribe the alteration in his character to the influence of this Englishwoman, and assumed that she had irritated him by her treatment. His sharp-sighted grandmother, who had spent the summer with the children, was of opinion that the boy's irritability had been provoked by the dissensions between the Englishwoman and the nurse. The Englishwoman had repeatedly called the nurse a witch, and had obliged her to leave the room; the little boy had openly taken the side of his beloved "Nanya" and let the governess see his hatred.

[2] Information of this kind may, as a rule, be employed as absolutely authentic material. It may seem tempting to take the easy course of filling up the gaps in a patient's memory by making inquiries from the older members of his family; but I cannot advise too strongly against such a technique. Any stories that may be told by relatives in reply to inquiries and requests are at the mercy of every critical misgiving that can come into play. One invariably regrets having made oneself dependent upon such information; at the same time confidence in the analysis is shaken and a court of appeal is set up over it. Whatever can be remembered at all will anyhow come to light in the further course of analysis.

However it may have been, the Englishwoman was sent away soon after the parents' return, without there being any consequent change in the child's unbearable behaviour.

The patient had preserved his memory of this naughty period. According to his belief he made the first of his scenes one Christmas, when he was not given a double quantity of presents—which were his due, because Christmas Day was at the same time his birthday. He did not spare even his beloved Nanya with his importunities and sensibilities, and even tormented her more remorselessly perhaps than any one. But the phase which brought with it this change in character was inextricably connected in his memory with many other strange and pathological phenomena which he was unable to arrange in a temporal sequence. He threw all the incidents that I am now about to relate (which cannot possibly have been contemporaneous, and which are full of internal contradictions) into one and the same period of time, to which he gave the name "still upon the first estate." He thought they must have left that estate by the time he was five years old. He could recollect, then, how he had suffered from a fear, which his sister exploited for the purpose of tormenting him. There was a particular picture-book, in which a wolf was represented, standing upright and striding along. Whenever he caught sight of this picture he began to scream like a lunatic that he was afraid of the wolf coming and eating him up. His sister, however, always succeeded in arranging so that he was obliged to see this picture, and was delighted at his terror. Meanwhile he was also frightened by other animals as well, big and little. Once he was running after a beautiful big butterfly, with striped yellow wings which ended in points, in the hope of catching it. (It was no doubt a "swallow-tail.") He was suddenly seized with a terrible fear of the creature, and, screaming, gave up the chase. He also felt fear and loathing of beetles and caterpillars. Yet he could also remember that at this very time he used to torment beetles and cut caterpillars to pieces. Horses, too, gave him an uncanny feeling. If a horse was beaten he began to scream, and he was once obliged to leave a circus on that account. On other occasions he himself enjoyed beating horses. Whether these contradictory sorts of attitudes towards animals were really in operation simultaneously, or whether they did not more probably replace one another, but if so in what order and when—to all these questions his memory could offer no decisive reply. He was also unable to say whether his naughty period was replaced by a phase of illness or whether it persisted right through the latter. But, in any case, the statements of his that follow justified the assumption that during these years of his childhood he went through an easily recognizable attack of obsessional neurosis. He related how during a long period he was very pious. Before he went to sleep he was obliged to pray for a long time and to make an endless series of signs of the cross. In the evening, too, he used to make the round of all the holy pictures that hung in the room, taking a chair with him, upon which he climbed, and used to kiss each one of them devoutly. There was another fact that was utterly inconsistent with this pious ceremonial—but perhaps it was, nevertheless, quite consistent with it—for he recollected some blasphemous thoughts which used to come into his head like an inspiration from the devil. He was obliged to think "God—swine" or "God—shit." Once while he was on a journey to a health-resort in Germany he was tormented by the obsession of having to think of the Holy Trinity whenever he saw three heaps of horse-dung or other excrement lying in the road. At that time he used to carry out another peculiar ceremonial when he saw people that he felt sorry for, such as beggars, cripples, or very old men. He had to breathe out noisily, so as not to become like them; and under certain other conditions he had to draw in his breath vigorously. I naturally assumed that these obvious symptoms of an obsessional neurosis belonged to a somewhat later time and stage of development than the signs of anxiety and the cruel treatment of animals.

The patient's maturer years were marked by a very unsatisfactory relation to his father, who, after repeated attacks of depression, was no longer able to conceal the pathological features of his character. In the earliest years of the patient's childhood this relation had been a very affectionate one, and the recollection of it had remained in his memory. His father was very fond of him, and liked playing with him. From an early age he was proud of his father, and was always declaring that he would like to be a gentleman like him. His Nanya told him that his sister was his mother's child, but that he was his father's—which had very much pleased him. Towards the end of his childhood there was an estrangement between him and his father. His father had an unmistakable preference for his sister, and he felt very much slighted by this. Later on fear of his father became the dominating factor.

All of the phenomena which the patient associated with the phase of his life that began with his naughtiness disappeared in about his eighth year. They did not disappear at a single blow, and made occasional reappearances, but finally gave way, in the patient's opinion, before the influence of the masters and tutors, who then took the place of the women who had hitherto looked after him. Here, then, in the briefest outline, are the riddles for which the analysis had to find a solution. What was the origin of the sudden change in the boy's character? What was the significance of his phobia and of his perversities? How did he arrive at his obsessive piety? And how are all these phenomena inter-related? I will once more recall the fact that our therapeutic work was concerned with a subsequent and recent neurotic illness, and that light could only be thrown upon these earlier problems when the course of the analysis led away for a time from the present, and forced us to make a *détour* through the prehistoric period of childhood.

III

The Seduction and Its Immediate Consequences

IT IS EASY TO understand that the first suspicion fell upon the English governess, for the change in the boy made its appearance while she was there. Two screen-memories had persisted, which were incomprehensible in themselves, and which related to her. Once, as she was walking on in front, she had said to the people coming behind her: "Do look at my little tail!" Another time, on a drive, her hat flew away, to the two children's great satisfaction. This pointed to the castration complex, and might permit of a construction being made to the effect that a threat uttered by her against the boy had been largely responsible for originating his abnormal conduct. There is no danger at all in communicating constructions of this kind to the person under analysis; they never do any damage to the analysis if they are mistaken; but at the same time they are not put forward unless there is some prospect of reaching a nearer approximation to the truth by means of them. The first effect of this supposition was the appearance of some dreams, which it was not possible to interpret completely, but all of which seemed to centre around the same material. As far as they could be understood, they were concerned with aggressive actions on the boy's part against his sister or against the governess and with energetic reproofs and punishments on account of them. It was as though . . . after her bath . . . he had tried . . . to strip his sister . . . to tear off her coverings . . . or veils—and so on. But it was not possible to get at the content with certainty from the interpretation; and since these dreams gave an impression of always working over the same material in various different ways, the correct reading of these ostensible reminiscences became assured. It could only be a question of phantasies, which the dreamer had made on the subject of his childhood at some time or other, probably at the age of puberty, and which had now come to the surface again in this unrecognizable form.

The explanation came at a single blow, when the patient suddenly called to mind the fact that, when he was still very small, "upon the first estate," his sister had seduced him into sexual practices. First came a recollection that in the watercloset, which the children used frequently to visit together, she had made this proposal: "Let's show one another our bottoms," and had proceeded from words to deeds. Subsequently the more essential part of the seduction came to light, with full particulars as to time and locality. It was in spring, at a time when his father was away; the children were in one room playing on the floor, while their mother was working in the next. His sister had taken hold of his member and played with it, at the same time telling him incomprehensible stories about his Nanya, as though by way of explanation. His Nanya, she said, used to do the same thing with all kinds of people—for instance, with the gardener: she used to stand him on his head, and then take hold of his genitals.

Here, then, was the explanation of the phantasies whose existence had already been divined. They were meant to efface the memory of an event which later on seemed offensive to the patient's masculine self-esteem, and they reached this end by putting an imaginary and desirable converse in the place of the historical truth. According to these phantasies it was not he who had played the passive part towards his sister, but, on the contrary, he had been aggressive, had tried to see his sister stripped, had been rejected and punished, and had for that reason got into the rage which the family tradition talked of so much. It was also appropriate to weave the governess into this imaginative composition, since the chief responsibility for his fits of rage had been ascribed to her by his mother and grandmother. These phantasies, therefore, corresponded exactly to the legends by means of which a nation that has become great and proud tries to conceal the insignificance and failure of its beginnings.

The governess can actually have had only a very remote share in the seduction and its consequences. The scenes with his sister took place in the early part of the same year in which, at the height of the summer, the Englishwoman arrived to take the place of his absent parents. The boy's hostility to the governess came about, rather, in another way. By abusing the nurse and slandering her as a witch, she was in his eyes following in the footsteps of his sister, who had first told him such monstrous stories about the nurse; and in this way she enabled him to express openly against herself the aversion which, as we shall hear, he had developed against his sister as a result of his seduction.

But his seduction by his sister was certainly not a phantasy. Its credibility was increased by some information which had never been forgotten and which dated from a later part of his life, when he was grown up. A cousin who was more than ten years his elder told him in a conversation about his sister that he very well remembered what a forward and sensual little thing she had been: once, when she was a child of four or five, she had sat on his lap and opened his trousers to take hold of his member.

I should like at this point to break off the story of my patient's childhood and say something of this sister, of her development and later fortunes, and of the influence she had upon him. She was two years older than he was, and had always remained ahead of him. As a child she was boyish and unmanageable, but she then entered upon a brilliant intellectual development and distinguished herself by her acute and realistic powers of mind; she inclined in her studies to the natural sciences, but also produced imaginative writings of which her father had a high opinion. She was mentally far superior to her numerous early admirers, and used to make jokes at their expense. In her early twenties, however, she began to be depressed, complained that she was not good-looking enough, and withdrew from all society. She was sent to travel in the company of an acquaintance, an elderly lady, and after her return told a number of most improbable stories of how she had been ill-treated by her companion, but remained with her affections obviously fixed upon her alleged tormentor. While she was on a second journey, soon afterwards, she poisoned herself and died far away from her home. Her disorder is probably to be regarded as the beginning of a dementia praecox. She was one of the proofs of the conspicuously neuropathic heredity in her family, but by no means the only one. An uncle, her father's brother, died after long years of life as an eccentric, with indications pointing to the presence of a severe obsessional neurosis; while a good number of collateral relatives were and are afflicted with less serious nervous complaints.

Leaving the seduction on one side for the moment—during his childhood our patient found in his sister an inconvenient competitor for the good opinion of his parents, and he felt very much oppressed by her merciless display of superiority. Later on he especially envied her the respect which his father showed for her mental capacity and intellectual achievements, while he, intellectually inhibited as he was since his obsessional neurosis, had to be content with a lower estimation. From his fourteenth year onwards the relations between the brother and sister began to improve; a similar disposition of mind and a common opposition to their parents brought them so close together that they got on with each other like the best of friends. During the tempestuous sexual excitement of his puberty he ventured upon an attempt at an intimate physical approach. She rejected him with equal decision and dexterity, and he at once turned away from her to a little peasant girl who was a servant in the house and had the same name as his sister. In doing so he was taking a step which had a determinant influence upon his heterosexual object-choice, for all the girls with whom he subsequently fell in love—often with the clearest indications of compulsion—were also servants, whose education and intelligence were necessarily far inferior to his own. If all of these objects of his love were substitutes for the figure of the sister whom he had to forgo, then it could not be denied that an intention of debasing his sister and of putting an end to her intellectual superiority, which he had formerly found so oppressive, had obtained the decisive control over his object-choice.

The sexual conduct of men, as well as everything else, has been subordinated by Alfred Adler to motive forces of this kind, which spring from the will to power, from the individual's self-assertive instinct. Without ever denying the importance of these motives of power and prerogative, I have never been convinced that they play the dominating and exclusive part that has been ascribed to them. If I had not pursued my patient's analysis to the end, I should have been obliged, on account of my observation of this case, to correct my preconceived opinion in a direction favourable to Adler. The conclusion of the analysis unexpectedly brought up new material which, on the contrary, showed that these motives of power (in this case the intention to debase) had determined the object-choice only in the sense of serving as a contributory cause and as a rationalization, whereas the true underlying determination enabled me to maintain my former convictions.[1]

When the news of his sister's death arrived, so the patient told me, he felt hardly a trace of grief. He had to force himself to show signs of sorrow, and was able quite coolly to rejoice at having now become the sole heir to the property. He had already been suffering from his recent illness for several years when this occurred. But I must confess that this one piece of information made me for a long time uncertain in my diagnostic judgement of the case. It was to be

[1] See below, p. 286.

assumed, no doubt, that his grief over the loss of the most dearly loved member of his family would meet with an inhibition in its expression, as a result of the continued operation of his jealousy of her and as a result of the interference of his incestuous love for her which had now become unconscious. But I could not do without some substitute for the missing outburst of grief. And this was at last found in another expression of feeling which had remained inexplicable to the patient. A few months after his sister's death he himself made a journey in the neighbourhood in which she had died. There he sought out the burial-place of a great poet, who was at that time his ideal, and shed bitter tears upon his grave. This reaction seemed strange to him himself, for he knew that more than two generations had passed by since the death of the poet he admired. He only understood it when he remembered that his father had been in the habit of comparing his dead sister's works with the great poet's. He gave me another indication of the correct way of interpreting the homage which he ostensibly paid to the poet, by a mistake in his story which I was able to detect at this point. He had repeatedly specified before that his sister had shot herself; but he was now obliged to make a correction and say that she had taken poison. The poet, however, had been shot in a duel.

I now return to the brother's story, but from this point I must proceed for a little upon thematic lines. The boy's age at the time at which his sister began her seductions turned out to be three and a quarter years. It happened, as has been mentioned, in the spring of the same year in whose summer the English governess arrived, and in whose autumn his parents, on their return, found him so fundamentally altered. It is very natural, then, to connect this transformation with the awakening of his sexual activity that had meanwhile taken place.

How did the boy react to the allurements of his elder sister? By a refusal, is the answer, but by a refusal which applied to the person and not to the thing. His sister was not agreeable to him as a sexual object, probably because his relation to her had already been determined in a hostile direction owing to their rivalry for their parents' love. He held aloof from her, and, moreover, her solicitations soon ceased. But he tried to win, instead of her, another person of whom he was fonder; and the information which his sister herself had given him, and in which she had claimed his Nanya as a model, directed his choice in that direction. He therefore began to play with his member in his Nanya's presence, and this, like so many other instances in which children do not conceal their onanism, must be regarded as an attempt at seduction. His Nanya disillusioned him; she made a serious face, and explained that that wasn't good: children who did that, she added, got a "wound" in the place.

The effect of this intelligence, which amounted to a threat, is to be traced in various directions. His dependence upon his Nanya was diminished in consequence. He might well have been angry with her; and later on, when his fits of rage set in, it became clear that he really was embittered against her. But it was characteristic of him that every position of the libido which he found himself obliged to abandon was at first obstinately defended by him against the new development. When the governess came upon the scene and abused his Nanya, drove her out of the room, and tried to destroy her authority, he, on the contrary, exaggerated his love for the victim of these attacks and assumed a brusque and defiant attitude towards the aggressive governess. Nevertheless, in secret he began to look about for another sexual object. His seduction had given him the passive sexual aim of being touched on the genitals; we shall presently hear in connection with whom it was that he tried to achieve this aim, and what paths led him to this choice.

It agrees entirely with our anticipations when we learn that, after his first genital excitations, his sexual inquiries began, and that he soon came upon the problem of castration. At this time he succeeded in observing two girls—his sister and a friend of hers—while they were micturating. His acumen might well have enabled him to gather the true facts from this spectacle, but he behaved as we know other male children behave in these circumstances. He rejected the idea that he saw before him a confirmation of the wound with which his Nanya had threatened him, and he explained to himself that this was the girls' "front bottom." The theme of castration was not settled by this decision: he found new allusions to it in everything that he heard. Once when the children were given some coloured sugar-sticks, the governess, who was inclined to disordered fancies, pronounced that they were pieces of chopped-up snakes. He remembered afterwards that his father had once met a snake while he was walking along a footpath, and had beaten it to pieces with his stick. He heard the story (out of *Reynard the Fox*) read aloud, of how the wolf wanted to go fishing in the winter, and used his tail as a bait, and how in that way his tail was broken off in the ice. He learned the different names by which horses are distinguished, according to the intactness of their sex. Thus he was occupied wtih thoughts about castration, but as yet he had no belief in it and no dread of it. Other sexual problems arose for him out of the fairy tales with which he became familiar at this time. In "Little Red Riding-Hood" and "The Seven Little Goats" the children were taken out of the wolf's body. Was the wolf a female creature, then, or could men have children in their bodies as well? At this time the question was not yet settled. Moreover, at the time of these inquiries he had as yet no fear of wolves.

One of the patient's pieces of information will make it easier for us to understand the alteration in his character which appeared during his parents' absence as a somewhat indirect consequence of his seduction. He said that he gave up onanism very soon after his Nanya's refusal and threat. *His sexual life, therefore, which was beginning to come under the sway of the genital zone, gave way before an external obstacle, and was thrown back by its influence into an earlier phase of pre-genital organization.* As a result of the suppression of his onanism, the boy's sexual life took on a sadistic-anal character. He became irritable and a tormentor, and gratified himself in this way at the expense of animals and men. His principal object was his beloved Nanya, and he knew how to cause her enough pain to make her burst into tears. In this way he revenged himself on her for the refusal he had met with, and at the same time gratified his sexual lust in the form which corresponded to his present regressive phase. He began to be cruel to small animals, to catch flies and pull out their wings, to crush beetles underfoot; in his imagination he liked beating large animals (horses) as well. All of these, then, were active and sadistic proceedings; we shall discuss his anal impulses at this period in a later connection.

It is a most important fact that some contemporary phantasies of quite another kind came up as well in the patient's memory. The content of these was of boys being chastised and beaten, and especially being beaten on the penis. And from other phantasies, which represented the heir to the throne being shut up in a narrow room and beaten, it was easy to guess for whom it was that the anonymous figures served as whipping-boys. The heir to the throne was evidently he himself; his sadism had therefore turned round in phantasy against himself, and had been converted into masochism. The detail of the sexual member itself receiving the beating justified the conclusion that a sense of guilt, which related to his onanism, was already concerned in this transformation.

No doubt was left in the analysis that these passive trends had made their appearance at the same time as the active-sadistic ones, or very soon after them.[2] This is in accordance with the unusually clear, intense, and constant *ambivalence* of the patient, which was shown here for the first time in the even development of both members of the pairs of contrary component instincts. Such behaviour was also characteristic of his later life, and so was this further trait: no position of the libido which had once been established was ever completely replaced by a later one. It was rather left in existence side by side with all the others, and this allowed him to maintain an incessant vacillation which proved to be incompatible with the acquisition of a fixed character.

---

[2] By passive trends I mean trends that have a passive sexual aim; but in saying this I have in mind a transformation not of the instinct but only of its aim.

The boy's masochistic trends lead on to another point, which I have so far avoided mentioning, because it can only be confirmed by means of the analysis of the subsequent phase of his development. I have already mentioned that after his refusal by his Nanya his libidinal expectation detached itself from her and began to contemplate another person as a sexual object. This person was his father, at that time away from home. He was no doubt led to this choice by a number of convergent factors, including such fortuitous ones as the recollection of the snake being cut to pieces; but above all he was in this way able to renew his first and most primitive object-choice, which, in conformity with a small child's narcissism, had taken place along the path of identification. We have heard already that his father had been his admired model, and that when he was asked what he wanted to be he used to reply: a gentleman like his father. This object of identification of his active current became the sexual object of a passive current in his present anal-sadistic phase. It looks as though his seduction by his sister had forced him into a passive rôle, and had given him a passive sexual aim. Under the persisting influence of this experience he pursued a path from his sister by way of his Nanya to his father—from a passive attitude towards women to the same attitude towards men—and had, nevertheless, by this means found a link with his earlier and spontaneous phase of development. His father was now his object once more; in conformity with his higher stage of development, identification was replaced by object-choice; while the transformation of his active attitude into a passive one was the consequence and the record of the seduction which had occurred meanwhile. It would naturally not have been so easy to achieve an active attitude in the sadistic phase towards his all-powerful father. When his father came home in the late summer or autumn his fits of rage and scenes of fury were put to a new use. They had served for active-sadistic ends in relation to his Nanya; in relation to his father their purpose was masochistic. By bringing his naughtiness forward he was trying to force punishments and beatings out of his father, and in that way to obtain from him the masochistic sexual satisfaction that he desired. His screaming fits were therefore simply attempts at seduction. In accordance, moreover, with the motives which underlie masochism, this beating would also have satisfied his sense of guilt. He had preserved a memory of how, during one of these scenes of naughtiness, he had redoubled his screams as soon as his father came towards him. His father did not beat him, however, but tried to pacify him by playing ball in front of him with the pillows of his cot.

I do not know how often parents and educators, faced with inexplicable naughtiness on the part of a child, might not have occasion to bear this typical state of affairs in mind. A child that behaves in this unmanageable way is making a confession and trying to provoke punishment. It hopes for a beating as a simultaneous means of setting its sense of guilt at rest and of satisfying its masochistic sexual trend.

For the further explanation of the case we have to thank a recollection which came up with the greatest distinctness to the effect that none of the patient's symptoms of anxiety were added to the indications of an alteration in his character until after the occurrence of a certain event. Previously, it seems, there was no anxiety, while directly after the event the anxiety expressed itself in the most tormenting shape. The date of this transformation can be stated with certainty; it was immediately before his fourth birthday. Taking this as a fixed point, we are able to divide the period of his childhood with which we are concerned into two phases: a first phase of naughtiness and perversity from his seduction at the age of three and a quarter up to his fourth birthday, and a longer subsequent phase in which the signs of neurosis predominated. But the event which makes this division possible was not an external trauma, but a dream, from which he awoke in a state of anxiety.

IV

The Dream and the Primal Scene

I HAVE ALREADY published this dream elsewhere,[1] on account of the quantity of material in it which is derived from fairy tales; and I will begin by repeating what I wrote on that occasion: " *'I dreamt that it was night and that I was lying in my bed. (My bed stood with its foot towards the window; in front of the window there was a row of old walnut trees. I know it was winter when I had the dream, and night-time.) Suddenly the window opened of its own accord, and I was terrified to see that some white wolves were sitting on the big walnut tree in front of the window. There were six or seven of them. The wolves were quite white, and looked more like foxes or sheep-dogs, for they had big tails like foxes and they had their ears pricked like dogs when they are attending to something. In great terror, evidently of being eaten up by the wolves, I screamed* and woke up. My nurse hurried to my bed, to see what had happened to me. It took quite a long while before I was convinced that it had only been a dream; I had had such a clear and life-like picture of the window opening

[1] "The Occurrence in Dreams of Material from Fairy Tales," *Character and Culture,* Collier Books edition BS 193V.

and the wolves sitting on the tree. At last I grew quieter, felt as though I had escaped from some danger, and went to sleep again.

" 'The only piece of action in the dream was the opening of the window; for the wolves sat quite still and without any movement on the branches of the tree, to the right and left of the trunk, and looked at me. It seemed as though they had riveted their whole attention upon me.—I think this was my first anxiety dream. I was three, four, or at most five years old at the time. From then until my eleventh or twelfth year I was always afraid of seeing something terrible in my dreams.'

"He added a drawing of the tree with the wolves, which confirmed his description (Fig. 2). The analysis of the dream brought the following material to light.

"He had always connected this dream with the recollection that during these years of his childhood he was most tre-

Fig. 2

mendously afraid of the picture of a wolf in a book of fairy tales. His elder sister, who was very much his superior, used to tease him by holding up this particular picture in front of him on some excuse or other, so that he was terrified and began to scream. In this picture the wolf was standing upright, striding out with one foot, with its claws stretched out and its ears pricked. He thought this picture must have been an illustration to the story of 'Little Red Riding-Hood.'

"Why were the wolves white? This made him think of the sheep, large flocks of which were kept in the neighbourhood of the estate. His father occasionally took him with him to visit these flocks, and every time this happened he felt very proud and blissful. Later on—according to inquiries that were made it may easily have been shortly before the time of the dream—an epidemic broke out among the sheep. His father sent for a follower of Pasteur's, who inoculated the animals, but after the inoculation even more of them died than before.

"How did the wolves come to be on the tree? This reminded him of a story that he had heard his grandfather tell. He could not remember whether it was before or after the dream, but its subject is a decisive argument in favour of the former view. The story ran as follows. A tailor was sitting at work in his room, when the window opened and a wolf leapt in. The tailor hit after him with his yard—no (he corrected himself), caught him by his tail and pulled it off, so that the wolf ran away in terror. Some time later the tailor went into the forest, and suddenly saw a pack of wolves coming towards him; so he climbed up a tree to escape from them. At first the wolves were in perplexity; but the maimed one, which was among them and wanted to revenge himself upon the tailor, proposed that they should climb one upon another till the last one could reach him. He himself—he was a vigorous old fellow—would be the base of the pyramid. The wolves did as he suggested, but the tailor had recognized the visitor whom he had punished, and suddenly called out as he had before: 'Catch the grey one by his tail!' The tailless wolf, terrified by the recollection, ran away, and all the others tumbled down.

"In this story the tree appears, upon which the wolves were sitting in the dream. But it also contains an unmistakable allusion to the castration complex. The *old* wolf was docked of his tail by the tailor. The fox-tails of the wolves in the dream were probably compensations for this taillessness.

"Why were there six or seven wolves? There seemed to be no answer to this question, until I raised a doubt whether the picture that had frightened him could be connected with the story of 'Little Red Riding-Hood.' This fairy tale only offers an opportunity for two illustrations—Little Red Riding-Hood's meeting with the wolf in the wood, and the scene in which the wolf lies in bed in the grandmother's nightcap. There must therefore be some other fairy tale behind his recollection of the picture. He soon discovered that it could only be the story of 'The Wolf and the Seven Little Goats.' Here the number seven occurs, and also the number six, for the wolf only ate up six of the little goats, while the seventh hid itself in the clock-case. The white, too, comes into this story, for the wolf had his paw made white at the baker's after the little goats had recognized him on his first visit by his grey paw. Moreover, the two fairy tales have much in common. In both there is the eating up, the cutting open of the belly, the taking out of the people who have been eaten and their replacement by heavy stones, and finally in both of them the wicked wolf perishes. Besides all this, in the story of the little goats the tree appears. The wolf lay down under a tree after his meal and snored.

"I shall have, for a special reason, to deal with this dream again elsewhere, and interpret it and consider its significance in greater detail. For it is the earliest anxiety dream that the dreamer remembered from his childhood, and its content, taken in connection with other dreams that followed it soon afterwards and with certain events in his earliest years, is of quite peculiar interest. We must confine ourselves here to the relation of the dream to the two fairy tales which have so much in common with each other, 'Little Red Riding-Hood' and 'The Wolf and the Seven Little Goats.' The effect produced by these stories was shown in the little dreamer by a regular animal phobia. This phobia was only distinguished from other similar cases by the fact that the anxiety-animal was not an object easily accessible to observation (such as a horse or a dog), but was known to him only from stories and picture-books.

"I shall discuss on another occasion the explanation of these animal phobias and the significance attaching to them. I will only remark in anticipation that this explanation is in complete harmony with the principal characteristic shown by the neurosis from which the present dreamer suffered in the later part of his life. His fear of his father was the strongest motive for his falling ill, and his ambivalent attitude towards every father-surrogate was the dominating feature of his life as well as of his behaviour during the treatment.

"If in my patient's case the wolf was merely a first father-surrogate, the question arises whether the hidden content in the fairy tales of the wolf that ate up the little goats and of 'Little Red Riding-Hood' may not simply be infantile fear of the father.[2] Moreover, my patient's father had the characteristic, shown by so many people in relation to their children, of indulging in *'affectionate abuse'*; and it is possible that during the patient's earlier years his father (though he grew severe later on) may more than once, as he caressed the little boy or played with him, have threatened in fun to 'gobble him up.' One of my patients told me that her two children could never get to be fond of their grandfather, because in the course of his affectionate romping with them he used to frighten them by saying he would cut open their tummies."

Leaving on one side everything in this quotation that anticipates the dream's remoter implications, let us return to its immediate interpretation. I may remark that this interpretation was a task that dragged on over several years. The patient related the dream at a very early stage of the analysis

[2] Compare the similarity between these two fairy tales and the myth of Cronos, which was pointed out by Rank in his paper, "Völkerpsychologische Parallelen zu den infantilen Sexualtheorien" (1912).

and very soon came to share my conviction that the causes of his infantile neurosis lay concealed behind it. In the course of the treatment we often came back to the dream, but it was only during the last months of the analysis that it became possible to understand it completely, and only then thanks to spontaneous work on the patient's part. He had always emphasized the fact that two factors in the dream had made the greatest impression upon him: first, the perfect stillness and immobility of the wolves, and secondly, the strained attention with which they all looked at him. The lasting sense of reality, too, which the dream left behind it, seemed to him to deserve notice.

Let us take this last remark as a starting-point. We know from our experience in interpreting dreams, that this sense of reality carries a particular significance along with it. It assures us that some part of the latent material of the dream is claiming in the dreamer's memory to possess the quality of reality, that is, that the dream relates to an occurrence that really took place and was not merely imagined. It can naturally only be a question of the reality of something unknown; for instance, the conviction that his grandfather really told him the story of the tailor and the wolf, or the stories of "Little Red Riding-Hood" and of "The Seven Little Goats" were really read aloud to him, would not be of a nature to be replaced by this sense of reality that outlasted the dream. The dream seemed to point to an occurrence the reality of which was in this way emphasized as being in marked contrast to the unreality of the fairy tales.

If we were led to assume that behind the content of the dream there lay some such unknown scene—one, that is, which had already been forgotten at the time of the dream— then it must have taken place very early. The dreamer, it will be recalled, said: "I was three, four, or at most five years old at the time I had the dream." And we can add: "And I was reminded by the dream of something that must have belonged to an even earlier period."

The parts of the manifest content of the dream which were emphasized by the dreamer, the factors of attentive looking and of motionlessness, must lead to the content of this scene. We must naturally expect to find that this material reproduces the unknown material of the scene in some distorted form, perhaps even distorted into its opposite.

There were several conclusions, too, to be drawn from the raw material which had been produced by the patient's first analysis of the dream, and these had to be fitted into the collocation of which we were in search. Behind the mention of the sheep-breeding, evidence was to be expected of his sexual inquiries, his interest in which he was able to gratify during his visits with his father; but there must also have been allusions to a fear of death, since the greater part of the sheep had died of the epidemic. The most obtrusive thing in the dream, the wolves on the tree, led straight to his grandfather's story; and what was fascinating about this story and capable of provoking the dream can scarcely have been anything but its connection with the theme of castration.

We also concluded from the first incomplete analysis of the dream that the wolf may have been a father-surrogate; so that, in that case, this first anxiety-dream would have brought to light the fear of his father which from that time forward was to dominate his life. This conclusion, indeed, was in itself not yet binding. But if we put together as the result of the provisional analysis what can be derived from the material produced by the dreamer, we then find before us for reconstruction some such fragments as these:

A real occurrence—dating from a very early period— looking — immobility — sexual problems — castration — his father—something terrible.

One day the patient began to proceed with the interpretation of the dream. He thought that the part of the dream which said that "suddenly the window opened of its own accord" was not completely explained by its connection with the window at which the tailor was sitting and through which the wolf came into the room. "It must mean: 'My eyes suddenly open.' I am asleep, therefore, and suddenly wake up, and as I wake I see something: the tree with the wolves." No objection could be made to this; but the point could be developed further. He had woken up and had seen something. The attentive looking, which in the dream is ascribed to the wolves, should rather be shifted on to him. At a decisive point, therefore, a transposition has taken place; and moreover this is indicated by another transposition in the manifest content of the dream. For the fact that the wolves were sitting on the tree was also a transposition, since in his grandfather's story they were underneath, and were unable to climb on to the tree.

What, then, if the other factor emphasized by the dreamer were also distorted by means of a transposition or reversal? In that case instead of immobility (the wolves sat there motionless; they looked at him, but did not move) the meaning would have to be: the most violent motion. That is to say, he suddenly woke up, and saw in front of him a scene of violent movement at which he looked with strained attention. In the one case the distortion would consist in an interchange of subject and object, of activity and passivity: being looked at instead of looking. In the other case it would consist in a transformation into the opposite: rest instead of motion.

On another occasion an association which suddenly occurred to him carried us another step forward in our understanding of the dream: "The tree was a Christmas-tree." He now knew that he had dreamed the dream shortly before Christmas and in expectation of it. Since Christmas Day was also his birthday, it now became possible to establish with certainty the date of the dream and of the transformation which proceeded from it. It was immediately before his fourth birthday. He had gone to sleep, then, in tense expectation of the day which ought to bring him a double quantity of presents. We know that in such circumstances a child may easily anticipate the fulfilment of his wishes. So it was already Christmas in his dream; the content of the dream showed him his Christmas box, the presents which were to be his were hanging on the tree. But instead of presents they had turned into—wolves, and the dream ended by his being overcome by fear of being eaten by the wolf (probably his father), and by his flying for refuge to his nurse. Our knowledge of his sexual development before the dream makes it possible for us to fill in the gaps in the dream and to explain the transformation of his satisfaction into anxiety. Of the wishes concerned in the formation of the dream the most powerful must have been the wish for the sexual satisfaction which he was at that time longing to obtain from his father. The strength of this wish made it possible to revive the long-forgotten traces in his memory of a scene which was able to show him what sexual satisfaction from his father was like; and the result was terror, horror of the fulfilment of the wish, the repression of the impulse which had manifested itself by means of the wish, and consequently a flight from his father to his less dangerous nurse.

The importance of this Christmas Day as a turning-point had been preserved in his supposed recollection of having had his first fit of rage because he was dissatisfied with his Christmas presents. The recollection combined elements of truth and of falsehood. It could not be entirely right, since according to the repeated declarations of his parents his naughtiness had already begun on their return in the autumn and it was not a fact that they had come on only at Christmas. But he had preserved the essential connection between his unsatisfied love, his rage, and Christmas.

But what picture can the nightly workings of his sexual desire have conjured up that could frighten him away so violently from the fulfilment for which he longed? The material of the analysis shows that there is one condition which this picture must satisfy. It must have been calculated to create a conviction of the reality of the existence of castration. Fear of castration could then became the motive power for the transformation of the affect.

I have now reached the point at which I must abandon the support I have hitherto had from the course of the analysis. I am afraid it will also be the point at which the reader's belief will abandon me.

What sprang into activity that night out of the chaos of the dreamer's unconscious memory-traces was the picture of a coitus between his parents, a coitus in circumstances which were not entirely usual and were especially favourable for observation. It gradually became possible to find satisfactory answers to all the questions that arose in connection with this scene; for in the course of the treatment the first dream returned in innumerable variations and new editions, the analysis of which produced the information that was required. Thus in the first place the child's age at the date of the observation was established as being about one and a half years.[3] He was suffering at the time from malaria, an attack of which used to come on every day at a particular hour.[4] From his tenth year onwards he was from time to time subject to moods of depression, which used to come on in the afternoon and reached their height at about five o'clock. This symptom still existed at the time of the analytic treatment. The recurring fits of depression took the place of the earlier attacks of fever or languor; five o'clock was either the time of the highest fever or of the observation of the coitus, unless the two times coincided.[5] Probably for the very reason of this illness, he was in his parents' bedroom. The illness, the occurrence of which is also corroborated by direct tradition, makes it reasonable to refer the event to the summer, and, since the child was born on Christmas Day, to assume that his age was $n + 1\frac{1}{2}$ years. He had been sleeping in his cot, then, in his parents' bedroom, and woke up, perhaps because of his rising fever, in the afternoon, possibly at five o'clock, the hour which was later marked out by depression. It harmonizes with our assumption that it was a hot summer's day, if we suppose that his parents had retired, half undressed,[6] for an afternoon *siesta*. When he woke up, he witnessed a coitus

[3] The age of six months came under consideration as a far less probable, and indeed scarcely tenable, alternative.

[4] Compare the subsequent metamorphoses of this factor during the obsessional neurosis. In the patient's dreams during the treatment it was replaced by a violent wind. (*"Aria"* = "air.")

[5] We may remark in this connection that the patient drew only *five* wolves in his illustration to the dream, although the text mentioned six or seven.

[6] In white underclothes: the *white* wolves.

a tergo, three times repeated;[7] he was able to see his mother's genitals as well as his father's member; and he understood the process as well as its significance.[8] Lastly he interrupted his parents' intercourse in a manner which will be discussed later.

There is at bottom nothing extraordinary, nothing to give the impression of being the product of an extravagant imagination, in the fact that a young couple who had only been married a few years should have ended a *siesta* on a hot summer's afternoon with a love-scene, and should have disregarded the presence of their little boy of one and a half, asleep in his cot. On the contrary, such an event would, I think, be something entirely commonplace and *banal*; and even the position in which we have inferred that the coitus took place cannot in the least alter this judgment—especially as the evidence does not require that the coitus should have been performed from behind each time. A single time would have been enough to give the spectator an opportunity for making observations which would have been rendered difficult or impossible by any other attitude of the lovers. The content of the scene cannot therefore in itself be an argument against its credibility. Doubts as to its probability will turn upon three minor points: whether a child at the tender age of one and a half could be in a position to take in the perceptions of such a complicated process and to preserve them so accurately in its unconscious; secondly, whether it could be possible for a deferred elaboration of the impressions thus received to force its way into comprehension at the age of four; and finally, whether any procedure could have succeeded in bring-

[7] Why three times? He suddenly one day produced the statement that I had discovered this detail by interpretation. This was not the case. It was a spontaneous association, exempt from further criticism; in his usual way he pressed it off on to me, and by this projection tried to make it seem more trustworthy.

[8] I mean that he understood it at the time of the dream when he was four years old, not at the time of the observation. He received the impressions when he was one and a half; his understanding of them was deferred, but became possible at the time of the dream owing to his development, his sexual excitations, and his sexual inquiries.

ing into consciousness coherently and convincingly the details of a scene of this kind which had been experienced and understood in such circumstances.[9]

Later on I shall carefully examine these and other doubts; but I can assure the reader that I am no less critically inclined than he towards an acceptance of this observation of the child's, and I will only ask him to join me in adopting a *provisional* belief in the reality of the scene. We will first proceed with the study of the relations between this *"primal scene"* and the patient's dream, his symptoms, and the history of his life; and we will trace separately the effects that followed from the essential content of the scene and from one of its visual impressions.

By the latter I mean the attitudes which he saw his parents adopt—the man upright, and the woman bent down like an animal. We have already heard that during his anxiety period his sister used to terrify him with a picture from the fairy-book, in which the wolf was shown standing upright, with one foot forward, with its claws stretched out and its ears pricked. He devoted himself with tireless perseverance during the treatment to the task of hunting in the second-hand bookshops till he had found the illustrated fairy-book of his childhood, and had recognized his bogy in an illustration to the story of "The Wolf and the Seven Little Goats." He thought that the attitude of the wolf in this picture might have reminded him of that of his father during the constructed primal scene. At all events the picture became the point of

[9] The first of these difficulties cannot be reduced by assuming that the child at the time of its observation was after all probably a year older, that is to say two and a half, an age at which it may perhaps have been perfectly capable of talking. All the minor details of my patient's case almost excluded the possibility of shifting the date in this way. Moreover, the fact should be taken into account that these scenes of observing a parental coitus are by no means rarely brought to light in analysis. The condition of their occurrence, however, is precisely that it should be in the earliest period of children. The older the child is, the more carefully, with parents above a certain social level, will the child be deprived of the opportunity for this kind of observation.

departure for further manifestations of anxiety. Once when he was in his seventh or eighth year he was informed that next day a new tutor was coming for him. That night he dreamt of this tutor in the shape of a lion that came towards his bed roaring loudly and in the attitude of the wolf in the picture; and once again he awoke in a state of anxiety. The wolf phobia had been overcome by that time, so he was free to choose himself a new anxiety-animal, and in this late dream he was recognizing the tutor as a father-surrogate. In the later years of his childhood each of his tutors and masters played the part of his father, and was endowed with the father's influence both for good and for evil.

While he was at his secondary school the Fates provided him with a remarkable opportunity of reviving his wolf phobia, and of using the relation which lay behind it as an occasion for severe inhibitions. The master who taught his form Latin was called Wolf. From the very first he felt cowed by him, and he was once taken severely to task by him for having made a stupid mistake in a piece of Latin translation. From that time on he could not get free from a paralysing fear of this master, and it was soon extended to other masters besides. But the occasion on which he made his blunder in the translation was also to the purpose. He had to translate the Latin word *"filius,"* and he did it with the French word *"fils"* instead of with the corresponding word from his own language. The wolf, in fact, was still his father.[10]

---

[10] After this reprimand from the schoolmaster-wolf he learnt that it was the general opinion of his companions that, in order to be pacified, the master—expected some money from him. We shall return to this later.—I can see that it would greatly facilitate a rationalistic view of such a history of a child's development as this if it could be supposed that his whole fear of the wolf had really originated from the Latin master of that name, that it had been projected back into his childhood, and, supported by the illustration to the fairy tale, had caused the phantasy of the primal scene. But this is untenable; the temporal priority of the wolf phobia and its reference to the period of his childhood spent upon the first estate is far too securely attested. And his dream at the age of four?

The first "transitory symptom"[11] which the patient produced during the treatment went back once more to the wolf phobia and to the fairy tale of "The Seven Little Goats." In the room in which the first sittings were held there was a large grandfather clock opposite the patient, who lay upon a sofa facing away from me. I was struck by the fact that from time to time he turned his face towards me, looked at me in a very friendly way as though to propitiate me, and then turned his look away from me to the clock. I thought at the time that he was in this way showing his eagerness for the end of the hour. A long time afterwards the patient reminded me of this piece of dumb show, and gave me an explanation of it; for he recalled that the youngest of the seven little goats hid himself in the case of the grandfather clock while his six brothers were eaten up by the wolf. So what he had meant was: "Be kind to me! Must I be frightened of you? Are you going to eat me up? Shall I hide myself from you in the clock-case like the youngest little goat?"

The wolf that he was afraid of was undoubtedly his father; but his fear of the wolf was conditional upon the creature being in an upright attitude. His recollection asserted most definitely that he had not been terrified by pictures of wolves going on all fours or, as in the story of "Little Red Riding-Hood," lying in bed. The attitude which, according to our construction of the primal scene, he had seen the woman assume, was of no less significance; though in this case the significance was limited to the sexual sphere. The most striking phenomenon of his erotic life after maturity was his liability to compulsive attacks of falling physically in love which came on and disappeared again in the most puzzling succession. These attacks released a tremendous energy in him even at times when he was otherwise inhibited, and they were quite beyond his control. I must for a specially important reason postpone a full consideration of this compulsive love; but I may mention here that it depended upon a definite condition, which was concealed from his consciousness, and

[11] Ferenczi, "Transitory Symptom-Formations during Analysis" (1912).

was discovered only during the treatment. It was necessary that the woman should have assumed the attitude which we have ascribed to his mother in the primal scene. From his puberty he had felt large and conspicuous buttocks as the most powerful attraction in a woman; to copulate except from behind gave him scarcely any enjoyment. At this point a criticism may justly be raised: it may be objected that a sexual preference of this kind for the hind parts of the body is a general characteristic of people who are inclined to an obsessional neurosis, and that its presence does not justify us in referring it back to a special impression in childhood. It is part of the fabric of the anal-erotic disposition and is one of the archaic traits which distinguish that constitution. Indeed, copulation from behind—*more ferarum*—may, after all, be regarded as phylogenetically the older form. We shall return to this point too in a later discussion, when we have brought forward the supplementary material which showed the basis of the unconscious condition upon which his falling in love depended.

Let us now proceed with our discussion of the relations between his dream and the primal scene. We should so far have expected the dream to present the child (who was rejoicing at Christmas in the prospect of the fulfilment of his wishes) with this picture of sexual satisfaction afforded through his father's agency, just as he had seen it in the primal scene, as a model of the satisfaction that he himself was longing to obtain from his father. Instead of this picture, however, there appeared the material of the story which he had been told by his grandfather shortly before: the tree, the wolves, and the taillessness (in the over-compensated form of the bushy tails of the alleged wolves). At this point some connection is missing, some associative bridge to lead from the content of the primal scene to that of the wolf story. This connection is provided once again by the attitudes and only by the attitudes. In his grandfather's story the tailless wolf asked the others *to climb upon him*. It was this detail that called up the recollection of the picture of the primal scene; and it was in this way that it became possible for the material of the primal scene to be represented by that of the wolf story, and at the same time for the *two* parents to be replaced, as was desirable, by *several* wolves. The content of the dream met with a further transformation, and the material of the wolf story was made to fit in with the content of the fairy tale of "The Seven Little Goats," by borrowing from it the number seven.[12]

The steps in the transformation of the material, "primal scene—wolf story—fairy tale of 'The Seven Little Goats,'" are a reflection of the progress of the dreamer's thoughts during the construction of the dream, "longing for sexual satisfaction from his father—realization that castration is a necessary condition of it—fear of his father." It is only at this point, I think, that we can regard the anxiety dream of this four-year-old boy as being exhaustively explained.[13]

[12] It says "six or seven" in the dream. Six is the number of the children that were eaten; the seventh escaped into the clock-case. It is always a strict law of dream interpretation that an explanation must be found for every detail.

[13] Now that we have succeeded in making a synthesis of the dream, I will try to give a comprehensive account of the relations between the manifest content of the dream and the latent dream thoughts.

It was night, I was lying in my bed. The latter is the beginning of the reproduction of the primal scene. "It was night" is a distortion of "I had been asleep." The remark, "I know it was winter when I had the dream, and night-time," refers to the patient's recollection of the dream and is not part of its content. It is correct, for it was one of the nights before his birthday, that is, Christmas Day.

Suddenly the window opened of its own accord. That is to be translated: "Suddenly I woke up of my own accord," a recollection of the primal scene. The influence of the wolf story, in which the wolf leapt in through the window, is making itself felt as a modifying factor, and transforms a direct expression into a plastic one. At the same time the introduction of the window serves the purpose of providing a contemporary reference for the subsequent content of the dream. On Christmas Eve the door opens suddenly and one sees before one the tree with the presents. Here therefore the influence of the actual expectation of Christmas (which comprises the wish for sexual satisfaction) is making itself felt.

After what has already been said I need only deal shortly with the pathogenic effect of the primal scene and the alteration which its revival produced in his sexual development. We will only trace that one of its effects to which the dream gave expression. Later on we shall have to make it clear that it was not only a single sexual current that started from the primal scene but a whole series of them, that his sexual life was positively splintered up by it. We shall further bear in mind that the activation of this scene (I purposely avoid the word "recollection") had the same effect as though it were a

---

The big walnut tree. The representative of the Christmas tree, and therefore belonging to the current situation. But also the tree out of the wolf story, upon which the tailor took refuge from pursuit, and under which the wolves were on the watch. Moreover, as I have often been able to satisfy myself, a high tree is a symbol of observing, of scoptophilia. A person sitting on a tree can see everything that is going on below him and cannot himself be seen. Compare Boccaccio's well-known story, and similar *facetiae*.

The wolves. Their number: *six or seven.* In the wolf story there was a pack, and no number was given. The fixing of the number shows the influence of the fairy tale of "The Seven Little Goats," six of whom were eaten up. The fact that the number two in the primal scene is replaced by a larger number, which would be absurd in the primal scene, is welcomed by the resistance as a means of distortion. In the illustration to the dream the dreamer brings forward the number five, which is probably meant to correct the statement "It was night."

They were sitting on the tree. In the first place they replace the Christmas presents hanging on the tree. But they are also transposed on to the tree because that can mean that they are looking. In his grandfather's story they were posted underneath the tree. Their relation to the tree has therefore been reversed in the dream; and from this it may be concluded that there are further reversals of the latent material to be found in the content of the dream.

They were looking at him with strained attention. This feature comes entirely from the primal scene, and has got into the dream at the price of being twisted completely round.

They were quite white. This feature is unessential in itself, but is strongly emphasized in the dreamer's narrative. It owes its intensity to a copious fusion of elements from all the strata of the

recent experience. The effects of the scene were deferred, but meanwhile it had lost none of its freshness in the interval between the ages of one and a half and four years. We shall perhaps find in what follows reason to suppose that it produced certain effects even at the time of its perception, that is, from the age of one and a half onwards.

When the patient entered more deeply into the situation of the primal scene, he brought to light the following pieces of self-observation. He seems to have assumed to begin with that the event of which he was a witness was an act of violence, but the expression of enjoyment which he saw upon his

---

material, and it combines unimportant details from the other sources of the dream with a fragment of the primal scene which is more significant. This last part of its determination goes back to the white of his parents' bedclothes and underclothes, and to this is added the white of the flocks of sheep, and of the sheepdogs, as an allusion to his sexual inquiries among animals, and the white in the fairy tale of "The Seven Little Goats," in which the mother is recognized by the white of her hand. Later on we shall see that the white clothes are also an allusion to death.

They sat there motionless. This contradicts the most striking feature of the observed scene, namely, its agitated movement, which, in virtue of the attitudes to which it led, constitutes the connection between the primal scene and the wolf story.

They had tails like foxes. This must be the contradiction of a conclusion which was derived from the action of the primal scene upon the wolf story, and which must be recognized as the most important result of the dreamer's sexual inquiries: "So there really is such a thing as castration." The terror with which this conclusion is received finally breaks out in the dream and brings it to an end.

The fear of being eaten up by the wolves. It seemed to the dreamer as though the motive force of this fear was not derived from the content of the dream. He said he need not have been afraid, for the wolves looked more like foxes or dogs, and they did not rush at him as though to bite him, but were very still and not at all terrible. We observe that the dream-work tries for some time to make the painful content harmless by transforming it into its opposite. ("They aren't moving, and, only look, they have the loveliest tails!") Until at last this expedient fails, and the fear breaks out. It expresses itself by the help of the fairy tale, in which the goat-children are eaten up by the wolf-father. This part of

mother's face did not fit in with this; he was obliged to recognize that what he was faced by was a process of gratification.[14] What was essentially new for him in his observation of his parents' intercourse was the conviction of the reality of castration—a possibility with which his thoughts had already been occupied previously. (The sight of the two girls micturating, his Nanya's threat, the governess's interpretation of the sugar-sticks, the recollection of his father having beaten a snake to pieces.) For now he saw with his own eyes the wound of which his Nanya had spoken, and understood that its presence was a necessary condition of intercourse with his father. He

---

the fairy tale may perhaps have acted as a reminder of threats made by the child's father in fun when he was playing with him; so that the fear of being eaten up by the wolf may be a reminiscence as well as a substitute by displacement.

The wishes which act as motive forces in this dream are obvious; first there are the superficial wishes of the day, that Christmas with its presents may already be here (a dream of impatience), and accompanying these is the deeper wish, now permanently present, for sexual satisfaction from the dreamer's father. This is immediately replaced by the wish to see once more what was then so fascinating. The mental process then continues its course from the fulfilment of this last wish by the conjuring up of the primal scene to what has now become inevitable—the repudiation of the wish and its repression.

The diffuseness and elaboration of this commentary have been forced upon me by the effort to present the reader with some sort of equivalent for the convincing power of an analysis carried through by oneself; perhaps they may also serve to discourage him from asking for the publication of analyses which have stretched over several years.

[14] The easiest way of meeting the patient's statement is perhaps to assume that the object of his observation was in the first instance a coitus in the normal attitude, which cannot fail to produce the impression of being a sadistic act. Only after this, we may suppose, was the attitude altered, so that he had an opportunity for making other observations and judgements. This hypothesis, however, was not confirmed with certainty, and moreover does not seem to me indispensable. We must not forget the actual situation which lies behind the abbreviated description given in the text: the patient under analysis, at an age of over twenty-five years, was lending words to the impressions and im-

could no longer confound it with the bottom, as he had in his observation of the little girls.[15]

The dream ended in a state of anxiety, from which he did not recover until he had his Nanya with him. He fled, therefore, from his father to her. His anxiety was a repudiation of the wish for sexual satisfaction from his father—the trend which had put the dream into his head. The form taken by the anxiety, the fear of "being eaten by the wolf," was only the (as we shall hear, regressive) transposition of the wish to be copulated with by his father, that is, to be given sexual satisfaction in the same way as his mother. His last sexual aim, the passive attitude towards his father, succumbed to repression, and fear of his father appeared in its place in the shape of the wolf phobia.

And the driving force of this repression? The circumstances of the case show that it can only have been his narcissistic genital libido, which, in the form of concern for his male organ, was fighting against a satisfaction whose attainment seemed to involve the renunciation of that organ. And it was from his threatened narcissism that he derived the masculinity

---

pulses of his fourth year which he would never have found at that time. If we fail to notice this, it may easily seem comic and incredible that a child of four should be capable of such technical judgements and learned notions. This is simply another instance of *deferred action*. At the age of one and a half the child receives an impression to which he is unable to react adequately; he is only able to understand it and to be moved by it when the impression is revived in him at the age of four; and only twenty years later, during the analysis, is he able to grasp with his conscious mental processes what was then going on in him. The patient justifiably disregards the three periods of time, and puts his present ego into the situation which is so long past. And in this we follow him, since with correct self-observation and interpretation the effect must be the same as though the distance between the second and third periods of time could be neglected. Moreover, we have no other means of describing the events of the second period.

[15] We shall learn later on, when we come to trace out his anal-erotism, how he further dealt with this portion of the problem.

with which he defended himself against his passive attitude towards his father.

We now observe that at this point in our narrative we must make an alteration in our terminology. During the dream he had reached a new phase in his sexual organization. Up to then the sexual opposites had been for him *active* and *passive*. Since his seduction his sexual aim had been a passive one, of being touched on the genitals; it was then transformed, by regression to the earlier stage of sadistic-anal organization, into the masochistic aim of being beaten or punished. It was a matter of indifference to him whether he reached this aim with a man or with a woman. He had wandered, without considering the difference of sex, from his Nanya to his father; he had longed to have his member touched by his Nanya, and had tried to provoke a beating from his father. In the process of this change his genitals were left out of account; though the connection which had been concealed by the regression was still expressed in his phantasy of being beaten on the penis. The activation of the primal scene in the dream now brought him back to the genital organization. He discovered the vagina and the biological significance of masculine and feminine. He understood now that active was the same as masculine, while passive was the same as feminine. His passive sexual aim should now have been transformed into a feminine one, and have expressed itself as "being copulated with by his father" instead of "being beaten by him on the genitals or on the bottom." This feminine aim, however, underwent repression and was obliged to let itself be replaced by fear of the wolf.

We must here break off the discussion of his sexual development until new light is thrown from the later stages of his history upon these earlier ones. For the proper appreciation of the wolf phobia we will only add that both his father and mother became wolves. His mother took the part of the castrated wolf, who let the others climb upon it; his father took the part of the wolf that climbed. But his fear, as we have heard him assure us, related only to the standing wolf, that is, to his father. It must further strike us that the fear with which

the dream ended had a model in his grandfather's story. For in this the castrated wolf, who had let the others climb upon it, was seized with fear as soon as he was reminded of the fact of his taillessness. It seems, therefore, as though he had identified himself with his castrated mother during the dream, and was now fighting against that fact. "If you want to be sexually satisfied by Father," we may perhaps represent him as saying to himself, "you must allow yourself to be castrated like Mother; but I won't have that." In short, a clear protest on the part of his masculinity! Let us, however, clearly understand that the sexual development of the case that we are now examining has a great disadvantage from the point of view of research, for it was by no means undisturbed. It was first decisively influenced by the seduction, and was then diverted by the scene of observation of the coitus, which in its deferred action operated like a second seduction.

V

A Few Discussions

THE WHALE and the polar bear, it has been said, cannot wage war upon each other, for since each is confined to his own element they cannot come together. It is just as impossible for me to argue with workers in the field of psychology or of the neuroses who do not recognize the postulates of psychoanalysis and who look upon its results as artifacts. But during the last few years there has also grown up another kind of opposition, among people who, in their own opinion at all events, take their stand upon the ground of analysis, who do not dispute its technique or results, but who merely think themselves justified in drawing other conclusions from the same material and in submitting it to other interpretations.

As a rule, however, theoretical controversy is unfruitful. No sooner has one begun to depart from the material upon which one ought to be relying, than one runs the risk of becoming intoxicated with one's own assertions and, in the end, of representing opinions which any observation would have contradicted. For this reason it seems to me to be incomparably more useful to combat dissentient interpretations by testing them upon particular cases and problems.

I have remarked above (see p. 223) that it will certainly be considered improbable that "a child at the tender age of

one and a half could be in a position to take in the perceptions of such a complicated process and to preserve them so
accurately in its unconscious; secondly, that it could be
possible for a deferred elaboration of this material to force
its way into comprehension at the age of four; and finally,
that any procedure could have succeeded in bringing into
consciousness coherently and convincingly the details of a
scene of this kind which had been experienced and understood
in such circumstances."

The last question is purely one of fact. Any one who will
take the trouble of pursuing an analysis into these depths by
means of the prescribed technique will convince himself that
it is decidedly possible. Any one who neglects this, and breaks
off the analysis in some higher stratum, has waived his right
of forming a judgement on the matter. But the interpretation
of what is arrived at in depth-analysis is not decided by this.

The two other doubts are based upon a low estimate of
the importance of early infantile impressions and an unwillingness to ascribe such enduring effects to them. The
supporters of this view look for the causes of neuroses almost
exclusively in the grave conflicts of later life; they assume
that the importance of childhood is only held up before our
eyes in analysis on account of the inclination of neurotics for
expressing their present interests in reminiscences and symbols
from the remote past. Such an estimate of the importance of
the infantile factor would involve the disappearance of much
that has formed part of the most intimate characteristics of
analysis, though also, no doubt, of much that raises resistance
to it and alienates the confidence of the outsider.

This, then, is the interpretation that we are bringing forward for discussion. It maintains that scenes from early
infancy, such as are brought up by an exhaustive analysis of
neuroses (as, for instance, in the present case), are not re-
productions of real occurrences, to which it is possible to
ascribe an influence over the course of the patient's later life
and over the formation of his symptoms. It considers them
rather as products of the imagination, which find their instigation in mature life, which are intended to serve as some

kind of symbolic representation of real wishes and interests, and which owe their origin to a regressive tendency, to an aversion from the problems of the present. If that is so, we can of course spare ourselves the necessity of making such bewildering demands upon the mental life and intellectual capacity of children of the tenderest age.

Besides the desire which we all share for the rationalization and simplification of our difficult problem, there are all sorts of facts that speak in favour of this interpretation. It is also possible to eliminate beforehand one objection to it which may arise, particularly in the mind of a practical analyst. It must be admitted that, if this interpretation of these scenes from infancy were the right one, the practice of analysis would not in the first instance be altered in any respect. If neurotics are endowed with the evil characteristic of diverting their interest from the present and of attaching it to these regressive substitutes, the products of their imagination, then there is absolutely nothing for it but to follow upon their tracks and bring these unconscious productions into consciousness; for, if we disregard their objective unimportance, they are of the utmost importance from our point of view, since they are for the moment the bearers and possessors of the interest which we want to set free so as to be able to direct it on to the problems of the present. The analysis would have to run precisely the same course as one which had a *naïf* faith in the truth of the phantasies. The difference would only come at the end of the analysis, after the phantasies had been laid bare. We should then say to the patient: "Very well, then; your neurosis proceeded *as though* you had received these impressions and spun them out in your childhood. You will see, of course, that that is out of the question. They were products of your imagination, and were intended to divert you from the real problems that lay before you. Let us now inquire what these problems were, and what lines of communication ran between them and your phantasies." After the infantile phantasies had been disposed of in this way, it would be possible to begin a second portion of the treatment, which would be concerned with the patient's real life.

Any shortening of this course, any alteration, that is, in psychoanalytic treatment as it has hitherto been practised, would be technically inadmissible. Unless the patient is made conscious of these phantasies to their fullest extent, he cannot obtain command of the interest which is attached to them. If his attention is diverted from them as soon as their existence and their general outlines are divined, support is simply being given to the work of repression, thanks to which they have been put beyond the patient's reach in spite of all his pains. If he is given a premature sense of their unimportance, by being informed, for instance, that it will only be a question of phantasies, which, of course, have no real significance, his co-operation will never be secured for the task of bringing them into consciousness. A correct procedure, therefore, would make no alteration in the technique of analysis, whatever estimate might be formed of these scenes from infancy.

I have already mentioned that there are a number of facts which can be brought up in support of the interpretation of these scenes as being regressive phantasies. And above all there is this one: so far as my experience hitherto goes, these scenes from infancy are not reproduced during the treatment as recollections, they are the products of construction. Many people will certainly think that this single admission decides the whole dispute.

I am anxious not to be misunderstood. Every analyst knows —and he has met with the experience on countless occasions —that in the course of a successful treatment the patient brings up a large number of spontaneous recollections from his childhood, for the appearance of which (a first appearance, perhaps) the physician feels himself entirely blameless, since he has not made any attempt at a construction which could have put any material of the sort into the patient's head. It does not necessarily follow that these previously unconscious recollections are always true. They may be; but they are often distorted from the truth, and interspersed with imaginary elements, just like the so-called screen-memories which are spontaneously preserved. All that I mean to say is this: scenes, like this one in my present patient's case, which date from such an early period and exhibit such a content, and which further lay claim to such an extraordinary significance for the history of the case, are as a rule not reproduced as recollections, but have to be divined—constructed—gradually and laboriously from an aggregate of indications. Moreover, it would be sufficient for the purposes of the argument if my admission that scenes of this kind do not become conscious in the shape of recollections applied only to cases of obsessional neurosis, or even if I were to limit my assertion to the case which we are studying here.

I am not of opinion, however, that such scenes must necessarily be phantasies because they do not reappear in the shape of recollections. It seems to me absolutely equivalent to a recollection if the memories are replaced (as in the present case) by dreams, the analysis of which invariably leads back to the same scene, and which reproduce every portion of its content in an indefatigable variety of new shapes. Indeed, dreaming is another kind of remembering, though one that is subject to the conditions that rule at night and to the laws of dream formation. It is this recurrence in dreams that I regard as the explanation of the fact that the patients themselves gradually acquire a profound conviction of the reality of these primal scenes, a conviction which is in no respect inferior to one based upon recollection.[1]

There is naturally no need for those who take the opposite view to abandon as hopeless their fight against such arguments. It is well known that dreams can be guided.[2] And the sense of conviction felt by the person analysed may be the result of suggestion, which is always having new parts as-

---

[1] A passage from the first edition of my *Traumdeutung* (1900) will show at what an early stage I was occupied with this problem. On p. 126 of that work there is an analysis of a remark occurring in a dream: *"that is no longer obtainable."* It is explained that the phrase originated from myself; a few days before, I had explained to the patient "that the earliest experiences of childhood are *no longer obtainable* as such, but are replaced in analysis by 'transferences' and dreams."

[2] The mechanism of dreaming cannot be influenced; but dream material is to some extent subject to orders.

signed to it in the play of forces involved in analytic treatment. The old-fashioned psychotherapeutist, it might be maintained, used to suggest to his patient that he was cured, that he had overcome his inhibitions, and so on; while the psychoanalyst, on this view, suggests to him that when he was a child he had some experience or other, which he must now recollect in order to be cured. This would be the difference between the two.

Let it be clearly understood that this last attempt at an explanation on the part of those who take the opposite view results in the scenes from infancy being disposed of far more fundamentally than was given out beforehand. What was argued at first was that they were not realities but phantasies. But what is argued now is evidently that they are phantasies not of the patient but of the analyst himself, who forces them upon the person under analysis on account of some complexes of his own. An analyst, indeed, who hears this reproach, will comfort himself by recalling how gradually the construction of this phantasy which he is supposed to have originated came about, and, when all is said and done, how independently of the physician's incentive many points in its development proceeded; how, after a certain phase of the treatment, everything seemed to converge upon it, and how later, in the synthesis, the most various and remarkable results radiated out from it; how not only the large problems but the smallest peculiarities in the history of the case were cleared up by this single assumption. And he will disclaim the possession of the amount of ingenuity necessary for the concoction of an occurrence which can fulfil all these demands. But even this plea will be without an effect upon an adversary who has not experienced the analysis himself. On the one side there will be a charge of refined self-deception, and on the other of obtuseness of judgement; it will be impossible to arrive at a decision.

Let us turn to another factor which supports the adverse interpretation of these constructed scenes from infancy. It is as follows: all the processes which have been brought forward in order to explain these dubious formations as phantasies really exist, and their importance must be recognized.

The diversion of interest from the problems of real life,[3] the existence of phantasies in the capacity of substitute-formations for unperformed actions, the regressive tendency which is expressed in these productions—regressive in more than one sense, in so far as there is involved simultaneously a shrinking-back from life and a harking-back to the past—all of this holds good, and is regularly confirmed by analysis. One would have thought that it would also suffice to explain the supposed reminiscences from early infancy which are under discussion; and in accordance with the economical principles of science such an explanation would have the advantage over another which is inadequate without the support of new and surprising assumptions.

I may here venture to point out that the repudiations which are to be found in the psychoanalytical literature of to-day are usually arrived at upon the principle of *pars pro toto*. From a highly composite unity one part of the operative factors is singled out and proclaimed as the truth; and for the sake of this one part, the other part, as well as the whole, is repudiated. If we look a little closer, to see which group of factors it is that has been given the preference, we shall find that it is the one that contains what is already known from other sources or what can be most easily related to it. Thus, with Jung, what is selected is actuality and regression, and with Adler, egoistic motives. What is left over, however, and rejected as false, is precisely what is new in psychoanalysis and peculiar to it. This is the easiest method by which to repel the revolutionary and embarrassing advance of psychoanalysis.

It is worth while remarking that none of the factors which are adduced by the adverse interpreters for their explanation of scenes from infancy required to wait for recognition until Jung brought them forward as novelties. The notion of a current conflict, of a turning away from reality, of a substitutive satisfaction obtained in phantasy, of a regression to material from the past—all of this (used, moreover, in the same con-

---

[3] I have good reasons for preferring to say "the diversion of the *libido* from current *conflicts*."

nection, though perhaps with a slightly different terminology) had for years formed an integral part of my own theory. It was not the whole of it, however. It was only that part of the causation of neurosis-formation which, starting from reality, operates in a regressive direction. Side by side with this I left room for another influence which, starting from the impressions of childhood, operates in a forward direction, which points out a path for the libido that is shrinking back from life, and which makes it possible to understand the otherwise inexplicable regression to childhood. Thus according to my interpretation the two factors operate together in the formation of symptoms, but an earlier co-operation seems to me to be of equal importance. I am of opinion that *the influence of childhood makes itself felt even in the situation at the beginning of the formation of a neurosis, since it plays a decisive part in determining whether and at what point the individual shall fail to master the real problems of life.*

What is in dispute, therefore, is the significance of the infantile factor. The problem is to find a case which can establish that significance beyond any doubt. Such, however, is the case which is being dealt with so exhaustively in these pages and which is distinguished by the characteristic that the neurosis in later life was preceded by a neurosis in early childhood. It is for that very reason, indeed, that I have chosen this case to report upon. In case any one should feel inclined to reject it because the animal phobia strikes him as not sufficiently serious to be recognized as an independent neurosis, I may mention that the phobia was succeeded without any interval by an obsessional ceremonial, and by obsessional acts and thoughts, which will be discussed in the following sections of this paper.

The occurrence of a neurotic disorder in the fourth and fifth years of childhood proves, first and foremost, that infantile experiences are by themselves in a position to produce a neurosis, without there being any need for the addition of a flight from some problem which has to be met in real life. It may be objected that even a child is constantly being confronted with problems, which it would perhaps be glad to evade. That is so; but the life of a child under school age is easily observable, and we can examine it to see whether any "problems" are to be found in it capable of determining the causation of a neurosis. But we discover nothing but instinctual trends which the child cannot satisfy and which it is not old enough to master, and the sources from which these trends arise.

As was to be expected, the enormous shortening of the interval between the outbreak of the neurosis and the date of the childhood experiences which are under discussion reduces to the narrowest limits the regressive part of the causation, while it brings into full view the portion of it which operates in a forward direction, the influence of earlier impressions. The present case history will, I hope, give a clear picture of this position of things. But there are other reasons why neuroses of childhood give a decisive answer to the question of the nature of primal scenes—the earliest experiences of childhood that are brought to light in analysis.

Let us assume as an uncontradicted premise that a primal scene of this kind has been correctly evolved technically, that it is indispensable to a comprehensive solution of all the conundrums that are set us by the symptoms of the infantile disorder, that all the consequences radiate out from it, just as all the threads of the analysis have led up to it. Then, in view of its content, it is impossible that it can be anything else than the reproduction of a reality experienced by the child. For a child, like an adult, can produce phantasies only from material which has been acquired from some source or other; and with children some of the means of acquiring it (by reading, for instance) are cut off, while the space of time at their disposal for acquiring it is short and can easily be searched with a view to the discovery of any such sources.

In the present case the content of the primal scene is a picture of sexual intercourse between the boy's parents in an attitude especially favourable for certain observations. Now it would be no evidence whatever of the reality of such a scene if we were to find it in a patient whose symptoms (the effects of the scene, that is) had appeared at some time or other in the later part of his life. A person in such a position might have acquired the impressions, the ideas, and the knowledge on a great number of different occasions in the course of the long interval; he might then have transformed them into an imaginary picture, have projected them back into his childhood, and have attached them to his parents. If, however, the effects of a scene of this sort appear in the child's fourth or fifth year, then he must have witnessed the scene at an even earlier age. But in that case we are still faced with all the bewildering consequences which have arisen from the analysis of this infantile neurosis. Some people may thus feel inclined to assume that the patient not only unconsciously imagined the primal scene, but also concocted the alteration in his character, his fear of the wolf, and his religious obsession; but such an expedient would be contradicted by his otherwise sober nature and by the direct tradition in his family. It must therefore be left at this—I can see no other possibility—: either the analysis based upon the neurosis in his childhood is all a piece of nonsense from start to finish, or everything took place just as I have described it above.

At an earlier stage in the discussion we were brought up against an ambiguity in regard to the patient's predilection for female nates and for coitus in the attitude in which they are especially prominent. It seemed necessary to trace this predilection back to the coitus which he had observed between his parents, while at the same time a preference of this kind is a general characteristic of archaic constitutions which are predisposed to an obsessional neurosis. But there is an easy way out of the difficulty in the solution of the contradiction as an over-determination. The person who was the subject of his observation of this position during coitus was, after all, his father in the flesh, and it may also have been from him that he had inherited this constitutional predilection. Neither his father's subsequent illness nor his family history contradicts this; as has been mentioned already, a brother of his father's died in a condition which must be regarded as the outcome of a severe obsessional disorder.

In this connection we may recall that, at the time of his

seduction as a boy of three and a quarter, his sister had uttered a remarkable calumny against his good old nurse, to the effect that she stood all kinds of people on their heads and then took hold of them by their genitals (see p. 202). We cannot fail to be struck by the idea that perhaps the sister, at a similar tender age, also witnessed the same scene as was observed by her brother later on, and that it was this that had suggested to her her notion about "standing people on their heads" during the sexual act. This hypothesis would also give us a hint of the reason for her own sexual precocity.

[Originally[4] I had no intention of pursuing the discussion of the reality of "primal scenes" any further in this place. Since, however, I have meanwhile had occasion in my *Introductory Lectures on Psycho-Analysis* to treat the subject on more general lines and with no polemical aim in view, it would be misleading if I omitted to apply the considerations which determined my other discussion of the matter to the case that is now before us. I therefore proceed as follows by way of supplement and rectification.—There remains the possibility of yet another interpretation of the primal scene underlying the dream,—of an interpretation, moreover, which obviates to a large extent the decision that has been arrived at above and relieves us of many of our difficulties. But the theory which seeks to reduce scenes from infancy to the level of regressive symbols will gain nothing even by this modification; and indeed that theory seems to me to be finally disposed of by this (as it would be by any other) analysis of an infantile neurosis.

I am of opinion, that is to say, that the state of affairs can also be explained in the following manner. It is true that we cannot dispense with the assumption that the child observed a coitus, the sight of which gave him a conviction that castration might be more than an empty threat. Moreover, the significance which he subsequently came to attach to the attitudes of men and women, in connection with the development of anxiety on the one hand, and as a condition upon which his

[4] [Author's square bracket. See end of footnote, p. 188.]

falling in love depended on the other hand, leaves us no choice but to conclude that it must have been a coitus *a tergo, more ferarum*. But there is another factor which is not so irreplaceable and which may be dropped. Perhaps what the child observed was not a coitus between his parents but an animal coitus, which he then displaced on to his parents, as though he had inferred that his parents did things in the same way.

Colour is lent to this interpretation above all by the fact that the wolves of the dream were actually sheep-dogs and, moreover, appear as such in the drawing. Shortly before the dream the boy was repeatedly taken to visit the flocks of sheep, and there he might see just such large white dogs and probably also observe them copulating. I should also like to bring into this connection the number three, which the dreamer introduced without adducing any further motive, and I would suggest that he had kept in his memory the fact that he had made three such observations with the sheep-dogs. What supervened during the expectant excitement of the night of his dream was the transference on to his parents of his recently acquired memory-picture, with *all* its details, and it was only thus that the powerful emotional effects which followed were made possible. He now arrived at a deferred understanding of the impressions which he may have received a few weeks or months earlier—a process such as all of us perhaps have been through in our own experiences. The transference from the copulating dogs on to his parents was accomplished not by means of his making an inference accompanied by words but by his searching out in his memory a real scene in which his parents had been together and which could be coalesced with the situation of the coitus. All of the details of the scene which were established in the analysis of the dream may have been accurately reproduced. It was really on a summer's afternoon while the child was suffering from malaria, the parents were both present, dressed in white, when the child woke up from its sleep, but—the scene was innocent. The rest had been added by the inquisitive child's subsequent wish, based upon his experiences with the dogs, to witness his parents as well in their love-making; and the scene which was thus imagined now produced all the effects that we have catalogued, just as though it had been entirely real and not fused together out of two components, the one earlier and indifferent, the other later and profoundly impressive.

It is at once obvious how greatly the demands upon our credulity are reduced. We need no longer suppose that the parents performed a coitus in the presence of their child (a very young one, it is true)—which was a disagreeable idea for many of us. The period of time during which the effects were deferred is very greatly diminished; it now covers only a few months of the child's fourth year and does not stretch back at all into the first dark years of childhood. There remains scarcely anything strange in the child's conduct in making the transference from the dogs on to his parents and in being afraid of the wolf instead of his father. He was in that phase of the development of his attitude towards the world which I have described in *Totem und Tabu* as the return of totemism. The theory which endeavours to explain the primal scenes found in neuroses as retrospective phantasies of a later date seems to obtain powerful support from the present observation, in spite of our patient being of the tender age of four years. Young though he was, he was yet able to succeed in replacing an impression of his fourth year by an imaginary trauma at the age of one and a half. This regression, however, seems neither mysterious nor tendentious. The scene which was to be made up had to fulfil certain conditions which, in consequence of the circumstances of the dreamer's life, could only be found in precisely this early period; such, for instance, was the condition that he should be in bed in his parents' bedroom.

But something that I am able to adduce from the analytic findings in other cases will seem to most readers to be the decisive factor in favour of the correctness of the interpretation here proposed. Scenes of observing sexual intercourse between parents at a very early age (whether they be real memories or phantasies) are as a matter of fact by no means rarities in the analyses of neurotic mortals. Possibly they are no less frequent among those who are not neurotics. Possibly they are part of the regular store in the—conscious or unconscious—treasury of their memories. But as often as I have been able by means of analysis to bring out a scene of this sort, it has shown the same peculiarity which startled us with our present patient too: it has related to coitus *a tergo*, which alone offers the spectator a possibility of inspecting the genitals. There is surely no need any longer to doubt that what we are dealing with is only a phantasy, which is invariably aroused, perhaps, by an observation of the sexual intercourse of animals. And yet more: I have hinted that my description of the "primal scene" has remained incomplete because I have reserved for a later moment my account of the way in which the child interrupted his parents' intercourse. I must now add that this method of interruption is also the same in every case.

I can well believe that I have now laid myself open to grave aspersions on the part of the readers of this case history. If these arguments in favour of such an interpretation of the "primal scene" were at my disposal, how could I possibly have taken it upon myself to begin by advocating one which seemed so absurd? Or have I made these new observations, which have obliged me to alter my original interpretation, in the interval between the first draft of the case history and this addition, and am I for some reason or other unwilling to admit the fact? I will admit something else instead: I intend on this occasion to close the discussion of the reality of the primal scene with a *non liquet*. This case history is not yet at an end; in its further course a factor will emerge which will shake the certainty which we seem at present to enjoy. Nothing, I think, will then be left but to refer my readers to the passages in my *Introductory Lectures* in which I have treated the problem of primal phantasies or primal scenes.]

VI

The Obsessional Neurosis

Now FOR THE THIRD TIME, the patient came under a new influence that gave a decisive turn to his development. When
he was four and a half years old, and as his state of irritability
and apprehensiveness had still not improved, his mother
determined to make him acquainted with the Bible story in
the hope of distracting and elevating him. Moreover, she
succeeded; his initiation into religion brought the previous
phase to an end, but at the same time it led to the anxiety
symptoms being replaced by obsessional symptoms. Up to
then he had not been able to get to sleep easily because he had
been afraid of having bad dreams like the one he had had
that night before Christmas; now he was obliged before he
went to bed to kiss all of the holy pictures in the room, to
recite prayers, and to make innumerable signs of the cross
upon himself and upon his bed.

His childhood now falls clearly into the following epochs:
first, the earliest period up to the seduction when he was three
and a quarter years old, during which the primal scene took
place; secondly, the period of the alteration in his character
up to the anxiety dream (four years old); thirdly, the period
of the animal phobia up to his initiation into religion (four
and a half years old); and from then onwards the period
of the obsessional neurosis up to a time later than his tenth

year. That there should be an instantaneous and clear-cut displacement of one phase by the next was not in the nature of things or of our patient; on the contrary, the preservation of all that had gone before and the coexistence of the most different sorts of currents were characteristic of him. His naughtiness did not disappear when the anxiety set in, and persisted with slowly diminishing force during the period of piety. But there was no longer any question of a wolf phobia during this last phase. The obsessional neurosis ran its course discontinuously; the first attack was the longest and most intense, and others came on when he was eight and ten, following each time upon exciting causes which stood in a clear relationship to the content of the neurosis. His mother told him the sacred story herself, and besides this made his Nanya read aloud to him about it out of a book which was adorned with illustrations. The chief emphasis in the narrative was naturally laid upon the story of the Passion. His Nanya, who was very pious and superstitious, added her own commentary upon it, but was also obliged to listen to all the little critic's objections and doubts. If the battles which now began to convulse his mind finally ended in a victory for faith, his Nanya's influence was not without its share in this result.

What he related to me as his recollection of his reactions to this initiation was met by me at first with complete disbelief. It was impossible, I thought, that these could have been the thoughts of a child of four and a half or five; he had probably referred back to this remote past the thoughts which had arisen from the reflections of a grown man of thirty.[1] But the patient would not hear of this correction;

[1] I also repeatedly attempted to throw the patient's whole story forward by one year at all events, and in that way to refer the seduction to an age of four and a quarter, the dream to his fifth birthday, etc. As regards the intervals between the events there was no possibility of gaining anything. But the patient remained obdurate on the point, though he did not succeed entirely in removing my doubts. A postponement like this for one year would obviously be of no importance as regards the impression made by the story and as regards the discussions and implications attached to it.

I could not succeed, as in so many other differences of opinion between us, in convincing him; and in the end the correspondence between the thoughts which he had recollected and the symptoms of which he gave particulars, as well as the way in which the thoughts fitted into his sexual development, compelled me on the contrary to come to believe him. And I then said to myself that this very criticism of the doctrines of religion, which I was unwilling to ascribe to the child, was only effected by an infinitesimal minority of adults.

I shall now bring forward the material of his recollections, and not until afterwards try to find some path that may lead to an explanation of them.

The impression which he received from the sacred story was, to begin with, as he reported, by no means an agreeable one. He set his face, in the first place, against the feature of suffering in the figure of Christ, and then against his story as a whole. He turned his critical dissatisfaction against God the Father. If he were almighty, then it was his fault that men were wicked and tormented others and were sent to Hell for it. He ought to have made them good; he was responsible himself for all wickedness and all torments. He took objection to the command that we should turn the other cheek if our right cheek is smitten, and to the fact that Christ had wished on the Mount of Olives that the cup might be taken away from him, as well as to the fact that no miracle had taken place to prove that he was the Son of God. Thus his acuteness was on the alert, and was able to search out with remorseless severity the weak points of the sacred poem.

But to this rationalistic criticism there were very soon added ruminations and doubts, which betray to us that hidden impulses were also at work. One of the first questions which he addressed to his Nanya was whether Christ had had a behind too. His Nanya informed him that he had been a god and also a man. As a man he had had and done all the same things as other men. Now this did not satisfy him at all, but he succeeded in finding his own consolation by saying to himself that the behind is really only a continuation of the legs. But hardly had he pacified his dread of having to humiliate the sacred figure, when it flared up again as the further question arose whether Christ used to shit too. He did not venture to put this question to his pious Nanya, but he himself found a way out, and she could not have shown him a better. Since Christ had made wine out of nothing, he could also have made food into nothing and in this way have avoided defaecating.

We shall be in a better position to understand these ruminations if we return to a piece of his sexual development which we have already mentioned. We know that, after his refusal by his Nanya and the consequent suppression of the beginnings of genital activity, his sexual life developed in the direction of sadism and masochism. He tormented and ill-treated small animals, imagined himself beating horses, and on the other hand imagined the heir to the throne being beaten.[2] In his sadism he maintained his ancient identification with his father; but in his masochism he chose him as a sexual object. He was deep in a phase of the pre-genital organization which I regard as the predisposition to obsessional neurosis. Through the operation of the dream, which brought him under the influence of the primal scene, he might have made the advance to the genital organization, and have transformed his masochism towards his father into a feminine attitude towards him—into homosexuality. But the dream did not bring about this advance; it ended in a state of anxiety. His relation to his father might have proceeded from the sexual aim of being beaten by him to the next aim, namely, that of being copulated with by him like a woman; but in fact, owing to the opposition of his narcissistic masculinity, this relation was thrown back to an even more primitive stage. It was displaced on to a father-surrogate, in the shape of fear of being eaten by the wolf, and was so split off; but this by no means disposed of it. On the contrary, we can only do justice to the apparent complexity of the state of affairs by bearing firmly in mind the coexistence of the three sexual trends which were directed by the boy towards his father. From the time of the

[2] Especially upon the penis (see p. 209).

dream onwards, in his unconscious he was homosexual, and in his neurosis he was at the level of cannibalism; while the earlier masochistic attitude remained the dominant one. All three currents had passive sexual aims; there was the same object, and the same sexual impulse, but they had become split up at three different levels.

His knowledge of the sacred story now gave him a chance of sublimating his predominant masochistic attitude towards his father. He became Christ—which was made specially easy for him on account of their having the same birthday. Thus he became something great and also (a fact upon which enough stress was not laid for the moment) a man. We catch a glimpse of his repressed homosexual attitude in his doubting whether Christ could have a behind, for these ruminations can have had no other meaning but the question whether he himself could be used by his father like a woman—like his mother in the primal scene. When we come to the solution of the other obsessional ideas, we shall find this interpretation confirmed. His reflection that it was insulting to bring the sacred figure into relation with such insinuations corresponded with the repression of his passive homosexuality. It will be noticed that he was endeavouring to keep his new sublimation free from the admixture which it derived from sources in the repressed. But he was unsuccessful.

We do not as yet understand why he also rebelled against the passive character of Christ and against his ill-treatment by his Father, and in this way began also to renounce his previous masochistic ideal, even in its sublimation. We may assume that this second conflict was especially favourable to the emergence of the humiliating obsessional thoughts from the first conflict (between the dominant masochistic and the repressed homosexual currents), for it is only natural that in a mental conflict all the currents upon one side or the other should combine with one another, even though they have the most diverse origins. We must await some fresh information which will tell us the motive of this rebelling and at the same time of the criticisms which he levelled at religion.

His sexual inquiries also gained something out of the information he was given upon the sacred story. So far he had had no reason for supposing that children only came from women. On the contrary, his Nanya had given him to believe that he was his father's child, while his sister was his mother's; and this closer connection with his father had been very precious to him. He now heard that Mary was called the Mother of God. So all children came from women, and what his Nanya had said to him was no longer tenable. Moreover, as a result of what he was told, he was bewildered as to who Christ's father really was. He was inclined to think it was Joseph, as he heard that he and Mary had always lived together, but his Nanya said that Joseph was only *like* his father and that his real father was God. He could make nothing of that. He only understood this much: if the question was one that could be argued at all, then the relation between father and son could not be such an intimate one as he had always imagined it to be.

The boy had some kind of inkling of the ambivalent feelings towards the father which are an underlying factor in all religions, and attacked his religion on account of the slackening which it implied in the relation between son and father. Naturally his opposition soon ceased to take the form of doubting the truth of the doctrine, and turned instead directly against the figure of God. God had treated his son harshly and cruelly, but he was no better towards men; he had sacrificed his own son and had ordered Abraham to do the same. He began to fear God.

If he was Christ, then his father was God. But the God which religion forced upon him was not a true substitute for the father whom he had loved and whom he did not want to have stolen from him. His love for this father of his gave him his critical acuteness. He resisted God in order to be able to cling to his father; and in doing this he was really upholding the old father against the new. He was faced by a trying part of the process of detaching himself from his father.

His old love for his father, which had been manifest in his earliest period, was therefore the source of his energy in struggling against God and of his acuteness in criticizing religion. But on the other hand this hostility to the new God was not an original reaction either; it had its prototype in a hostile impulse against his father, which had come into existence under the influence of the anxiety-dream, and it was at bottom only a revival of that impulse. The two opposing currents of feeling, which were to rule the whole of his later life, met here in the ambivalent struggle over the question of religion. It followed, moreover, that what this struggle produced in the shape of symptoms, the blasphemous ideas, the obsession which came over him of thinking "God—shit," "God—swine," were genuine compromise-products, as we shall see from the analysis of these ideas in connection with his anal-erotism.

Some other obsessional symptoms of a less typical sort pointed with equal certainty to his father, but at the same time showed the connection between the obsessional neurosis and the earlier occurrences.

A part of the pious ritual by means of which he eventually atoned for his blasphemies was the command to breathe in a ceremonious manner under conditions. Each time he made the sign of the cross he was obliged to breathe in deeply or to exhale forcibly. In his native tongue "breath" is the same word as "spirit," so that here the Holy Ghost came in. He was obliged to breathe in the Holy Spirit, or to breathe out the evil spirits which he had heard and read about.[3] He ascribed too to these evil spirits the blasphemous thoughts for which he had to inflict such heavy penance upon himself. He was, however, also obliged to exhale when he saw beggars, or cripples, or ugly, old, or wretched-looking people; but he could think of no way of connecting this obsession with the spirits. The only account he could give to himself was that he did it so as not to become like them.

Eventually, in connection with a dream, the analysis elicited the information that the breathing out at the sight of pitiable-looking people had begun only after his sixth year and was

---

[3] This symptom, as we shall hear, had developed after he had reached his sixth year and could already read.

related to his father. He had not seen his father for many months, when one day his mother said she was going to take the children with her to the town and show them something that would very much please them. She then took them to a sanatorium, where they saw their father again; he looked ill, and the boy felt very sorry for him. His father was thus the prototype of all the cripples, beggars, and poor people in whose presence he was obliged to breathe out; just as a father is the prototype of the bogies that people see in anxiety-states, and of the caricatures that are drawn to bring derision upon some one. We shall learn elsewhere that this attitude of pity was derived from a particular detail of the primal scene, a detail which only became operative in the obsessional neurosis at this late moment.

Thus his determination (which was the motive of his breathing out in the presence of cripples) not to become like them was his old identification with his father transformed into the negative. But in so doing he was also copying his father in the positive sense, for the heavy breathing was an imitation of the noise which he had heard coming from his father during the coitus.[4] He had derived the Holy Ghost from this manifestation of male sensual excitement. Repression had turned this breathing into an evil spirit, which had another genealogy as well: namely, the malaria from which he had been suffering at the time of the primal scene.

His repudiation of these evil spirits corresponded to an unmistakable strain of asceticism in him which also found expression in other reactions. When he heard that Christ had once cast out some evil spirits into a herd of swine which then rushed down a precipice, he thought of how his sister in the earliest years of her childhood, before he could remember, had rolled down on to the beach from the cliff-path above the harbour. She too was an evil spirit and a swine. It was a short road from here to "God—swine." His father himself had shown that he was no less of a slave to sensuality. When he was told the story of the first of mankind he was struck by

---

[4] Assuming the reality of the primal scene.

the similarity of his lot to Adam's. In conversation with his Nanya he professed hypocritical surprise that Adam should have allowed himself to be dragged into misfortune by a woman, and promised her that he would never marry. A hostility towards women, due to his seduction by his sister, found strong expression at this time. And it was destined to disturb him often enough in his later erotic life. His sister came to be the permanent embodiment for him of temptation and sin. After he had been to confession he seemed to himself pure and free from sin. But then it appeared to him as though his sister were lying in wait to drag him again into sin, and in a moment he had provoked a quarrel with her which made him sinful once more. Thus he was obliged to keep on reproducing the fact of his seduction over and over again. Moreover, he had never given away his blasphemous thoughts at confession, in spite of their being such a weight on his mind.

We have been led unawares into a consideration of the symptoms of the later years of the obsessional neurosis; and we shall therefore pass over the events of the intervening period and shall proceed to describe its termination. We already know that, apart from its permanent strength, it underwent occasional intensifications: once—though the episode must for the present remain obscure to us—at the time of the death of a boy living in the same street with whom he was able to identify himself. When he was ten years old he had a German tutor, who very soon obtained a great influence over him. It is most instructive to observe that the whole of his strict piety dwindled away, never to be revived, after he had noticed and had learnt from enlightening conversations with his tutor that this father-surrogate attached no importance to piety and set no store by the truth of religion. His piety sank away with his dependence upon his father, who was now replaced by a new and more sociable father. This did not take place, however, without one last flicker of the obsessional neurosis; and from this he particularly remembered the obsession of having to think of the Holy Trinity whenever he saw three heaps of dung lying together in the road. In fact he never gave way to a new instigation without making one last attempt at clinging to what had lost its value for him. When his tutor discouraged him from his cruelties to small animals he also put an end to those misdeeds, but not until he had again cut up caterpillars for a last time to his thorough satisfaction. Once more he behaved in just the same way during the analytic treatment, for he showed a habit of producing a transitory "negative reaction"; every time something had been conclusively cleared up he attempted to contradict the effect for a short while by an aggravation of the symptom which had been cleared up. It is quite the rule, as we know, for children to treat prohibitions in the same kind of way. When they have been rebuked for something (for instance, because they are making an unbearable din), they repeat it once more after the prohibition before stopping it. In this way they gain the point of apparently stopping of their own accord and of disobeying the prohibition.

Under the German tutor's influence there arose a new and better sublimation of the patient's sadism, which, with the approach of puberty, had then gained the upper hand over his masochism. He developed an enthusiasm for military affairs, for uniforms, arms, and horses, and used them as food for continual day-dreams. Thus, under a man's influence, he had got free from his passive attitudes, and found himself for the time being on fairly normal lines. It was as an after-effect of his affection for the tutor, who left him soon afterwards, that in his later life he preferred German things (as, for instance, physicians, sanatoriums, women) to those belonging to his native country (representing his father)—a fact which was incidentally of great advantage to the transference during the treatment.

There was another dream, which belongs to the period before his emancipation by the tutor, and which I mention because it was forgotten until its appearance during the treatment. He saw himself riding on a horse and pursued by a gigantic caterpillar. He recognized in this dream an allusion to an earlier one from the period before the tutor, which we had interpreted long before. In this earlier dream he saw the

Devil dressed in black and in the upright attitude with which the wolf and the lion had terrified him so much in their day. He was pointing with his outstretched finger at a gigantic snail. The patient had soon guessed that this Devil was the Demon out of a well-known poem, and that the dream itself was a version of a very popular picture representing the Demon in a love-scene with a girl. The snail was in the woman's place, as being a perfect female sexual symbol. Guided by the Demon's pointing gesture, we were soon able to give as the dream's meaning that the patient was longing for some one who should give him the last pieces of information that were still missing upon the riddle of sexual intercourse, just as his father had given him the first in the primal scene long before.

In connection with the later dream, in which the female symbol was replaced by the male one, he remembered a particular event which had occurred a short time before the dream. Riding on the estate one day, he passed a peasant who was lying asleep with his little boy beside him. The latter woke his father and said something to him, whereupon the father began to abuse the rider and to pursue him till he rode off hastily. There was also a second recollection, that on the same estate there were trees that were quite white, spun all over by caterpillars. We can see that he took flight from the realization of the phantasy of the son lying with his father, and that he brought in the white trees in order to make an allusion to the anxiety dream of the white wolves on the walnut tree. It was thus a direct outbreak of dread of the feminine attitude towards men against which he had at first protected himself by his religious sublimation and was soon to protect himself still more effectively by the military one.

It would, however, be a great mistake to suppose that after the obsessional symptoms had been removed no permanent effects of the obsessional neurosis remained behind. The process had led to a victory for the faith of piety over the rebelliousness of critical research, and had presupposed the repression of the homosexual attitude. Lasting disadvantages resulted from both these factors. His intellectual activity remained seriously impaired after this first great defeat. He developed no zeal for learning, he showed no more of the acuteness with which at the tender age of five he had criticized and dissected the doctrines of religion. The repression of his over-powerful homosexuality, which was accomplished during the anxiety-dream, reserved that important impulse for the unconscious, kept it directed towards its original aim, and withdrew it from all the sublimations to which it is susceptible in other circumstances. For this reason the patient was without all those social interests which give a content to life. It was only when, during the analytic treatment, it became possible to liberate his shackled homosexuality that this state of affairs showed any improvement; and it was a most remarkable experience to see how (without any direct advice from the physician) each piece of the homosexual libido which was set free sought out some application in life and some attachment to the great common concerns of mankind.

VII

Anal Erotism and the Castration Complex

I MUST BEG THE READER to bear in mind that I obtained this history of an infantile neurosis as a by-product, so to speak, during the analysis of an illness in mature years. I was therefore obliged to put it together from even smaller fragments than are usually at one's disposal for purposes of synthesis. This task, which is not difficult in other respects, finds a natural limit when it is a question of forcing a structure which is itself in many dimensions on to the two-dimensional descriptive plane. I must therefore content myself with bringing forward fragmentary portions, which the reader can then put together into a living whole. The obsessional neurosis that has been described grew up, as has been repeatedly emphasized, upon the basis of a sadistic-anal constitution. But we have hitherto discussed only one of the two chief factors—the patient's sadism and its transformations. Everything that concerns his anal erotism has intentionally been left on one side so that it might be brought together and discussed at this later stage.

Analysts have long been agreed that the multifarious instinctual trends which are comprised under the name of anal erotism play an extraordinarily important part, which it would be quite impossible to overestimate, in building up sexual life and mental activity in general. It is equally agreed that one of the most important manifestations of the transformed erotism derived from this source is to be found in the treatment of money; for in the course of life this precious material attracts on to itself the psychical interest which was originally proper to faeces, the product of the anal zone. We have accustomed ourselves to trace back interest in money, in so far as it is of a libidinal and not of a rational character, to excremental pleasure, and to require a normal man to keep his relations to money entirely free from libidinal influences and to regulate them according to the demands of reality.

In our patient, at the time of his later illness, these relations were disturbed to a particularly severe degree, and this fact was not the least considerable element in his lack of independence and his incapacity for dealing with life. He had become very rich through legacies from his father and uncle; it was obvious that he attached great importance to being taken for rich, and he was liable to feel very much hurt if he was undervalued in this respect. But he had no idea how much he possessed, what his expenditure was, or what balance was left over. It was hard to say whether he ought to be called a miser or a spendthrift. He behaved now in this way and now in that, but never in a way that seemed to show any consistent intention. Some striking traits, which I shall further discuss below, might have led one to regard him as a hardened plutocrat, who considered his wealth as his greatest personal advantage, and who would never for a moment allow emotional interests to weigh against pecuniary ones. Yet he did not value other people by their wealth, and, on the contrary, showed himself upon many occasions unassuming, helpful, and charitable. Money, in fact, had been withdrawn from his conscious control, and meant for him something quite different.

I have already mentioned (on p. 206) that I viewed with

grave suspicion the way in which he consoled himself for the loss of his sister, who had become his closest companion during her latter years, with the reflection that now he would not have to share his parents' inheritance with her. But what was perhaps even more striking was the calmness with which he was able to relate this, as though he had no comprehension of the coarseness of feeling to which he was thus confessing. It is true that analysis rehabilitated him by showing that his grief for his sister had merely undergone a displacement; but only then did it become quite inexplicable why he should have tried to find a substitute for his sister in an increase of wealth.

He himself was puzzled by his behaviour in another connection. After his father's death the property that was left was divided between him and his mother. His mother administered it, and, as he himself admitted, met his pecuniary claims irreproachably and liberally. Yet every discussion of money matters that took place between them used to end with the most violent reproaches on his side, to the effect that she did not love him, that she was trying to economize at his expense, and that she would probably rather see him dead so as to have sole control over the money. His mother used then to protest her disinterestedness with tears, and he would thereupon grow ashamed of himself and declare with justice that he thought nothing of the sort of her; but he was sure to repeat the same scene at the first opportunity.

Many incidents, of which I will relate two, show that, for a long time before the analysis, faeces had had the significance of money for him. At a time when his bowel as yet played no part in his complaint, he once paid a visit to a poor cousin of his in a large town. As he left him he reproached himself for not giving this relative financial support, and immediately afterwards had what was "perhaps the most urgent need for relieving his bowels that he had experienced in his life." Two years later he really settled an annuity upon this cousin. Here is the other case. At the age of eighteen, while he was preparing for his leaving-examination at school, he visited a friend and came to an agreement with him upon a plan which seemed advisable on account of the dread which they shared of failing in the examination.[1] It had been decided to corrupt the school servant, and the patient's share of the sum to be provided was naturally the largest. On the way home he thought to himself that he should be glad to give even more if only he could succeed in getting through, if only he could be sure that nothing would happen to him in the examination —and an accident of another sort really did happen to him[2] before he reached his own front door.

We shall be prepared to hear that during his later illness he suffered from disturbances of his intestinal function which were very obstinate, though various circumstances caused them to fluctuate in intensity. When he came under my treatment he had become accustomed to enemas, which were given him by an attendant; spontaneous evacuations did not occur for months at a time, unless a sudden excitement from some definite direction intervened, as a result of which normal activity of the bowels might set in for a few days. His principal subject of complaint was that for him the world was hidden in a veil, or that he was cut off from the world by a veil. This veil was torn only at one moment—when, after an enema, the contents of the bowel left the intestinal canal; and he then felt well and normal again.[3]

The colleague to whom I referred the patient for a report upon his intestinal condition was perspicacious enough to explain it as being a functional one, or even psychically determined, and to abstain from any active medicinal treatment. Moreover, neither this nor dieting were of any use. During the years of analytic treatment there was no spontaneous move-

---

[1] [The German word *"Durchfall"* means literally "falling through"; it is used in the sense of "failing," as in an examination, and also of "diarrhoea."] The patient informed me that his native tongue has no parallel to the familiar German use of *"Durchfall"* as a description for disturbances of the bowels.

[2] This expression has the same meaning in the patient's native tongue as in German. [The German idiom refers euphemistically to the excretory processes. Compare *Dora—An Analysis of a Case of Hysteria*, Collier Books edition AS 581V.]

[3] The effect was the same whether he had the enema given him by some one else or whether he managed it himself.

ment—apart from the sudden influences that I have mentioned. The patient allowed himself to be convinced that if the intractable organ received more intensive treatment things would only be made worse, and contented himself with bringing on an evacuation once or twice a week by means of an enema or a purgative.

In discussing these intestinal troubles I have given more space to the patient's later illness than has been my plan elsewhere in this work, which is concerned with his infantile neurosis. I have done so for two reasons: first, because the intestinal symptoms were in point of fact carried forward from the infantile neurosis into the later one with little alteration, and secondly, because they played a principal part in the conclusion of the treatment.

We know how important doubt is to the physician who is analysing an obsessional neurosis. It is the patient's strongest weapon, the favourite expedient of his resistance. This same doubt enabled our patient to lie entrenched behind a respectful indifference and to allow the efforts of the treatment to slip past him for years together. Nothing changed, and there was no way of convincing him. At last I recognized the importance of the intestinal trouble for my purposes; it represented the small trait of hysteria which is regularly to be found at the root of an obsessional neurosis. I promised the patient a complete recovery of his intestinal activity, and by means of this promise made his incredulity manifest. I then had the satisfaction of seeing his doubt dwindle away, as in the course of the work his bowel began, like a hysterically affected organ, to "join in the conversation," and in a few weeks time recovered its normal functions after their long impairment.

I now turn back to the patient's childhood—to a time at which it was impossible that faeces could have had the significance of money for him.

Intestinal disorders set in very early with him, and especially in the form which is the most frequent and, among children, the most normal—namely, incontinence. We shall certainly be right, however, in rejecting a pathological explanation of these earliest occurrences, and in regarding them only as evidence of the patient's intention not to let himself be disturbed or checked in the pleasure attached to the function of evacuation. He found a great deal of enjoyment (such as would tally with the natural coarseness of many classes of society, though not of his) in anal jokes and exhibitions, and this enjoyment had been retained by him until after the beginning of his later illness.

During the time of the English governess it repeatedly happened that he and his Nanya had to share that obnoxious lady's bedroom. His Nanya noticed with comprehension the fact that precisely on those nights he made a mess in his bed, though otherwise this had ceased to happen a long time before. He was not in the least ashamed of it; it was an expression of defiance against the governess.

A year later (when he was four and a half), during the anxiety period, he happened to make a mess in his knickerbockers in the daytime. He was terribly ashamed of himself, and as he was being cleaned he moaned that he could not go on living like that. So that in the meantime something had changed; and by following up his lament we came upon the traces of this something. It turned out that the words "he could not go on living like that" were repeated from some one else. His mother had once[4] taken him with her when she was walking down to the station with the doctor who had come to visit her. During this walk she had lamented over her pains and haemorrhages and had broken out in the same words, "I cannot go on living like this," without imagining that the child whose hand she was holding would keep them in his memory. Thus his lament (which, moreover, he was to repeat on innumerable occasions during his later illness) had the significance of—an identification with his mother.

There soon appeared in his recollection what was evidently, in respect both of its date and of its content, a missing

[4] When this happened was not exactly fixed; but in any case before the anxiety-dream when he was four, and probably before his parents' absence from home.

middle term between these two events. It once happened at the beginning of his anxiety period that his apprehensive mother gave orders that precautions were to be taken to protect the children from dysentery, which had made its appearance in the neighbourhood of the estate. He made inquiries as to what that might be; and after hearing that when you have dysentery you find blood in your stool he became very nervous and declared that there was blood in his own stool; he was afraid he would die of dysentery, but allowed himself to be convinced by an examination that he had made a mistake and had no need to be frightened. We can see that in this dread he was trying to put into effect an identification with his mother, whose haemorrhages he had heard about in the conversation with her doctor. In his later attempt at identification (when he was four and a half) he had dropped any mention of the blood; he no longer understood himself, for he imagined that he was ashamed of himself and was not aware that he was being shaken by a dread of death, though this was unmistakably revealed in his lament.

At that time his mother, suffering as she was from an abdominal affection, was in general nervous, both about herself and the children; it is most probable that his own nervousness, besides its other motives, was based upon an identification with his mother.

Now what can have been the meaning of this identification with his mother?

Between the impudent use he made of his incontinence when he was three and a half, and the horror with which he viewed it when he was four and a half, there lies the dream with which his anxiety period began—the dream which gave him a deferred comprehension of the scene he had experienced when he was one and half (see p. 232), and an explanation of the part played by women in the sexual act. It is only another step to connect the change in his attitude towards defaecation with this same great revulsion. Dysentery was evidently his name for the illness which he had heard his mother lamenting about, and which it was impossible to go on living with; he did not regard his mother's disease as being abdominal but as being intestinal. Under the influence of the primal scene he came to the conclusion that his mother had been made ill by what his father had done to her;[5] and his dread of having blood in his stool, of being as ill as his mother, was his repudiation of being identified with his mother in this sexual scene—the same repudiation with which he awoke from the dream. But the dread was also a proof that in his later elaboration of the primal scene he had put himself in his mother's place and had envied her this relation with his father. The organ by which his identification with women and his passive homosexual attitude to men was able to express itself was the anal zone. The disorders in the function of this zone had acquired the significance of feminine impulses of tenderness, and they retained it during the later illness as well.

At this point we must consider an objection, the discussion of which may contribute much to the elucidation of the apparent confusion of the circumstances. We have been driven to assume that during the process of the dream he understood that women are castrated, that instead of a male organ they have a wound which serves for sexual intercourse, and that castration is the necessary condition of femininity; we have been driven to assume that the threat of this loss induced him to repress his feminine attitude towards men, and that he awoke from his homosexual sentimentalizing in dread. Now how can this comprehension of sexual intercourse, this recognition of the vagina, be brought into harmony with the selection of the bowel for the purpose of identification with women? Are not the intestinal symptoms based upon what is probably an older notion, and one which in any case completely contradicts the dread of castration—the notion, namely, that sexual intercourse takes place at the anus?

To be sure, this contradiction is present; and the two views are entirely inconsistent with each other. The only question is whether they need be consistent. Our bewilderment arises only because we are always inclined to treat unconscious

---

[5] A conclusion which was probably not far from the truth.

mental processes like conscious ones and to forget the profound differences between the two psychical systems.

When his Christmas dream, with its excitement and expectancy, conjured up before him the picture of the sexual intercourse of his parents as it had once been observed (or constructed) by him, there can be no doubt that the first view of it to come up was the old one, according to which the part of the female body which received the male organ was the anus. And, indeed, what else could he have supposed when at the age of one and a half he was a spectator of the scene?[6] But now came a new event, now that he was four years old. What he had learnt in the meantime, the allusions which he had heard to castration, awoke and cast a doubt upon the "cloacal theory"; they suggested to him a recognition of the difference between the sexes and of the sexual part played by women. In this contingency he behaved as children in general behave when they are given an unwished-for piece of information—whether sexual or of any other kind. He rejected what was new (in our case from motives connected with his fear of castration) and clung fast to what was old. He decided in favour of the intestine and against the vagina in the same way as he later on took his father's side against God, and in both cases his motives were similar. He rejected the new information and clung to the old theory; it fell to the latter to provide the material for his identification with women, which made its appearance later as a dread of death in connection with the bowels, and for his first religious scruples, about whether Christ had had a behind, and so on. It is not as though his new insight remained without any effect; quite the reverse. It developed an extraordinarily powerful effect, for it became a motive for maintaining the whole process of the dream in repression and for excluding it from later conscious elaboration. But with that its effect was exhausted; it had no influence upon the decision of the sexual problem. That it should have been possible from that time onwards for a fear

6 Or so long as he did not understand the copulation of the dogs.

of castration to exist side by side with an identification with women by means of the bowel admittedly involved a contradiction. But it was only a logical contradiction—which is not saying much. On the contrary, the whole process is characteristic of the way in which the unconscious works. A repression is something very different from a condemning judgement.

When we were studying the genesis of the wolf phobia, we followed the effect of his new insight into the sexual act; but now that we are investigating the disturbances of the intestinal function, we find ourselves working on the basis of the old cloacal theory. The two points of view remained separated from each other by a stage of repression. His feminine attitude towards men, which had been repudiated by means of the act of repression, drew itself back, as it were, into the intestinal symptoms, and expressed itself in the attacks of diarrhoea, constipation, and intestinal pain, which were so frequent during the patient's childhood. His later sexual phantasies, which were based upon a correct sexual knowledge, were thus able to express themselves regressively as intestinal troubles. But we cannot understand them until we have explained the modifications which take place in the significance of faeces from the first years of childhood onward.[7]

I have already hinted at an earlier point in my story that one portion of the content of the primal scene has been kept back. I am now in a position to produce this missing portion. The child finally interrupted his parents' intercourse by passing a stool, which gave him an excuse for screaming. All the considerations which I have raised above in discussing the rest of the content of the same scene apply equally to the criticism of this additional piece. The patient accepted this concluding act when I had constructed it, and appeared to confirm it by producing "transitory symptoms." A further additional piece which I had proposed, to the effect that his father was annoyed at the interruption and gave vent to his

---

[7] Cf. "On the Transformation of Instincts with Special Reference to Anal Erotism," *Character and Culture,* Collier Books edition BS 193V.

ill-humour by scolding him, had to be dropped. The material of the analysis did not react to it.

The additional detail which I have now brought forward cannot of course be put on a level with the rest of the content of the scene. Here it is not a question of an impression from outside, which must be expected to re-emerge in a number of later indications, but of a reaction on the part of the child himself. It would make no difference to the story as a whole if this demonstration had not occurred, or if it had been taken from a later period and inserted into the course of the scene. But there can be no question of how we are to regard it. It is the sign of an excitement of the anal zone (in the widest sense of the words). In other similar cases an observation like this of sexual intercourse has ended with a discharge of urine; a grown-up man in the same circumstances would feel an erection. The fact that our little boy passed a stool as a sign of his sexual excitement is to be regarded as a characteristic of his congenital sexual constitution. He at once assumed a passive attitude; and showed more inclination towards a subsequent identification with women than with men.

At the same time, like every other child, he was making use of the content of the intestines in one of its earliest and most primitive meanings. Faeces are the child's first *gift*, the first sacrifice of his affection, a portion of his own body which he is ready to part with, but only for the sake of some one he loves.[8] To use faeces as an expression of defiance, as our patient did against the governess when he was three and a

[8] I believe there can be no difficulty in substantiating the statement that infants only soil with their excrement people whom they know and are fond of; they do not consider strangers worthy of this distinction. In my *Drei Abhandlungen zur Sexualtheorie* I mentioned the very first purpose to which faeces are put—namely, the auto-erotic stimulation of the intestinal mucous membrane. We now reach a further stage, at which a decisive part in the process of defaecation is played by the child's attitude to some object to whom it thus shows itself obedient or agreeable. This relation is one that persists; for even older children will only allow themselves to be assisted in defaecating and urinating by particular privileged persons, though in this connection the prospect of other forms of gratification is also involved.

half, is merely to turn this earlier "gift" meaning into the negative. The *"grumus merdae"* left behind by criminals upon the scene of their misdeeds seems to have both these meanings: contumacy, and a regressive expression of amends. It is always possible, when a higher stage has been reached, for use still to be made of the lower one in its negative and debased sense. The contrariety is a manifestation of repression.[9]

At a later stage of sexual development faeces take on the meaning of a *child*. For children, like faeces, are born through the anus. The "gift" meaning of faeces readily admits of this transformation. It is a common usage to speak of a child as a "gift." The more frequent expression is that the woman has "presented" the man with a child; but in the usage of the unconscious equal attention is justly paid to the other aspect of the relation, namely, to the woman having "received"[10] the child as a gift from the man.

The *"money"* meaning of faeces branches off from the "gift" meaning in another direction.

The deeper meaning of our patient's early screen-memory, to the effect that he had his first fit of rage because he was not given enough presents one Christmas, is now revealed to us. What he was feeling the want of was sexual satisfaction, which he had taken as being anal. His sexual inquiries discovered definitely during the course of the dream what they had been prepared for finding before the dream, namely, that the sexual act solved the problem of the origin of babies. Even before the dream he had disliked babies. Once, when he had come upon a small unfledged bird that had fallen out of its nest, he had taken it for a human baby and been horrified at it. The analysis showed that all small animals, such as caterpillars and insects, that he had been so enraged with, had had the meaning of babies to him.[11] His position in regard

---

[9] In the unconscious, as we are aware, "No" does not exist, and there is no distinction between contraries. Negation is only introduced by the process of repression.

[10] [The word *"empfangen"* in the German means both "received" and "conceived."—*Trans.*]

[11] Just as vermin often stand for babies in dreams and phobias.

to his elder sister had given him every opportunity for reflecting upon the relation between elder and younger children. His Nanya had once told him that his mother was so fond of him because he was the youngest, and this gave him good grounds for wishing that no younger child might come after him. His dread of this youngest child was revived under the influence of the dream, for it brought up before him his parent's intercourse.

To the sexual currents that are already known to us we must therefore add a further one, which, like the rest, started from the primal scene reproduced in the dream. In his identification with women (that is, with his mother) he was ready to present his father with a child, and was jealous of his mother, who had already done so and would perhaps do so again.

In a roundabout way, then, through their common relation to the "gift" meaning of faeces, money can come to have the meaning "child," and can thus become the means of expressing feminine (homosexual) satisfaction. This was what occurred with our patient when—he and his sister were staying at a German sanatorium at the time—he saw his father give his sister two large bank-notes. In imagination he had always had suspicions of his father's relations with his sister; and at this his jealousy awoke. He rushed at his sister as soon as they were alone, and demanded a share of the money with so much vehemence and such reproaches that his sister, in tears, threw him the whole of it. What had excited him was not merely the actual money, but rather the child—anal sexual satisfaction from his father. And he was able to console himself with this when, in his father's lifetime, his sister died. The revolting thought which occurred to him when he heard the news of her death in fact meant no more than this: "Now I am the only child. Now Father will have to love me only." But though this reflection was in itself perfectly capable of becoming conscious, yet its homosexual background was so intolerable that it was possible for its disguise in the shape of the most sordid avarice to come as a great relief.

Similarly, too, when after his father's death he reproached his mother so unjustifiably with wanting to cheat him out of the money and of being fonder of the money than of him. His old jealousy of her for having loved another child besides him, the possibility of her having wanted another child after him, drove him into making charges which he himself knew were unwarranted.

This analysis of the meaning of faeces makes it clear that the obsessive thoughts which obliged him to connect God with faeces had a further significance beyond the disparagement which he saw in them himself. They were in fact true compromise-products, in which a part was played no less by a tender current of devotion than by a hostile current of abuse. "God—shit" was probably an abbreviation for an offering that one occasionally hears mentioned in its unabbreviated form. "Shitting to God" ["*auf Gott scheissen*"], or "shitting something to God" [*"Gott etwas scheissen"*], also means presenting him with a child or getting him to present one with a child. The old "gift" meaning in its negative and debased form and the "child" meaning that was later developed from it are combined with each other in the obsessional phrase. In the latter of these meanings a feminine tenderness finds expression: a readiness to give up one's masculinity if in exchange for it one can be loved like a woman. Here, then, we have precisely the same impulse towards God which was expressed in unambiguous words in the delusional system of the paranoic Senatspräsident Schreber.[12]

When later on I come to describing the final clearing up of my patient's symptoms, the way in which the intestinal disorder had put itself at the service of the homosexual current and had given expression to his feminine attitude towards his father will once again become evident. Meanwhile we shall mention a further meaning of faeces, which will lead us on to a discussion of the castration complex.

Since the column of faeces stimulates the erotogenic mucous membrane of the intestine, it plays the part of an active organ in regard to it; it behaves just as the penis does to the vaginal

[12] See the second paper in this volume.

mucous membrane, and acts as it were as its precursor during the cloacal epoch. The handing over of faeces for the sake of (out of love for) some one else becomes a prototype of castration; it is the first occasion upon which an individual gives up a piece of his own body[13] in order to gain the favour of some other person whom he loves. So that a person's love of his own penis, which is in other respects narcissistic, is not without an element of anal erotism. "Faeces," "child," and "penis" thus form a unity, an unconscious concept (*sit venia verbo*)—the concept, namely, of a little thing that can become separated from one's body. Along these paths of association the libidinal cathexis[14] may become displaced or intensified in ways which are pathologically important and which are revealed by analysis.

We are already acquainted with the attitude which our patient first adopted to the problem of castration. He rejected castration, and held to his theory of intercourse by the anus. When I speak of his having rejected it, the first meaning of the phrase is that he would have nothing to do with it, in the sense of having repressed it. This really involved no judgement upon the question of its existence, but it was just as though it did not exist. Such an attitude, however, could not have been his final one, even at the time of his infantile neurosis. We find good subsequent evidence of his having recognized castration as a fact. In this connection, once again, he behaved in the manner which was so characteristic of him, but which makes it so difficult to give a clear account of his mental processes or to feel one's way into them. First he resisted and then he yielded; but the one reaction was not supplanted by the other. In the end there were to be found in him two contrary currents side by side, of which one abominated the idea of castration, while the other was prepared to accept it and console itself with femininity as a compensation. But beyond any doubt a third current, the oldest

---

[13] It is as such that faeces are invariably treated by children.
[14] [See footnote 32, p. 54.]

and deepest, which did not as yet even raise the question of the reality of castration, was still capable of coming into activity. I have elsewhere[15] reported a hallucination which this same patient had at the age of five and upon which I need only add a brief commentary here.

" 'When I was five years old I was playing in the garden near my nurse, and was carving with my pocket-knife in the bark of one of the walnut trees that also come into my dream.[16] Suddenly, to my unspeakable terror, I noticed that I had cut through the little finger of my (right or left?) hand, so that it was only hanging on by its skin. I felt no pain, but great fear. I did not venture to say anything to my nurse, who was only a few paces distant, but I sank down on the nearest seat and sat there incapable of casting another glance at my finger. At last I grew calm, took a look at the finger, and saw that it was entirely uninjured.' "

After he had received his instruction in the Bible story at the age of four and a half he began, as we know, to make the intense effort of thought which ended in his obsessional piety. We may therefore assume that this hallucination belongs to the period in which he brought himself to recognize the reality of castration, and it is perhaps to be regarded as actually marking this step. Even the small correction made by the patient is not without interest. If he had a hallucination of the same dreadful experience which Tasso, in his *Gerusalemme Liberata,* tells of his hero Tancred, we shall perhaps be justified in reaching the interpretation that the tree meant a woman to my little patient as well. Here, then, he was playing the part of his father, and was connecting his mother's

[15] *"Fausse Reconnaissance ("Déjà Raconté")* in Psychoanalytic Treatment," *Therapy and Technique,* Collier Books edition BS 189V.

[16] "Cf. 'The Occurrence in Dreams of Material from Fairy Tales' (1913), *Character and Culture,* Collier Books edition BS 193V. In telling the story again on a later occasion he made the following correction: 'I don't believe I was cutting the tree. That was a confusion with another recollection, which must also have been hallucinatorily falsified, of having made a cut upon a tree with my knife and of *blood* having come out of the tree.' "

familiar haemorrhages with the castration of women, which he now recognized—with the "wound."

His hallucination of the severed finger was instigated, as he reported later on, by the story that a female relation of his had been born with six toes and that the extra one had immediately afterwards been chopped off with an axe. Women, then, had no penis because it was taken away from them at birth. In this manner he came, at the period of the obsessional neurosis, to accept what he had already learned during the dream but had at the time rejected by means of repression. He must also have become acquainted, during the readings and discussions of the sacred story, with the ritual circumcision of Christ and of the Jews in general.

There is no doubt whatever that at this time his father was turning into the terrifying figure that threatened him with castration. The cruel God with whom he was then struggling —who made men sinful, only to punish them afterwards, who sacrificed his own son and the sons of men—this God threw back his character on to the patient's father, though, on the other hand, the boy was at the same time trying to defend his father against the God. At this point the boy had to fit himself into a phylogenetic schema, and he did so, although his personal experiences may not have agreed with it. The threats or hints of castration which he had come across had, on the contrary, emanated from women,[17] but this could not hold up the final result for long. In spite of everything it was his father from whom in the end he came to fear castration. In this respect heredity triumphed over accidental experience; in man's prehistory it was unquestionably the father who practised castration as a punishment and who later softened it down into circumcision. The further the patient went in repressing sensuality during the course of the development of the obsessional neurosis,[18] the more natural it must have become to him to attribute these evil intentions to his father, who was the true representative of sensual activity.

[17] We already know this as regards his Nanya, and we shall hear of it again as coming from another woman.

[18] For evidence of this see p. 256.

His identification of his father with the castrator[19] became important as being the source of an intense unconscious hostility towards him (which reached the extent of a death-wish) and of a sense of guilt which reacted against it. Up to this point, however, he was behaving normally—that is to say, like every neurotic who is possessed by a positive Oedipus complex. But the astonishing thing was that even against this there was a counter-current working in him, which, on the contrary, regarded his father as the person castrated and as calling, therefore, for his sympathy.

When I analysed his ceremonial of breathing out whenever he saw cripples, beggars, and such people, I was able to show that that symptom could also be traced back to his father, whom he had felt sorry for when he visited him as a patient in the sanatorium. The analysis made it possible to follow this thread even further back. At a very early period, probably before his seduction (at the age of three and a quarter), there had been upon the estate an old day-labourer whose business it was to carry the water into the house. He could not speak, ostensibly because his tongue had been cut out. (He was probably a deaf mute.) The little boy was very fond of him and pitied him deeply. When he died, he looked for him in the sky.[20] Here, then, was the first of the cripples for whom he had felt sympathy, and, as was shown by the context and the point at which the episode came out in the analysis, an undoubted father-surrogate.

[19] Among the most tormenting, though at the same time the most grotesque, symptoms of his later illness was his relation to every tailor from whom he ordered a suit of clothes: his deference and timidity in the presence of this high functionary, his attempts to get into his good books by giving him extravagant tips, and his despair over the results of the work however it might in fact have turned out. [The German word for "tailor" is *"Schneider,"* from the verb *"schneiden"* ("to cut"), a compound of which, *"beschneiden,"* means "to circumcise."—*Trans.*]

[20] In this connection I may mention some dreams which he had, later than the anxiety-dream, but while he was still upon the first estate. These dreams represented the coitus scene as an event taking place between heavenly bodies.

In the analysis this man was associated with the recollection of other servants whom the patient had liked and of whom he emphasized the fact that they had been either sickly or Jews (which implied circumcision). The footman, too, who had helped to clean him after his accident when he was four and a half, had been a Jew and a consumptive and had been an object of his compassion. All of these figures belong to the period before his visit to his father at the sanatorium, that is, before the formation of the symptom; the latter must therefore rather have been intended to ward off (by means of the breathing out) any identification with the object of the patient's pity. Then suddenly, in connection with a dream, the analysis plunged back into the prehistoric period, and led him to assert that during the coitus in the primal scene he had observed the penis disappear, that he had felt sympathy with his father on that account, and had rejoiced at the reappearance of what he thought had been lost. So here was a fresh emotional trend, starting once again from the primal scene. Moreover, the narcissistic origin of sympathy (which is confirmed by the word itself) is here quite unmistakably revealed.

VIII

Fresh Material from the Primal Period—Solution

IT HAPPENS in many analyses that as one approaches their end new recollections emerge which have hitherto been kept carefully concealed. Or it may be that on one occasion some unpretentious remark is thrown out in an indifferent tone of voice as though it were superfluous; that then, on another occasion, something further is added, which begins to make the physician prick his ears; and that at last he comes to recognize this despised fragment of a memory as the key to the weightiest secrets that the patient's neurosis has screened.

Early in the analysis my patient had told me of a memory of the period in which his naughtiness had been in the habit of suddenly turning into anxiety. He was chasing a beautiful big butterfly with yellow stripes and large wings which ended in pointed projections—a swallow-tail, in fact. Suddenly, when the butterfly had settled on a flower, he was seized with a dreadful fear of the creature, and ran away screaming.

This memory recurred occasionally during the analysis, and required an explanation; but for a long time none was to be found. Nevertheless it was to be assumed as a matter of course that a detail like this had not kept its place in his recollection on its own account, but that it was a screen-memory, representing something of more importance with which it was in some way connected. One day he told me that in his language a butterfly was called *"babushka,"* "granny." He added that in general butterflies had seemed to him like women and girls, and bettles and caterpillars like boys. So there could be little doubt that in his anxiety scene a recollection of some female person had been aroused. I will not conceal the fact that at the time I put forward the possibility that the yellow stripes on the butterfly had reminded him of similar stripes upon a piece of clothing worn by some women. I only mention this as an illustration to show how inadequate the physician's constructive efforts usually are for clearing up questions that arise, and how unjust it is to attribute the results of analysis to the physician's imagination and suggestion.

Many months later, in quite another connection, the patient remarked that the opening and shutting of the butterfly's wings while it was settled on the flower had given him an uncanny feeling. It had looked, so he said, like a woman opening her legs, and the legs then made the shape of a Roman V, which, as we know, was the hour at which, in his boyhood, and even up to the time of the treatment, he used to fall into a depressed state of mind.

This was an association which I could never have arrived at myself, and which gained importance from a consideration of the thoroughly infantile nature of the train of association which it revealed. The attention of children, as I have often noticed, is attracted far more readily by movements than by forms at rest; and they frequently base associations upon a similarity of movement which is overlooked or neglected by adults.

After this the little problem was once more left untouched for a long time; but I may mention the facile suspicion that the points or stick-like projections of the butterfly's wings might have had the meaning of genital symbols.

One day there emerged, timidly and indistinctly, a kind of recollection that at a very early age, even before the time of the nurse, he must have had a nursery-maid who was very fond of him. Her name had been the same as his mother's. He had no doubt returned her affection. It was, in fact, a first love that had faded into oblivion. But we agreed that something must have occurred at that time that became of importance later on.

Then on another occasion he emended this recollection. She could not have had the same name as his mother; that had been a mistake on his part, and it showed, of course, that in his memory she had become fused with his mother. Her real name, he went on, had occurred to him in a roundabout way. He had suddenly thought of a store-room, on the first estate, in which fruit was kept after it had been picked, and of a particular sort of pear with a most delicious taste—a big pear with yellow stripes on its skin. The word for "pear" in his language was *"grusha,"* and that had also been the name of the nursery-maid.

It thus became clear that behind the screen-memory of the hunted butterfly the memory of the nursery-maid lay concealed. But the yellow stripes were not upon her dress, but upon the pear whose name was the same as hers. What, however, was the origin of the anxiety which had arisen when the memory of her had been activated? The obvious answer to this might have been the crude hypothesis that it had been this girl whom, when he was a small child, he had first seen making the movements with her legs which he had fixed in his mind with the Roman V,—movements which allow access to the genitals. We spared ourselves such theorizing as this and waited for more material.

Very soon after this there came the recollection of a scene, incomplete, but, so far as it was preserved, definite. Grusha was kneeling on the floor, and beside her a pail and a short broom made of a bundle of twigs; he was also there, and she was teasing him or scolding him.

The missing elements could easily be supplied from other directions. During the first months of the treatment he had told me of how he had suddenly fallen in love in a compulsive manner with a peasant girl from whom he had contracted the exciting cause of his later illness (at the age of eighteen). When he told me this he had displayed a most extraordinary unwillingness to give me the girl's name. It was an entirely isolated instance of resistance, for apart from it he obeyed the fundamental rule of analysis unreservedly. He asserted, however, that the reason for his being so much ashamed of mentioning the name was that it was a purely peasant name and that no girl of gentle birth could possibly be called by it. When eventually the name was produced, it turned out to be Matrona, which has a motherly ring about it. The shame was evidently displaced. He was not ashamed of the fact that these love-affairs were invariably concerned with girls of the humblest origin; he was ashamed only of the name. If it should turn out that the affair with Matrona had something in common with the Grusha scene, then the shame would have to be transferred back to that early episode.

He had told me another time that when he heard the story of John Huss he had been greatly moved, and that his attention had been held by the bundles of firewood that were dragged up when he was burnt at the stake. Now his sympathy for Huss created a perfectly definite suspicion in my mind, for I have often come upon this sympathy in youthful patients and I have always been able to explain it in the same way. One such patient even went so far as to produce a dramatized version of Huss's career; he began to write his play on the day upon which he lost the object with whom he was secretly in love. Huss perished by fire, and (like others who possess the same qualification) he becomes the hero of people who have at one time suffered from enuresis. My patient himself connected the bundles of firewood used for the execution of Huss with the nursery-maid's broom or bundle of twigs.

This material fitted together spontaneously and served to fill in the gaps in the patient's memory of the scene with Grusha. When he saw the girl scrubbing the floor he had urinated in the room and she had rejoined, no doubt jokingly, with a threat of castration.[1]

----

[1] It is very remarkable that the reaction of shame should be so intimately connected with involuntary emptying of the bladder (whether in the daytime or at night) and not equally so, as one would have expected, with incontinence of the bowels. Experience

I do not know if my readers will have already guessed why it is that I have given such a detailed account of this episode from the patient's early childhood.[2] It provides an important link between the primal scene and the later love-compulsion which came to be of such decisive significance in his subsequent career, and it further shows us a condition upon which his falling in love depended and which elucidates that compulsion.

When he saw the girl upon the floor engaged in scrubbing it, and kneeling down, with her buttocks projecting and her back horizontal, he was faced once again with the attitude which his mother had assumed in the coitus scene. She became his mother to him; he was seized with sexual excitement owing to the activation of this picture;[3] and, like his father (whose action he can only have regarded at the time as urination), he behaved in a masculine way towards her. His urinating on the floor was in reality an attempt at a seduction, and the girl replied to it with a threat of castration, just as though she had understood what he meant.

The compulsion, which took its origin from the primal scene, was transferred on to the scene with Grusha and was carried forward by it. But the condition upon which his falling in love depended underwent a change which showed the influence of the second scene: it was transferred from the woman's attitude to the occupation upon which she was engaged while in that attitude. This was clear, for instance, in the episode of Matrona. He was walking through the village which formed part of the (second) estate, when he saw a

---

leaves no room for doubt upon the point. The regular relation that is found to exist between incontinence of the bladder and fire also provides food for reflection. It is possible that these reactions and relations represent precipitates from the history of human civilization derived from a lower stratum than anything that is preserved for us in the traces surviving in myths or folk-lore.

[2] It may be assigned to a time at which he was about two and a half: between his supposed observation of coitus and his seduction.

[3] This was *before* the dream.

peasant girl kneeling by the pond and employed in washing clothes in it. He fell in love with the girl instantly and with irresistible violence, although he had not yet been able to get even a glimpse of her face. By her posture and occupation she had taken the place of Grusha for him. We can now see how it was that the shame which properly related to the content of the scene with Grusha could become attached to the name of Matrona.

Another attack of falling in love, dating from a few years earlier, shows even more clearly the compelling influence of the Grusha scene. A young peasant girl, who was a servant in the house, had long attracted him, but he succeeded in keeping himself from approaching her. One day, when he came upon her in a room by herself, he was overwhelmed by his love. He found her kneeling on the floor and engaged in scrubbing it, with a pail and a broom beside her—in fact, exactly as he had seen the girl in his childhood.

Even his final object-choice, which played such an important part in his life, is shown by its details (though they cannot be adduced here) to have been dependent upon the same condition and to have been an offshoot of the compulsion which, starting from the primal scene and going on to the scene with Grusha, had dominated his love-choice. I have remarked on an earlier page that I recognize in the patient an endeavour to debase his love-object. This is to be explained as a reaction against pressure from the sister who was so much his superior. But I promised at the same time (see p. 205) to show that this self-assertive motive was not the only determinant, but that it concealed another and deeper one based upon purely erotic motives. These were brought to light by the patient's memory of the nursery-maid scrubbing the floor—physically debased too, by the by. All his later love-objects were surrogates for this one person, who through the accident of her attitude had herself become his first mother-surrogate. The patient's first association in connection with the problem of his fear of the butterfly can now easily be explained retrospectively as a distant allusion to the primal scene (the hour of five). He confirmed the connection between the

Grusha scene and the threat of castration by a particularly ingenious dream, which he himself succeeded in deciphering. "I had a dream," he said, "of a man tearing off the wings of an *Espe*."—"*Espe?*" I asked; "what do you mean by that?"—"You know; that insect with yellow stripes on its body, that stings."—I could now put him right: "So what you mean is a *Wespe* [wasp]."—"Is it called a *Wespe*? I really thought it was called an *Espe*." (Like so many other people, he used his difficulties with a foreign language as a screen for symptomatic acts.) "But *Espe*, why, that's myself: S. P." (which were his initials). The *Espe* was of course a mutilated *Wespe*. The dream said clearly that he was avenging himself on Grusha for her threat of castration.

The action of the two-and-a-half-year-old boy in the scene with Grusha is the earliest effect of the primal scene which has come to our knowledge. It represents him as copying his father, and shows us a tendency towards development in a direction which would later deserve the name of masculine. His seduction drove him into passivity—for which, in any case, the way was prepared by his behaviour when he was a witness of his parents' intercourse.

I must here turn for a moment to the history of the treatment. When once the Grusha scene had been assimilated—the first experience that he could really remember, and one which he had remembered without any conjectures or intervention on my part—the problem of the treatment had every appearance of having been solved. From that time forward there were no more resistances; all that remained to be done was to collect and to co-ordinate. The old trauma theory, which was after all built up upon impressions gained from psychoanalytic practice, had suddenly come to the front once more. Out of critical interest I made one more attempt to force upon the patient another view of his story, which might commend itself more to sober common sense. It was true that there could be no doubt about the scene with Grusha, but, I suggested, in itself that scene meant nothing; it had been emphasized *ex post facto* by a regression from the circumstances of his object-choice, which, as a result of his intention to debase, had been diverted from his sister on to servant girls. On the other hand, his observation of coitus, I argued, was a phantasy of his later years; its historical nucleus may perhaps have been an observation or an experience by the patient of the administration of an innocent enema. Some of my readers will possibly be inclined to think that with such hypotheses as these I was for the first time beginning to approach an understanding of the case; but the patient looked at me uncomprehendingly and a little contemptuously when I put this view before him, and he never reacted to it again. I have already stated my own arguments against any such rationalization at their proper point in the discussion.

[Thus[4] the Grusha scene, by explaining the conditions governing the patient's object-choice—conditions which were of decisive importance in his life—prevents our over-estimating the significance of his intention to debase women. But it does more than this. It affords me a justification for having refused on an earlier page (see p. 248) to adopt unhesitatingly, as the only tenable explanation, the view that the primal scene was derived from an observation made upon animals shortly before the dream. The Grusha scene emerged in the patient's memory spontaneously and through no effort of mine. His fear of the yellow-striped butterfly, which went back to that scene, proved that it had had a significant content, or that it had been possible to attach this significance to its content subsequently. By means of the accompanying associations and the inferences that followed from them, it was possible with certainty to supply this significant element which was lacking in the patient's memory. It then appeared that his fear of the butterfly was in every respect analogous to his fear of the wolf; in both cases it was a fear of castration, which was, to begin with, referred to the person who had first uttered the threat of castration, but was then transposed on to another person to whom it was bound to become attached in accordance with phylogenetic precedent. The scene with Grusha had occurred when the patient was two and a half,

[4] [Author's square bracket. See end of footnote, p. 188.]

but the anxiety-episode with the yellow butterfly was certainly subsequent to the anxiety-dream. It was easy to understand how the patient's later comprehension of the possibility of castration had retrospectively brought out the anxiety in the scene with Grusha. But that scene in itself contained nothing objectionable or improbable; on the contrary, it consisted entirely of commonplace details which gave no grounds for scepticism. There was nothing in it which could lead one to attribute its origin to the child's imagination; such a supposition, indeed, seemed scarcely possible.

The question now arises whether we are justified in regarding the fact that the boy urinated, while he stood looking at the girl on her knees scrubbing the floor, as a proof of sexual excitement on his part. If so, the excitement would be evidence of the influence of an earlier impression, which might equally have been the actual occurrence of the primal scene or an observation made upon animals before the age of two and a half. Or are we to conclude that the situation as regards Grusha was entirely innocent, that the child's emptying his bladder was purely accidental, and that it was not until later that the whole scene became sexualized in his memory, after he had come to recognize the importance of similar situations?

On these issues I can venture upon no decision. I must confess, however, that I regard it as greatly to the credit of psychoanalysis that it should even have reached the stage of raising such questions as these. Nevertheless, I cannot deny that the scene with Grusha, the part it played in the analysis, and the effects that followed from it in the patient's life can be most naturally and completely explained if we consider that the primal scene, which may in other cases be a phantasy, was a reality in the present one. After all, there is nothing impossible about it; and the hypothesis of its reality is entirely compatible with the instigating action of the observations upon animals which are suggested by the sheep-dogs in the dream-picture.

I will now turn from this unsatisfactory conclusion to a consideration of the problem which I have attempted in my

Introductory Lectures on Psychoanalysis. I should myself be glad to know whether the primal scene in my present patient's case was a phantasy or a real experience; but, taking other similar cases into account, I must admit that the answer to this question is not in reality a matter of very great importance. These scenes of observing parental intercourse, of being seduced in childhood, and of being threatened with castration are unquestionably an inherited endowment, a phylogenetic inheritance, but they may just as easily be acquired by personal experience. With my patient, his seduction by his elder sister was an indisputable reality; why should not the same have been true of his observation of his parents' intercourse?

All that we find in the prehistory of neuroses is that a child catches hold of this phylogenetic experience where his own experience fails him. He fills in the gaps in individual truth with prehistoric truth; he replaces occurrences in his own life by occurrences in the life of his ancestors. I fully agree with Jung[5] in recognizing the existence of this phylogenetic inheritance; but I regard it as a methodological error to seize upon a phylogenetic explanation before the ontogenetic possibilities have been exhausted. I cannot see any reason for obstinately disputing the importance of infantile prehistory while at the same time freely acknowledging the importance of ancestral prehistory. Nor can I overlook the fact that phylogenetic motives and productions themselves stand in need of elucidation, and that in quite a number of instances this is afforded by factors in the childhood of the individual. And, finally, I cannot feel surprised that what was originally produced by certain circumstances in prehistoric times and was then transmitted in the shape of a predisposition to its re-acquirement should, since the same circumstances persist, emerge once more as a concrete event in the experience of the individual.]

Room must also be found in the interval between the primal scene and the seduction (from the age of one and a

[5] *Die Psychologie der unbewussten Prozesse,* 1917. This was published too late for it to have influenced my *Introductory Lectures.*

half to the age of three and a quarter) for the dumb water-carrier. He served the patient as a father-surrogate just as Grusha served him as a mother-surrogate. I do not think there is any justification for regarding this as an example of the intention to debase, even though it is true that both parents have come to be represented by servants. A child pays no regard to social distinctions, which have little meaning for it as yet; and it classes people of inferior rank with its parents if they love it as its parents do. Nor is the intention to debase any more responsible for the substitution of animals for a child's parents, for children are very far indeed from taking a disparaging view of animals. Uncles and aunts are used as parent-surrogates without any regard to the question of debasing, and this was in fact done by our present patient, as many of his recollections showed.

There also belongs in this period a phase, which was obscurely remembered, in which he would not eat anything except sweet things, until alarm was felt on the score of his health. He was told about one of his uncles who had refused to eat in the same way and had wasted away to death while he was still young. He was also informed that when he himself was three months old he had been so seriously ill (with pneumonia?) that his winding-sheet had been got ready for him. In this way they succeeded in alarming him, so that he began eating again; and in the later years of his childhood he used actually to overdo this duty, as though to guard himself against the threat of death. The fear of death, which was evoked at that time for his own protection, made its reappearance later when his mother warned him of the danger of dysentery; later still, it brought on an attack of his obsessional neurosis (see p. 257). We shall attempt further on to go into its origins and meanings.

I am inclined to the opinion that this disturbance of appetite should be regarded as the very first of the patient's neurotic illnesses. If so, the disturbance of appetite, the wolf phobia, and the obsessional piety would constitute the complete series of infantile disorders which laid down the predisposition for his neurotic collapse after he had passed the age of puberty. It will be objected that few children escape such disorders as a temporary loss of appetite or an animal phobia. But this argument is exactly what I should wish for. I am ready to assert that every neurosis in an adult is built upon a neurosis which has occurred in his childhood but has not invariably been severe enough to strike the eye and be recognized as such. This objection only serves to emphasize the theoretical importance of the part which infantile neuroses must play in our view of those later disorders which we treat as neuroses and endeavour to attribute entirely to the effects of adult life. If our present patient had not suffered from obsessional piety in addition to his disturbance of appetite and his animal phobia, his story would not have been noticeably different from that of other children, and we should have been the poorer by the loss of precious material which may guard us against certain plausible errors.

The analysis would be unsatisfactory if it failed to explain the phrase used by the patient for summing up the troubles of which he complained. The world, he said, was hidden from him by a veil; and our psychoanalytic training forbids our assuming that these words can have been without significance or have been chosen at haphazard. The veil was torn, strange to say, in one situation only; and that was at the moment when, as a result of an enema, he passed a motion through his anus. He then felt well again, and for a very short while he saw the world clearly. The interpretation of this "veil" progressed with as much difficulty as we met with in clearing up his fear of the butterfly. Nor did he keep to the veil. It evaporated into a sense of twilight, into *"ténèbres,"* and into other impalpable things.

It was not until just before taking leave of the treatment that he remembered having been told that he was born with a caul.[6] He had for that reason always looked on himself as a special child of fortune whom no ill could befall. He did not lose that conviction until he was forced to realize that his gonorrhoeal infection constituted a serious injury to his body. The blow to his narcissism was too much for him and he

---

[6] [The German *"Glückshaube,"* like the corresponding Scots expression "sely how," means literally "lucky hood."—*Trans.*]

collapsed. It may be said that in so doing he was repeating a mechanism that he had already brought into play once before. For his wolf phobia had broken out when he found himself faced by the fact that such a thing as castration was possible; and he clearly classed his gonorrhoea as castration.

Thus the caul was the veil which hid him from the world and hid the world from him. The complaint that he made was in reality a fulfilled wish-phantasy: it exhibited him as back once more in the womb, and was, in fact, a wish-phantasy of flight from the world. It can be translated as follows: "Life makes me so unhappy! I must get back into the womb!"

But what can have been the meaning of the fact that this veil, which was now symbolic but had once been real, was torn at the moment at which he evacuated his bowels after an enema, and that under this condition his illness left him? The context enables us to reply. If this birth-veil was torn, then he saw the world and was re-born. The stool was the child, as which he was born a second time, to a happier life. Here, then, we have the phantasy of re-birth, to which Jung has recently drawn attention and to which he has assigned such a dominating position in the imaginative life of neurotics.

This would be very agreeable, if it were all. But certain details of the situation, and a due regard for the connection between it and this particular patient's life-history, compel us to pursue the interpretation further. The necessary condition of his re-birth was that he should have an enema administered to him by a man. (It was not until later on that he was driven by necessity to take this man's place himself.) This can only have meant that he had identified himself with his mother, that the man was acting as his father, and that the enema was repeating the act of copulation, as the fruit of which the excrement-baby (which was once again himself) would be born. The phantasy of re-birth was therefore bound up closely with the necessary condition of sexual satisfaction from a man. So that the translation now runs to this effect: only on condition that he took the woman's place and substituted himself for his mother, and thus let himself be sexually satisfied by his father and bore him a child—only on that condition would his illness leave him. Here, therefore, the phantasy of re-birth was simply a mutilated and censored version of the homosexual wish-phantasy.

If we look into the matter more closely we cannot help remarking that in this condition which he laid down for his recovery the patient was simply repeating the state of affairs at the time of the so-called primal scene. At that moment he had wanted to substitute himself for his mother; and, as we assumed long ago, it was he himself who, in the scene in question, had produced the excrement-baby. He still remained fixed as though by a spell to the scene which had such a decisive effect upon his sexual life, and the return of which during the night of the dream brought the onset of his illness. The tearing of the veil was analogous to the opening of his eyes and to the opening of the window. The primal scene had become transformed into the necessary condition for his recovery.

It is easy to make a unified statement of what was expressed on the one hand by the complaint he made and on the other hand by the single exceptional condition under which the complaint no longer held good, and thus to make clear the whole meaning that underlay the two factors. He wished he could be back in the womb, not simply in order that he might then be re-born, but in order that he might be copulated with there by his father, might obtain sexual satisfaction from him, and might bear him a child.

The wish to be born of his father (as he had at first believed was the case), the wish to be sexually satisfied by him, the wish to present him with a child—and all of this at the price of his own masculinity, and expressed in the language of anal erotism—these wishes complete the circle of his fixation upon his father: in them homosexuality has found its furthest and most intimate expression.[7]

---

[7] A possible subsidiary explanation, namely that the veil represented the hymen which is torn at the moment of intercourse with a man, does not harmonize completely with the necessary condition of his recovery. Moreover it has no bearing upon the life of the patient, for whom virginity carried no significance.

This instance, I think, throws light upon the meaning and origin of the womb-phantasy as well as that of re-birth. The former, the womb-phantasy, is frequently derived (as it was in the present case) from an attachment to the father. There is a wish to be inside the mother's womb in order to replace her during coitus—in order to take her place in regard to the father. The phantasy of re-birth, on the other hand, is in all probability regularly a softened substitute (a euphemism, one might say) for the phantasy of incestuous intercourse with the mother; to make use of Silberer's expression, it is an *anagogic* abbreviation of it. There is a wish to be back in a situation in which one was in the mother's genitals; and in this connection the man is identifying himself with his own penis and is using it to represent himself. Thus the two phantasies are revealed as one another's counterparts: they give expression, according as the subject's attitude is feminine or masculine, to his wish for sexual intercourse with his father or with his mother. We cannot dismiss the possibility that in the complaint made by our present patient and in the necessary condition laid down for his recovery the two phantasies, that is to say the two incestuous wishes, were united.

I will make a final attempt at re-interpreting the last findings of this analysis in accordance with the scheme of my opponents. The patient lamented his flight from the world in a typical womb-phantasy and viewed his recovery as a typically conceived re-birth. In accordance with the predominant side of his disposition, he expressed the latter in anal symptoms. He next concocted, upon the model of his anal phantasy of re-birth, a childhood scene which repeated his wishes in an archaic-symbolic medium of expression. His symptoms were then strung together as though they had been derived from a primal scene of this kind. He was driven to embark upon this long backward course either because he had come up against some problem in life which he was too lazy to solve, or because he had every reason to be aware of his own inferiority and thought he could best protect himself from being slighted by elaborating such arrangements as these.

All this would be very nice and pretty, if only the unlucky

wretch had not had a dream when he was no more than four years old, which brought the beginning of his neurosis, which was instigated by his grandfather's story of the tailor and the wolf, and the interpretation of which necessitates the assumption of this primal scene. But all the alleviations which the theories of Jung and Adler seek to afford us come to grief, alas, upon such paltry but unimpeachable facts as these. As things stand, it seems to me that the phantasy of re-birth was a derivative of the primal scene rather than that the primal scene was, on the contrary, a reflection of the phantasy of re-birth. And we may perhaps even suppose that the patient, at a time only four years after his birth, may still have been too young to be already wishing to be born again. But no, I must take this last argument back; for my own observations show that we have rated the powers of children too low and that there is no knowing what they cannot be given credit for.[8]

[8] I admit that this is the most ticklish question in the whole domain of psychoanalysis. I did not require the contributions of Adler to Jung to induce me to consider the matter with a critical eye, and to bear in mind the possibility that what analysis puts forward as being forgotten experiences of childhood (and of an improbably early childhood) may on the contrary be based upon phantasies brought about upon occasions occurring late in life. According to this view, wherever we seemed in analyses to see traces of the after-effects of an infantile impression of the kind in question, we should rather have to assume that we were faced by the manifestation of some constitutional factor or of some predisposition that had been phylogenetically maintained. On the contrary, no doubt has troubled me more; no other uncertainty has been more decisive in holding me back from publishing my conclusions. I was the first—a point to which none of my opponents have referred—to recognize both the part played by phantasies in symptom-formation and also the "phantasying back" of late impressions into childhood and their sexualization after the event. (See *Traumdeutung*, First Edition, 1900, p. 49, and "Notes upon a Case of Obsessional Neurosis," 1908 [p. 64 of this volume].) If, in spite of this, I have held to the more difficult and more improbable view, it has been as a result of arguments such as are forced upon the investigator by the case described in these pages or by any other infantile neurosis. These arguments I once again lay before my readers for their decision.

IX

Recapitulations and Problems

I DO NOT KNOW if the reader of this report of an analysis will have succeeded in forming a clear picture of the origin and development of the patient's illness. I fear that, on the contrary, this will not have been the case. But though on other occasions I have said very little on behalf of my powers in the art of exposition, I should like in the present instance to plead mitigating circumstances. The description of such early phases and of such deep strata of mental life has been a problem which has never before been attacked; and it is better to solve that problem badly than to take flight before it—a proceeding which would moreover (or so we are told) involve the coward in risks of a particular kind. I prefer, therefore, to put a bold face on it and show that I have not allowed myself to be held back by a sense of my own inferiority.

The case itself was not a particularly favourable one. The advantages of having a wealth of information about the patient's childhood (an advantage which was made possible by the fact that the child could be studied through the medium of the adult) had to be purchased at the expense of the analysis being most terribly disjointed and of the exposition showing corresponding gaps. Personal peculiarities in the patient and a national character that was foreign to ours made the task of feeling one's way into his mind a laborious one. The contrast between the patient's agreeable and affable personality, his acute intelligence and his nice-mindedness on the one hand, and his completely unbridled instinctual life on the other, necessitated an excessively long process of preparatory education, and this made a general perspective more difficult. But the patient himself has no responsibility for that feature of the case which put the severest obstacles in the way of any description of it. In the psychology of adults we have fortunately reached the point of being able to divide mental processes into conscious and unconscious and of being able to give a clearly worded description of both. With children this distinction leaves us almost completely in the lurch. It is often embarrassing to decide what one would choose to call conscious and what unconscious. Processes which have become the dominant ones, and which from their subsequent behaviour must be equated with conscious ones, have nevertheless not been conscious in the child. It is easy to understand why. In children the conscious has not yet acquired all its characteristics; it is still in process of development, and it does not as yet fully possess the capacity for transposing itself into verbal images. We are constantly guilty of making a confusion between the phenomenon of emergence as a perception in consciousness and the fact of belonging to a hypothetical psychical system to which we ought to assign some conventional name, but which we in fact also call "consciousness" (the system Cs.). This confusion does no harm when we are giving a psychological description of an adult, but it is misleading when we are dealing with that of a young child. Nor should we be much assisted here if we introduced the "preconscious," for a child's preconscious may, in just the same way, fail to coincide with an adult's. We must be content, therefore, with having clearly recognized the obscurity.

It is obvious that a case such as that which is described in these pages might be made an excuse for dragging into the discussion every one of the findings and problems of psycho-analysis. But this would be an endless and unjustifiable labour. It must be recognized that everything cannot be learnt from a single case and that everything cannot be decided by it; we must content ourselves with exploiting whatever it may happen to show most clearly. There are in any case narrow limits to what a psychoanalysis is called upon to explain. For, while it is its business to explain the striking symptom-formations by revealing their origin, the psychical mechanisms and instinctual processes to which one is led by that means do not require to be explained but merely to be described. In order to derive fresh generalizations from what has thus been established with regard to the mechanisms and instincts, it would be essential to have at one's disposal numerous cases as thoroughly and deeply analysed as the present one. But they are not easily to be had, and each one of them requires years of labour. So that advances in these spheres of knowledge must necessarily be slow. There is no doubt a great temptation to content oneself with "scratching" the mental surface of a number of people and of replacing what is left undone by speculation—the latter being put under the patronage of some school or other of philosophy. Practical requirements may also be adduced in favour of this procedure; but no substitute can satisfy the requirements of science.

I shall now attempt to sketch out a synthetic survey of my patient's sexual development, beginning from its earliest indications. The first that we hear of it is in the disturbance of his appetite; for, taking other observations into account, I am inclined, though with due reservations, to regard this as a result of some process in the sphere of sexuality. I have been driven to regard as the earliest recognizable sexual organization the so-called "cannibalistic" or "oral" phase, during which the original attachment of sexual excitation to the nutritional instinct still dominates the scene. It is not to be expected that we should come upon direct manifestations of this phase, but only upon indications of it where disturbances have been set up. Impairment of the nutritional instinct (though this can of course have other causes) draws our attention to a failure on the part of the organism to master its sexual excitation. In this phase the sexual aim could only be cannibalism—eating; it makes its appearance with our present patient by means of regression from a higher stage, in the form of fear of "being eaten by the wolf." We were, indeed, obliged to translate this into a fear of being copulated with by his father. It is well known that there is a neurosis which occurs at a much later age, in girls at the time of puberty or soon afterwards, and which expresses aversion to sexuality by means of anorexia. This neurosis will have to be brought into relation with the oral phase of sexual life. The erotic aim of the oral organization further makes its appearance at the height of a lover's paroxysm (in such phrases as "I could devour you with love") and in affectionate intercourse with children, when the grown-up person is pretending to be a child himself. I have elsewhere given voice to a suspicion that the father of our present patient used himself to indulge in "affectionate abuse," and may have played at wolf or dog with the little boy and have threatened as a joke to gobble him up (see p. 217). The patient confirmed this suspicion by his curious behaviour in the transference. Whenever he shrank back on to the transference from the difficulties of the treatment, he used to threaten me with eating me up and later with all kinds of other ill-treatment—all of which was merely an expression of affection.

Permanent marks have been left by this oral phase of sexuality upon the usages of language. People commonly speak, for instance, of an "appetizing" love-object, and describe persons they are fond of as "sweet." It will be remembered, too, that our little patient would only eat sweet things. In dreams sweet things and sweetmeats stand regularly for caresses or sexual gratifications.

It appears, moreover, that there is an anxiety belonging to this phase (only, of course, where some disturbance has arisen) which manifests itself as a fear of death and may be attached to anything that is pointed out to the child as being suitable for the purpose. With our patient it was employed to induce him to overcome his loss of appetite and indeed to overcompensate for it. A way will be pointed in the direction of the possible origin of this disturbance of his appetite, if we bear in mind (basing ourselves upon the hypothesis that we have so often discussed) that his observation of coitus at the age of one and a half, which produced so many deferred effects, certainly occurred before the time of these difficulties in his eating. So we may perhaps suppose that it accelerated the processes of sexual maturing and consequently did in fact also produce direct effects, though these were insignificant-looking.

I am of course aware that it is possible to explain the symptoms of this period (the wolf-anxiety and the disturbance of appetite) in another and simpler manner, without any reference to sexuality or to a pregenital stage of its organization. Those who like to neglect the indications of neurosis and the interconnections between events will prefer this other explanation, and I shall not be able to prevent their doing so. It is hard to discover any cogent evidence in regard to these beginnings of sexual life except by such roundabout paths as I have indicated.

In the scene with Grusha (at the age of two and a half) we see the little boy at the beginning of a development which, except perhaps for its prematureness, deserves to be considered normal; thus we find in it identification with his father, and urethral erotism representing masculinity. It was also completely under the sway of the primal scene. We have hitherto regarded his identification with his father as being narcissistic; but if we take the content of the primal scene into account we cannot deny that it had already reached the stage of genital organization. His male genital organ had begun to play its part and it continued to do so under the influence of his seduction by his sister.

But his seduction gives the impression not merely of having encouraged his sexual development but of having, to an even greater extent, disturbed and diverted it. It offered him a passive sexual aim, which was ultimately incompatible with the action of his male genital organ. At the first external obstacle, the threat of castration from his Nanya (at the age of three and a half), his genital organization, half-hearted as it still was, broke down and regressed to the stage which had preceded it, namely to that of the sadistic-anal organization, which he might otherwise have passed through, perhaps, with as slight indications as other children.

The sadistic-anal organization can easily be regarded as a continuation and development of the oral one. The violent muscular activity, directed upon the object, by which it is characterized, is to be explained as an action preparatory to eating. The eating then ceases to be a sexual aim, and the preparatory action becomes a sufficient aim in itself. The essential novelty, as compared with the previous stage, is that the receptive passive function becomes disengaged from the oral zone and attached to the anal zone. In this connection we can hardly fail to think of biological parallels or of the theory that the pregenital organizations in man should be regarded as vestiges of conditions which have been permanently retained in several classes of animals. The building up of the instinct of inquiry out of its various components is another characteristic feature of this stage of development.

The boy's anal erotism was not particularly noticeable. Under the influence of his sadism the affectionate significance of faeces gave place to an offensive one. A sense of guilt, the presence of which points to developmental processes in spheres other than the sexual one, played a part in the transformation of his sadism into masochism.

His seduction continued to make its influence felt, by maintaining the passivity of his sexual aim. It transformed his sadism to a great extent into its passive counterpart, masochism. But it is questionable whether the seduction can be made entirely responsible for this characteristic of passivity, for the child's reaction to his observation of coitus at the age of one and a half was already preponderantly a passive one. His sympathetic sexual excitement expressed itself by his passing a stool, though it is true that in this behaviour an active element is also to be distinguished. Side by side with the masochism which dominated his sexual tendencies and also found expression in phantasies, his sadism, too, persisted and was directed against small animals. His sexual inquiries had set in from the time of the seduction and had been concerned, in essence, with two problems: the origin of children and the possibility of losing the genitals. These inquiries wove themselves into the manifestations of his instinctual activities, and directed his sadistic propensities on to small animals as being representatives of small children.

We have now carried our account down to about the time of the boy's fourth birthday, and it was at that point that the dream brought into deferred operation his observation of coitus at the age of one and a half. The processes which now ensued can neither be completely grasped nor adequately described. The activation of the picture, which, thanks to the advance in his intellectual development, he was now able to understand, operated like a fresh event, but also like a new trauma, like an interference from outside analogous to the seduction. The genital organization which had been broken off was re-established at a single blow; but the advance that was achieved in the dream could not be maintained. On the contrary, there came about, by means of a process that can only be likened to a repression, a repudiation of the new element and its replacement by a phobia.

Thus the sadistic-anal organization continued to exist during the phase of the animal phobia which now set in, only it suffered an admixture of anxiety-phenomena. The child persisted in his sadistic as well as in his masochistic activities, but he reacted with anxiety to a portion of them; the conversion of his sadism into its opposite probably made further progress.

The analysis of the anxiety-dream shows us that the repression was connected with his recognition of the existence of castration. The new element was rejected because its acceptance would have cost him his penis. Closer consideration leads us to some such conclusion as the following. What was repressed was the homosexual attitude understood in the genital sense, an attitude which had been formed under the influence of this recognition of castration. But that attitu was retained as regards the unconscious and constituted into a dissociated and deeper stratum. The motive force of the repression seems to have been the narcissistic masculinity which attached to the boy's genitals, and which had come into a long-prepared conflict with the passivity of his homosexual sexual aim. The repression was thus a result of his masculinity.

One might be tempted at this point to introduce a slight alteration into psychoanalytical theory. It would seem palpably obvious that the repression and the formation of the neurosis must have originated out of the conflict between masculine and feminine tendencies, that is out of bisexuality. This view of the situation, however, is incomplete. Of the two conflicting sexual impulses one was ego-syntonic, while the other offended the boy's narcissistic interest and for that reason underwent repression. So that in this case, no less than in others, it was the ego that put the repression into operation, for the benefit of one of the sexual tendencies. In other cases there is no such conflict between masculinity and femininity; there is only a single sexual tendency present, which seeks for admission, but offends against certain forces of the ego and is consequently expelled. Conflicts between sexuality and the moral ego-tendencies are indeed far more common than such as take place within the sphere of sexuality, though a moral conflict of the former kind is lacking in our present case. To assert that bisexuality is the motive force leading to repression is to make an insufficiently wide generalization; whereas if we assert the same of the conflict between the ego and the sexual tendencies (that is, the libido) we shall have covered all possible cases.

The theory of the "masculine protest," as it has been developed by Adler, is faced by the difficulty that repression by no means always takes the side of masculinity against femininity; there are quite large classes of cases in which it is masculinity that has to submit to repression by the ego.

Moreover, a juster appreciation of the process of repression in our present case would lead us to deny that narcissistic masculinity was the sole motive force. The homosexual attitude which came into being during the dream was of such over-whelming intensity that the little boy's ego found itself unable to cope with it and so defended itself against it by the process of repression. The narcissistic masculinity which attached to his genitals, being opposed to the homosexual attitude, was drawn in, in order to assist the ego in carrying out the task. Merely to avoid misunderstandings, I will add that all narcissistic impulses operate from the ego and have their permanent seat in the ego, and that repressions are directed against libidinal object-cathexes.

Let us now leave the process of repression, though we have perhaps not succeeded in dealing with it exhaustively, and let us turn to the boy's state when he awoke from the dream. If it had really been his masculinity that had triumphed over his homosexuality (or femininity) during the dream-process, then we should necessarily find that the dominant tendency was an active sexual tendency of a character already explicitly masculine. But there is no question of this having happened. The essentials of the sexual organization had not been changed; the sadistic-anal phase persisted, and remained the dominant one. The triumph of his masculinity was shown only in this: that thenceforward he reacted with anxiety to the passive sexual aims of the dominant organization—aims which were masochistic but not feminine. We are not confronted by a triumphant masculine sexual tendency, but only by a passive one and a struggle against it.

I can well imagine the difficulties that the reader must find in the sharp distinction (unfamiliar but essential) which I have drawn between "active" and "masculine" and between "passive" and "feminine." I shall therefore not hesitate to repeat myself. The state of affairs, then, after the dream, may be described as follows. The sexual tendencies had been split up; in the unconscious the stage of the genital organization had been reached, and a very intense homosexuality set up; on the top of this (virtually in the conscious) there persisted the earlier sadistic and predominantly masochistic sexual current; the ego had upon the whole changed its attitude towards sexuality, for it now repudiated sexuality and rejected the dominant masochistic aims with anxiety, just as it had reacted to the deeper homosexual aims with the formation of a phobia. Thus the result of the dream was not so much the triumph of a masculine current, as a reaction against a feminine and passive one. It would be very forced to ascribe the quality of masculinity to this reaction. The truth is that the ego has no sexual currents, but only an interest in its own self-protection and in the preservation of its narcissim.

Let us now consider the phobia. It came into existence on the level of the genital organization, and shows us the relatively simple mechanism of any anxiety-hysteria. The ego, by developing anxiety, was protecting itself against what it regarded as an overwhelming danger, namely, homosexual gratification. But the process of repression left behind it a trace which cannot be overlooked. The object to which the dangerous sexual aim had been attached had to have its place taken in consciousness by another one. What became conscious was fear not of the *father* but of the *wolf*. Nor did the process stop at the formation of a phobia with a single content. A considerable time afterwards the wolf was replaced by the lion. Simultaneously with sadistic impulses against small animals there was a phobia directed towards them, in their capacity of representatives of the boy's rivals, the possible small children. The origin of the butterfly phobia is of especial interest. It was like a repetition of the mechanism that produced the wolf phobia in the dream. Owing to a chance stimulus an old experience, the scene with Grusha, was activated; her threat of castration thus produced deferred effects, though at the time it was uttered it had made no impression.[1]

---

[1] The Grusha scene was, as I have said, a spontaneous product of the patient's memory, and no construction or stimulation on the part of the physician played any part in evoking it. The gaps in it were filled up by the analysis in a fashion which must be regarded as unexceptionable, if any value at all is attached to the analytic method of work. The only possible rationalistic explanation of the phobia would be the following. There is nothing extraordinary, it might be said, in a child that was inclined to be nervous having had an anxiety attack in connection with a

It may truly be said that the anxiety that was concerned in the formation of these phobias was a fear of castration. This statement involves no contradiction of the view that the anxiety originated from the repression of homosexual libido. Both modes of expression refer to the same process: namely, the withdrawal of libido by the ego from the homosexual conative tendency, the libido having then become converted into free anxiety and subsequently bound in phobias. The first method of statement merely mentions in addition the motive power by which the ego was actuated.

If we look into the matter more closely we shall see that our patient's first illness (leaving the disturbance of appetite out of account) is not exhausted when we have extracted the phobia from it. It must be regarded as a true hysteria showing not merely anxiety-symptoms but also conversion-phenomena. A portion of the homosexual impulse was retained by the organ concerned in it; from that time forward, and equally during his adult life, his bowel behaved like a hysterically affected organ. The unconscious repressed homosexuality withdrew into his bowel. It was precisely this trait of hysteria

---

yellow-striped butterfly, probably as a result of some inherited tendency to anxiety. (See Stanley Hall, "A Synthetic Genetic Study of Fear," 1914.) In ignorance of the true causation of his fear, this explanation would proceed, the patient looked about for something in his childhood on to which he could connect it; he made use of the chance similarity of names and the recurrence of the stripes as a ground for the construction of an imaginary adventure with the nursery-maid whom he still remembered. When, however, we observe that the trivial details of this event (which, according to this view, was in itself an innocent one)— the scrubbing, the pail and the broom—had enough power over the patient's later life to determine his object-choice permanently and compulsively, then the butterfly phobia seems to have acquired an inexplicable importance. The state of things upon this hypothesis is thus seen to be at least as remarkable as upon mine, and any advantage that might be claimed for a rationalistic reading of the scene has melted away. The Grusha scene is of particular value to us, since in relation to it we can prepare our judgement upon the less certain primal scene.

which was of such great service in helping to clear up his later illness.

We must now summon up our courage to attack the still more complicated structure of the obsessional neurosis. Let us once more bear the situation in mind: a dominant masochistic sexual current and a repressed homosexual one, and an ego deep in hysterical repudiation of them. What processes transformed this condition into one of obsessional neurosis?

The transformation did not occur spontaneously, through internal development, but through an outside influence. Its visible effect was that the patient's relation to his father, which stood in the foreground, and which had so far found expression in the wolf phobia, was now manifested in obsessional piety. I cannot refrain from pointing out that the course of events in this part of the patient's history affords an unmistakable confirmation of an assertion which I made in *Totem und Tabu* upon the relation of the totem animal to the deity.[2] I there decided in favour of the view that the idea of God was not a development from the totem, but replaced it after arising independently from a root common to both ideas. The totem, I maintained, was the first father-surrogate, and God was a later one, in which the father had regained his human form. And we find the same thing with our patient. In his wolf phobia he had gone through the stage of the totemistic father-surrogate; but that stage was now broken off, and, as a result of new relations between him and his father, was replaced by a phase of religious piety.

The influence that provoked this transformation was the acquaintance which he obtained through his mother's agency with the doctrines of religion and with the Bible story. This educational measure had the desired effect. The sadistic-masochistic sexual organization came slowly to an end, the wolf phobia quickly vanished, and, instead of sexuality being repudiated with anxiety, a higher method of suppressing it made its appearance. Piety became the dominant force in the child's life. These victories, however, were not won without

[2] *Totem und Tabu* (1913), Third Edition, 1922, p. 137.

struggles, of which his blasphemous thoughts were an indication, and of which the establishment of an obsessive exaggeration of religious ceremonial was the result.

Apart from these pathological phenomena, it may be said
that in the present case religion achieved all the aims for the
sake of which it is included in the education of the individual.
It put a restraint upon his sexual tendencies by affording them
a sublimation and a safe mooring; it lowered the importance
of his family relationships, and thus protected him from the
threat of isolation by giving him access to the great com-
munity of mankind. The untamed and fear-ridden child became social, well-behaved, and amenable to education.

The chief motive force of the influence which religion had
upon him was his identification with the figure of Christ,
which came particularly easily to him owing to the accident
of the date of his birth. Along this path his extravagant love
of his father, which had made the repression necessary, found
its way at length to an ideal sublimation. As Christ, he could
love his father, who was now called God, with a fervour
which had sought in vain to discharge itself so long as his
father had been a mortal. The means by which he could bear
witness to this love were laid down by religion, and they were
not haunted by that sense of guilt from which his individual
feelings of love could not set themselves free. In this way it
was still possible for him to drain off his deepest sexual current, which had already been precipitated in the form of
unconscious homosexuality; and at the same time his more
superficial masochistic tendency found an incomparable sublimation, without much renunciation, in the story of the
Passion of Christ, who, at the behest of his divine Father and
for his honour, had let himself be ill-treated and sacrificed.
So it was that religion did its work for the hard-pressed child
—by the combination which it afforded the believer of satisfaction, of sublimation, of diversion from sensual processes to
purely spiritual ones, and of access to social relationships.

The opposition which he at first offered to religion had
three different points of origin. To begin with, there was, in
general, his characteristic (which we have seen exemplified

already) of fending off all novelties. Any position of the libido which he had once taken up was obstinately defended by him from fear of what he would lose by giving it up and from distrust of the probability of a complete substitute being afforded by the new position that was in view. This is an important and fundamental psychological peculiarity, which I described in my *Drei Abhandlungen zur Sexualtheorie* as capacity for "fixation." Under the name of psychical "inertia" Jung has attempted to erect it into the principal cause of all the failures of neurotics. I think he is wrong in this; for this factor has a far more general application and plays an important part in the lives of the non-neurotic as well. Instability and inertness of the libidinal cathexes (as well as of other kinds of energic cathexes) are special characteristics which attach to many normal persons and by no means to all neurotics, and which have hitherto not been brought into relation with other qualities. They are, as it were, like prime numbers, not further divisible. We only know one thing about them, and that is that mobility of the mental cathexes is a quality which shows striking diminution with the advance of age. This has given us one of the indications of the limits within which psychoanalytic treatment is effective. There are some people, however, who retain this mental plasticity far beyond the usual age-limit, and others who lose it very prematurely. If the latter are neurotics, we make the unwelcome discovery that it is impossible to undo developments in them which, in apparently similar circumstances, have been easily dealt with in other people. So that in considering the conversion of psychical energy no less than of physical, we must make use of the concept of an *entropy,* which opposes the undoing of what has already occurred.

A second point of attack was afforded by the circumstance that religious doctrine is itself based upon a by no means unambiguous relation to God the Father, and in fact bears the stamp of the ambivalent attitude which presided over its origin. The patient's own ambivalence, which he possessed in a high degree of development, helped him to detect the same quality in religion, and he associated with it those acute powers of criticism whose presence could not fail to astonish us in a child of four and a half. But there was a third factor at work, which was certainly the most important of all, and to the operation of which we must ascribe the pathological products of his struggle against religion. The truth was that the mental current which impelled him to turn to men as sexual objects and which should have been sublimated by religion was no longer free; a portion of it was cut off by repression and so withdrawn from the possibility of sublimation and attached to its original sexual aim. In virtue of this state of things, the repressed portion kept struggling to forge its way through to the sublimated portion or to drag down the latter to itself. The first ruminations which he wove round the figure of Christ already involved the question whether that sublime son could also fulfil the sexual relationship to his father which the patient had retained in his unconscious. The only result of his attempts at repudiating this tendency was the production of apparently blasphemous obsessive thoughts, in which his physical affection for God asserted itself in the form of disparagement. A violent defensive struggle against these compromise-formations then inevitably led to an obsessive exaggeration of all the activities which are prescribed for giving expression to piety and a pure love of God. Religion won in the end, but its instinctual foundations proved themselves to be incomparably stronger than the durability of the products of their sublimation. As soon as the course of events presented him with a new father-surrogate, who threw his weight into the scale against religion, it was dropped and replaced by something else. Let us further bear in mind, as an interesting complication, that his piety originated under the influence of women (his mother and his nurse), while it was a masculine influence that set him free from it.

The origin of this obsessional neurosis upon the basis of the sadistic-anal organization confirms on the whole what I have said elsewhere upon the predisposition to obsessional neurosis.[3] The previous existence, however, of a severe hysteria in

[3] "The Predisposition to Obsessional Neurosis." *Sexuality and the Psychology of Love,* Collier Books edition BS 192V.

the present case makes it more obscure in this respect. I will conclude my survey of the patient's sexual development by giving some brief glimpses of its later vicissitudes. During the years of puberty a markedly sensual, masculine current, with a sexual aim suitable to the genital organization, made its appearance in him; it must be regarded as normal, and its history occupied the period up to the time of his later illness. It was connected directly with the Grusha scene, from which it borrowed its characteristic feature—a compulsive falling in love that came on and passed off by sudden fits. This current had to struggle against the inhibitions that were derived from his infantile neurosis. There had been a violent revulsion in the direction of women, and he had thus won his way to complete masculinity. From that time forward he retained women as his sexual object; but he did not enjoy this possession, for a powerful, and now entirely unconscious, inclination towards men, in which were united all the forces of the earlier phases of his development, was constantly drawing him away from his female objects and compelling him in the intervals to exaggerate his dependence upon women. He kept complaining during the treatment that he could not bear having to do with women, and all our labours were directed towards disclosing to him his unconscious relation to men. The whole situation might be summarized in the shape of a formula. His childhood had been marked by a wavering between activity and passivity, his puberty by a struggle for masculinity, and the period after he had fallen ill by a fight for the object of his masculine desires. The exciting cause of his illness was not one of the types of neurotic nosogenesis which I have been able to put together as special cases of "frustration,"[4] and it thus draws attention to a gap in that classification. He broke down after an organic affection of the genitals had revived his fear of castration, shattered his narcissism, and compelled him to abandon his hope of being personally favoured by destiny. He fell ill, therefore, as the result

[4] "Types of Neurotic Nosogenesis" (1912), ibid.

of a narcissistic "frustration." This excessive strength of his narcissism was in complete harmony with the other indications of an inhibited sexual development: with the fact that so few of his psychical tendencies were concentrated in his heterosexual object-choice, in spite of all its energy, and that his homosexual attitude, standing so much nearer to narcissism, persisted in him as an unconscious force with such very great tenacity. Naturally, where disturbances like these are present, psychoanalytic treatment cannot bring about any instantaneous revolution or put matters upon a level with a normal development; it can only get rid of the obstacles and clear the path, so that the influences of life may be able to further development along better lines.

I shall now bring together some peculiarities of the patient's mentality which were revealed by the psychoanalytic treatment but were not further elucidated and were accordingly not susceptible to direct influence. Such were his tenacity of fixation, which has already been discussed, his extraordinary propensity to ambivalence, and (as a third trait in a constitution which deserves the name of archaic) his power of maintaining simultaneously the most various and contradictory libidinal cathexes, all of them capable of functioning side by side. His constant wavering between these (a characteristic which for a long time seemed to block the way to recovery and progress in the treatment) dominated the clinical picture during his adult illness, which I have scarcely been able to touch upon in these pages. This was undoubtedly a trait belonging to the general character of the unconscious, which in his case had persisted into processes that had become conscious. But it showed itself only in the products of affective impulses; in the region of pure logic he betrayed, on the contrary, a peculiar skill in unearthing contradictions and inconsistencies. So it was that his mental life impressed one in much the same way as the religion of ancient Egypt, which is so unintelligible to us because it preserves the earlier stages of its development side by side with the end-products, retains the most ancient gods and their significations along with the most modern ones, and thus, as it were, spreads out upon a two-dimensional surface what other instances of evolution show us in the solid.

I have now come to the end of what I had to say upon this case. There remain two problems, of the many that it raises, which seem to me to deserve special emphasis. The first relates to the phylogenetically inherited schemata, which, like the categories of philosophy, are concerned with the business of "placing" the impressions derived from actual experience. I am inclined to take the view that they are precipitates from the history of human civilization. The Oedipus complex, which comprises a child's relation to its parents, is one of them—is, in fact, the best known member of the class. Wherever experiences fail to fit in with the hereditary schema, they become remodelled in the imagination—a process which might very profitably be followed out in detail. It is precisely such cases that are calculated to convince us of the independent existence of the schema. We are often able to see the schema triumphing over the experience of the individual; as when in our present case the boy's father became the castrator and the menace to his infantile sexuality in spite of what was in other respects an inverted Oedipus complex. A similar process is at work where a nurse comes to play the mother's part or where the two become fused together. The contradictions between experience and the schema seem to introduce an abundance of material into the conflicts of childhood.

The second problem is not far removed from the first, but it is incomparably more important. If one considers the behaviour of the four-year-old child towards the re-activated primal scene,[5] or even if one thinks of the far simpler re-

---

[5] I may disregard the fact that it was not possible to put this behaviour into words until twenty years afterwards; for all the effects that we traced back to the scene had already been manifested in the form of symptoms, obsessions, etc., in the patient's childhood and long before the analysis. It is also a matter of indifference in this connection whether we choose to regard it as a primal scene or as a primal phantasy.

actions of the one-and-a-half-year-old child when the scene was actually experienced, it is hard to dismiss the view that some sort of hardly definable knowledge, something, as it were, preparatory to an understanding, was at work in the child at the time.[6] What this may have consisted in we can form no conception; we have nothing at our disposal but the single analogy—and it is an excellent one—of the far-reaching *instinctive* knowledge of animals.

If human beings too possessed an instinctive endowment such as this, it would not be surprising that it should be very particularly concerned with the processes of sexual life, even though it could not be by any means confined to them. This instinctive factor would then be the nucleus of the unconscious, a primitive kind of mental activity, which would later be dethroned and overlaid by human reason, when that faculty came to be acquired, but which in some people, perhaps in every one, would retain the power of drawing down to it the higher mental processes. Repression would be the return to this instinctive stage, and man would thus be paying for his great new acquisition with his liability to neurosis, and would be bearing witness by the possibility of the neuroses to the existence of those earlier, instinct-like, preliminary stages. But the significance of the traumas of early childhood would lie in the fact that to this unconscious they would contribute material which would save it from being worn away by the subsequent course of development.

I am aware that expression has been given in many quarters to thoughts like these, which emphasize the hereditary, phylogenetically acquired factor in mental life. In fact, I am of opinion that people have been far too ready to find room for them and ascribe importance to them in psychoanalysis. I consider that they are only admissible when psychoanalysis strictly observes the correct order of precedence, and, after forcing its way through the strata of what has been acquired

---

[6] I must once more emphasize the fact that these reflections would be vain if the dream and the neurosis had not themselves occurred in infancy.

by the individual, comes at last upon traces of what has been inherited.[7]

[7] (*Additional Note*, 1923.)—I will once more set out here the chronology of the events mentioned in this case history.

Born on Christmas Day.

1½ years old: Malaria. Observation of his parents' coitus or of the interview between them into which he later introduced his coitus phantasy.

Just before 2½: Scene with Grusha.

2½: Screen memory of his parents' departure with his sister. This showed him alone with his Nanya and so disowned Grusha and his sister.

Before 3¼: His mother's laments to the doctor.

3¼: Beginning of his seduction by his sister. Soon afterwards the threat of castration from his Nanya.

3½: The English governess. Beginning of the change in his character.

4: The wolf dream. Origin of the phobia.

4½: Influence of the Bible story. Appearance of the obsessional symptoms.

Just before 5: Hallucination of the loss of his finger.

5: Departure from the first estate.

After 6: Visit to his sick father.

8:
10: } Final outbreaks of the obsessional neurosis.

It will have been easy to guess from my account that the patient was a Russian. I parted from him, regarding him as cured, a few weeks before the unexpected outbreak of the Great War; and I did not see him again until the shifting chances of the war had given the Central European Powers access to South Russia. He then came to Vienna and reported that immediately after the end of the treatment he had been seized with a longing to tear himself free from my influence. After a few months' work a piece of the transference which had not hitherto been overcome was successfully dealt with. Since then the patient has felt normal and has behaved unexceptionably, in spite of the war having robbed him of his home, his possessions, and all his family relationships. It may be that his very misery, by gratifying his sense of guilt, contributed to the consolidation of his recovery.

List of Books and Papers Referred to in the Text

Abraham, Karl, "Die psychosexuellen Differenzen der Hysterie und der Dementia praecox." First published in *Centralblatt für Nervenheilkunde und Psychiatrie,* Neue Folge, Bd. 19, 1908; reprinted in Abraham, *Klinische Beiträge zur Psychoanalyse,* Vienna, 1921.

Adler, Alfred, "Der psychische Hermaphroditismus im Leben und in der Neurose." *Fortschritte der Medizin,* 1910.

Ferenczi, S., "Transitory Symptom-Foundations during Analysis." (Chapter vii. of Ferenczi, *Contributions to Psychoanalysis,* Boston, 1916.) Translated by Ernest Jones from "Über passagère Symptombildungen während der Analyse," *Zentralblatt für Psychoanalyse,* Bd. II., 1912.

Freud, Sigm., *Der Witz und seine Beziehung zum Unbewussten,* Vienna, 1905; Fourth Edition, 1925.

Die Traumdeutung, Vienna, 1900; Seventh Edition, 1922.

Drei Abhandlungen zur Sexualtheorie, Vienna, 1905; Sixth Edition, 1925.

Eine Kindheitserinnerung des Leonardo da Vinci, Vienna, 1910; Third Edition, 1923.

Introductory Lectures on Psychoanalysis, London, 1922. Translated by Joan Riviere from *Vorlesungen zur Einführung in die Psychoanalyse,* Vienna, 1917-18; Fourth Edition, 1923.

Totem und Tabu, Vienna, 1913; Third Edition, 1922.

Zur Psychopathologie des Alltagslebens. First published in *Monatsschrift für Psychiatrie und Neurologie,* Bd. X., 1901; reprinted in book form, Berlin, 1904; Tenth Edition, Vienna, 1924.

Hall, Stanley, "A Synthetic Genetic Study of Fear," *American Journal of Psychology,* vol. xxv., 1914.

Jones, Ernest, "Rationalization in Every-day Life," *Journal of Abnormal Psychology,* vol. iii., 1908; reprinted in Jones, *Papers on Psychoanalysis,* London, 1913; Third Edition, 1923.

Jung, C. G., *Die Psychologie der unbewussten Prozesse,* Zurich, 1917.

"Ein Beitrag zur Psychologie des Gerüchtes," *Zentralblatt für Psychoanalyse,* Bd. I., 1911.

Über die Psychologie der Dementia praecox, Halle, 1907.

"Wandlungen und Symbole der Libido," *Jahrbuch für psychoanalytische und psychopathologische Forschungen,* Bd. III., 1912.

Loewenfeld, L., *Die psychischen Zwangserscheinungen,* Wiesbaden, 1904.

Maeder, A., "Psychologische Untersuchungen an Dementia praecox-Kranken," *Jahrbuch für psychoanalytische und psychopathologische Forschungen,* Bd. II., 1910.

Rank, Otto, *Der Mythus von der Geburt des Helden,* Vienna, 1909; Second Edition, 1922.

"Völkerpsychologische Parallelen zu den infantilen Sexualtheorien," *Zentralblatt für Psychoanalyse,* Bd. II., 1912.

Reinach, Salomon, *Cultes, Mythes et Religions,* Paris, 1905-8.

Riklin, F., "Über Versetzungsbesserungen," *Psychiatrisch-neurologische Wochenschrift,* 1905.

Sadger, I., "Ein Fall von multipler Perversion mit hysterischen Absenzen," *Jahrbuch für psychoanalytische und psychopathologische Forschungen*, Bd. II., 1910.

Schreber, Daniel Paul, *Denkwürdigkeiten eines Nervenkranken*, Leipzig, 1903.

Spielrein, S., "Über den psychologischen Inhalt eines Falles von Schizophrenie (Dementia praecox)," *Jahrbuch für psychoanalytische und psychopathologische Forschungen*, Bd. III., 1912.

Weininger, Otto, *Geschlecht und Charakter*, Vienna, 1903.